Policy Failures and the Irish Economic Crisis

Ciarán Michael Casey

Policy Failures and the Irish Economic Crisis

palgrave
macmillan

Ciarán Michael Casey
University of Oxford
Oxford, UK

ISBN 978-3-030-07954-3 ISBN 978-3-319-90182-4 (eBook)
https://doi.org/10.1007/978-3-319-90182-4

Cover illustration: Simon Burt/Alamy Stock Photo

Printed on acid-free paper

This Palgrave Macmillan imprint is published by the registered company Springer International Publishing AG part of Springer Nature
The registered company address is: Gewerbestrasse 11, 6330 Cham, Switzerland

To Bróna

Preface

This book examines the public discourse on the Irish economy in the years immediately prior to the Great Recession. The purpose is to understand why almost all commentators on the Irish economy were unprepared for the scale of the crisis. There have been several very worthwhile books on the crisis itself, particularly those on the bank guarantee and Anglo Irish Bank. However, misplaced confidence in the Irish economy and financial system was far from the preserve of bankers and senior policymakers. Contemporary survey evidence and the source material examined here demonstrate that almost nobody understood the degree of the risk. The book is structured around key institutions, including formal organisations, academia, the newspapers and politics. This allows us to examine the interlinkages and intellectual dependencies between these institutions, as well as their structural limitations. These core institutional shortcomings remain essentially intact, and some are so systemic that nothing short of radical restructuring will address them. The relatively modest reforms implemented since the crisis have been entirely insufficient.

The subject of this book should appeal to anyone with an interest in contemporary Ireland. It will also be of interest to political scientists and economists internationally, with an approach that could readily be applied to other countries and contexts. Methodologically, the book is first a foremost a work of history, and the study is based almost entirely on primary source material. This adds a dimension to the existing literature on the crisis and will hopefully resonate strongly with readers who lived in or were familiar with Ireland in the period. Now that the economy is growing strongly again, many of the themes dealt with here have returned to the fore. The treatment of the property market in the newspapers alone should cause unease. The crisis represented a lost opportunity for significant and genuine reform across many of the key institutions in Irish life. The recovery presents its own opportunities, which we will ignore to our cost.

Oxford, UK Ciarán Michael Casey

Acknowledgements

I owe very heartfelt thanks to the Clarendon Fund and Wadham College for funding my doctoral scholarship, without which this book would likely never have been written. I genuinely loved the three and a half years of my DPhil. I was uniquely lucky in terms of my supervisors, Roy Foster and Kevin O'Rourke, for their shared knowledge, insight, encouragement and forbearance during early draft chapters as I relearnt how to write history and unlearnt how to write reports. There have been many academics who encouraged and helped me along the way, all of whom have helped me more than they know. I owe particular thanks to Cormac Ó Gráda, David Vines, Jane Garnett, Frank Barry, Niamh Hardiman, Morgan Kelly, Sean Barrett, Mary Daly, Lindsey Earner Byrne, Diarmaid Ferriter and Andy Storey. I am also indebted to Jemima Warren and Oliver Foster at Palgrave Macmillan for being so enthusiastic and proactive in publishing this book. My family and friends have been a constant support throughout, which I try not to take for granted. The book is dedicated to Bróna, who was and remains the highlight at the end of every day.

Contents

Acronyms

AIB	Allied Irish Bank
BEPGs	Broad Economic Policy Guidelines
BOI	Bank of Ireland
CBFSAI	Central Bank and Financial Services Authority of Ireland
CORI	Conference of Religious of Ireland
CPI	Consumer Price Index
DCU	Dublin City University
EC	European Commission
ECB	European Central Bank
EMH	Efficient Market Hypothesis
EMU	European Monetary Union
ESM	European Stability Mechanism
ESR	Economic and Social Review
ESRI	Economic and Social Research Institute
EU15	European Union of 15 Countries
FDI	Foreign Direct Investment
FSAP	Financial Sector Assessment Programme
FSR	Financial Stability Report
FSSA	Financial System Stability Assessment
GDP	Gross Domestic Product
GNP	Gross National Product
IBEC	Irish Business and Employers Confederation
ICTU	Irish Congress of Trade Unions
IDA	Industrial Development Agency
IEA	Irish Exporters Association
IFSRA	Irish Financial Services Regulatory Authority

IIB	Irish Intercontinental Bank
IMF	International Monetary Fund
INBS	Irish Nationwide Building Society
INM	Independent News and Media
IT	The Irish Times
NPRF	National Pensions Reserve Fund
PTSB	Permanent Trustee Savings Bank

List of Figures

List of Tables

CHAPTER 1

Introduction

The Irish recession that began in 2008 has understandably received enormous public, official and academic attention. To date there have been five official reports, including the parliamentary Banking Inquiry. There have also been several authoritative academic examinations, notably those by Patrick Honohan (2009), Morgan Kelly (2009), Philip Lane (2011) and Karl Whelan (2013). The most comprehensive academic analysis to date has been Donovan and Murphy's 2013 book, 'The Fall of the Celtic Tiger'. There is a strong consensus about what happened to the Irish economy, and the systemic weaknesses that left it so exposed. While these works pay some attention to the discourse on the economy in the years preceding the crash, in no instance is it the core focus. This gap has been filled to some extent, and analysts such as Daniel Kanda (2010), Jim O'Leary (2011) and Michael Breen (2012) have scrutinised the external surveillance of the Irish economy during the boom years. Similarly, Julien Mercille (2014) and Mark O'Brien (2014) have both examined the role played by the newspapers in the period. Nonetheless, there has been little focused analysis on the contemporary publications by domestic organisations like the ESRI, of the political debates, or of the contribution made by academics.

This leaves a significant gap in the literature. If the economic roots of the Irish crisis have proven to be relatively mundane, the sociopolitical issues it has raised are much more challenging. Key questions that are yet to be fully answered include:

C. M. Casey, *Policy Failures and the Irish Economic Crisis*,
https://doi.org/10.1007/978-3-319-90182-4_1

1. Why were most commentators so unaware of the scale of the risks to the Irish economy?
2. What was distinctive about the analysis conducted by those who warned about systemic threats?
3. Did the newspapers intentionally downplay the risks to the property market and the economy?
4. What role did academics and politicians play in the discourse?
5. Was the Irish crash ultimately attributable to poor policy, flawed analysis, or both?

A systematic analysis of the public discourse on the Irish economy goes a significant way towards answering these questions. The core study of this book is based on an examination of the relevant publications by four formal international and domestic organisations, the ESRI (Economic and Social Research Institute), academic economists, the two main Irish daily broadsheet newspapers, *The Economist* and the contemporary Dáil (parliamentary) debates. This amounts to over 130 reports, a similar number of academic journal articles, thousands of newspaper articles and seven years of political debates. It is certainly sufficient to provide an insight into the mentalities of contemporary observers of the Irish economy. There are of course many additional sources that would be worthy of scrutiny in the future, including the contributions made by private-sector analysts, the international ratings agencies, additional newspapers, television and the Dáil committee debates.

It is important to clarify the necessary limits of the study. While those writing the officially commissioned reports were given access to the internal files of the banks and the regulatory authorities, these records are not publicly available and are not expected to be for the foreseeable future. We therefore cannot examine the mentalities underpinning the decisions that senior bank officials made in the period. The testimonies made to the parliamentary Banking Inquiry are available, and in some cases have been very useful. But these are best regarded as supplements to the source material from the period. Statements made after the crash need to be treated with a degree of caution. Given the paucity of internal documentation published to date it is difficult to conclude whether senior bank executives were aware of the extent of the risks they were taking. Bill Black, as a former director of the US Institute of Fraud Prevention, has argued that bankers must have been cognisant of the danger because similar actions had been so closely associated with disaster in the past. However, this is to attribute Irish bankers with a knowledge of financial history that they may well not have possessed. The fact that many staff and several non-executive directors from Anglo Irish Bank had equity holdings in the institution is highly suggestive in this respect. Similarly, Sean Fitzpatrick, as CEO and later chairman of Anglo, invested €16 million of his own money in AIB and Bank of Ireland shares. Accusing bankers of incompetence rather than intentional fraudulence may actually be appropriate in many cases.[1]

As we will see in Chapter 2, it is far from unusual for large numbers of people to arrive at unduly positive conclusions about future market developments. In a global historical context, the fact that the prevailing view was so wrong is therefore less surprising than it first appears. Of primary interest then, are the analytical shortcomings that underpinned the majority view, particularly flawed assumptions and illogical reasoning processes. The consensus view was overly sanguine in two key respects. Firstly, commentators were unduly optimistic about what they considered to be the most likely outcome for the boom. Secondly, and much more interestingly, even when commentators did try to consider worst-case scenarios they clearly had difficult envisaging a crisis on the scale of what subsequently materialised. The intellectual perspectives and historical horizons evident in the key publications offer considerable guidance in this respect, and will be a core focus of the study.

The millennial year marked an important juncture for the Irish economy. This is generally considered the point at which the export-led boom of the 1990s mutated into a credit-driven bubble. While there are inevitable problems with defining economic periods in this way, it does seem like a good starting point for our study. Similarly, 2006 is significant because it represented the peak of the residential property boom. There is some agreement that at this stage 'the die was largely cast', and it is difficult to imagine how a significant economic crisis could have been averted. The time span of interest is therefore the bubble period prior to the onset of the global financial crisis. In some cases the focus

[1] Houses of the Oireachtas, *Joint Committee of Inquiry into the Banking Crisis*, vol. 1, no. 6, William Black, 5 February 2015, 261–263; Newstalk, 'Sinn Féin calls on Fianna Fáil to Apologise for Lenihan's "We all partied" line', at www.newstalk.com, 28 January 2016. Available from https://www.newstalk.com/Dil-debate-on-Banking-Inquiry-report-today. Accessed 3 February 2016; Tom Lyons and Brian Carey, *The Fitzpatrick Tapes* (Dublin, 2011), 42–43, 230; and Nyberg Commission, *Misjudging Risk* (2011), 2, 11.

will extend beyond this period, for example to incorporate some of the concern expressed about the decision to join the European Monetary Union in the late 1990s.[2]

The treatment of a period that ended just over a decade ago as history is worthy of discussion. Opinions about how long ago events need to have happened to be considered historical are inevitably subjective. The frequently cited difficulties that arise from studying the recent past as history are that not enough material has been made available and that the researcher faces additional difficulties in terms of achieving sufficient dispassion and historical perspective. This book deals with the first problem by deliberately concentrating on the sources that are already available as its primary focus. It is up to the reader to decide whether the study is sufficiently objective, though of course the passage of time is clearly not a guaranteed safeguard in this respect either.[3]

Our focus on the recent past offers opportunities as well as challenges. Since much of the primary material is already digitised it is possible to study it quite quickly, and therefore to be more comprehensive than if it was only available in physical archives. As will be observed, search engines and online databases also allow for some quantitative analysis that would be prohibitively time-consuming otherwise. There are invariably trade-offs in some cases. One pertinent example is that by using digital archives of the newspapers one gets less of a sense of the physical positioning and prominence that an article was given. Even this will become less of an issue in the future: as newspapers are increasingly read

[2]Honohan Commission, *The Irish Banking Crisis: Regulatory and Financial Stability Policy 2003–2008. A Report to the Minister of Finance by the Governor of the Central Bank* (2010), 10, 21–22, 96; Morgan Kelly, 'The Irish Credit Bubble', UCD Centre for Economic Research Working Paper, WP 9, 32 (December 2009), 1–3; Philip R. Lane, 'The Irish Crisis', IIIS Discussion Paper no. 356, February 2011, 2–3, 6; Klaus Regling and Max Watson, *A Preliminary Report on the Sources of Ireland's Banking Crisis* (2010), 22; Jim O'Leary, 'External Surveillance of Irish Fiscal Policy During the Boom', July 2010, 4. Available from http://www.irisheconomy.ie/Notes/IrishEconomyNote11.pdf; Houses of the Oireachtas, *Joint Committee of Inquiry into the Banking Crisis*, vol. 1, no. 7, John Fitzgerald, 11 February 2015, 326; and Patrick Honohan, 'What Went Wrong in Ireland?' Prepared for the World Bank (May 2009b), 1–2.

[3]Matt Elton, 'History? It Started a Second Ago', 28 October 2009. Available from http://www.historyextra.com/feature/history-it-started-second-ago and Matt Elton, 'When Does History End?', 28 October 2009. Available from http://www.historyextra.com/feature/when-does-history-end.

online, the readership figures for individual articles will provide a fascinating resource.

Although the house price crash has garnered enormous attention since the start of the crisis, it was far from the most destructive element in its own right. The collapse of the construction sector had a much greater impact in terms of job losses, and Ireland's reliance on the sector for employment was both a cause and effect of the cost competitiveness losses observed during the boom. The human impact of the house price crash would have been far less severe had workers, the Exchequer and the banks been less exposed to the fortunes of the construction sector. It is therefore vital to examine what commentators said about all of the key economic vulnerabilities. Each chapter will examine the analysis conducted under four categories: property and construction, fiscal policy, competitiveness and the financial sector. Of course, there was often a great deal of overlap, and the boundaries between each were quite permeable. Nonetheless, by using this framework we can come to a more comprehensive understanding of how contemporaries understood the risks.[4]

It is also important to stress that the analysts involved were certainly not working in silos, and it is clear from the discourse that commentators influenced each other very significantly. For example, reports from the international agencies often incorporated analysis conducted by Irish commentators, including those working in the private sector, the ESRI and the Central Bank. Key findings by the official organisations were frequently cited in the media and by politicians. This is significant for our immediate purposes for two reasons. Firstly, it means that it is possible to gauge approximately how much of an impact a particular report or piece of analysis had on the discourse. Secondly, it reduces the chance of our analysis missing anything particularly influential. If a contribution had a significant impact it was likely to be cited elsewhere. In many instances it is impossible to definitively prove that the discourse had a direct impact on policy, and even if policymakers did cite a piece of research it does not necessarily mean that they were swayed by it. Nonetheless, it is difficult to imagine that the property price bubble could have been sustained in a climate where most commentators were predicting its

[4] Donovan and Murphy, *The Fall of the Celtic Tiger* (2013), 106 and Houses of the Oireachtas, *Report of the Joint Committee of Inquiry into the Banking Crisis*, vol. 1 (January 2016), 173.

imminent demise. Similarly, it is quite likely that successive Governments would have adopted more prudent policies if there had been more public concern. Contemporary survey data convincingly demonstrate how unprepared the public was for a house price crash at the peak of the boom.[5]

There is an understandable tendency to focus on those individuals and organisations who dissented from the prevailing view and made accurate predictions. The pessimists are of such significant interest because their critiques suggest that the crash was foreseeable, and this offers guidance about what analysts should pay particular attention to in the future. Perhaps more important in terms of contemporary policy, however, were the analysts who bolstered and sustained the consensus view. Just studying the pessimists tells us little about why they failed to convince most commentators of the imminent dangers. We need to examine the broader discourse in order to understand how such optimism was sustained in the face of the warnings issued.

Dissent is defined for the purposes of this book as the expression of opinions at variance with those commonly or officially held. It is important to establish from the outset the various levels at which dissent could exist. Early in the decade in particular, senior policymakers did appreciate that the rates of general and house price inflation were undesirably high. If a commentator stressed the associated risks this therefore did not necessarily constitute dissent, although criticising Government policy clearly did. There was considerably less consensus that housing was substantially overpriced, and arguments to that effect can be considered dissent. Far more contentious were warnings that prices were liable to fall significantly. However, on their own even these did not equate to an appreciation of anything like the extent of the macroeconomic risk. The strongest examples of dissent were warnings of significant property price falls and serious attendant implications for construction activity, employment and the Exchequer.[6]

There are many examples of commentators pointing to property prices or construction activity as risks, but not appreciating anything like the scale of the problem. Quantification, or implied quantification, was

[5] Paul Melia, 'Survey Sees No End to Boom in Property', *The Irish Independent*, 21 March 2005.

[6] http://www.oxforddictionaries.com/definition/english/dissent. Accessed 24 March 2016.

crucial. If an Opposition politician rebuked the Government about the risks emanating from the property market but continued to demand tax cuts in tandem with spending increases, then the warning was clearly undermined. One striking aspect of the discourse is that commentators were distinctly more prepared to warn that existing trends were unsustainable than they were to suggest that the point of danger had already been reached. Conversely, there were several conspicuous occasions when analysts expressed concern early on but then became more sanguine as the boom progressed. The positions that analysts took were sometimes fluid, and we can gain considerable insight from both the individuals who changed their minds and those who did not.

On a final point, it is tempting as the economy recovers to conclude that the crisis was less serious than it appeared at the time. As of 2018 Irish GDP has surpassed its pre-crash peak, and the country is growing at the fastest rate in Europe. Many of the human costs have been far more permanent, however, particularly those related to job losses and cutbacks to social supports. A particularly unwelcome and historically resonant aspect of the crisis was the return of mass emigration. The poor policies pursued during the boom must shoulder much of the blame, but they were not created in a vacuum. The broader context in which policy was formed was vital, particularly in terms of the intellectual and the institutional shortfalls that will become evident throughout the book. Improving our understanding of these limitations is a significant first step towards addressing them.[7]

[7]GDP and Emigration data from www.cso.ie; Suzanne Lynch, 'Ireland Remains Fastest-Growing Economy in Europe', *The Irish Times*, 4 February 2016 and Eoin Burke-Kennedy, 'Ireland Set for Fastest Euro Zone Growth for Fourth Year in a Row', *The Irish Times*, 8 May 2017.

CHAPTER 2

An Irish Depression

Nations have their ego, just like individuals.
James Joyce, 1907

In 2006 Alan Ahearne, Finn Kyland and Mark Wynne published a paper in the Economic and Social Review entitled 'Ireland's Great Depression'. The thesis was that the 1980s in Ireland constituted a depression comparable to those experienced internationally in the interwar period. By way of justification the authors pointed to the fact that the episode met the criteria of an output decline of at least 20% below trend, and of at least 15% below trend in the first decade. By this measure the Irish crisis from late 2007 easily constituted a depression. In just over three years the country experienced a cumulative GDP decline of 21% and a decline in nominal GNP of 20%. Even this experience paled in comparison with the American Great Depression, where unemployment reached 25% and GNP fell by a third. However, the widespread reticence to label the recent Irish crisis a depression has little definitional justification.[1]

[1]Alan Ahearne, Finn Kyland, and Mark A. Wynne, 'Ireland's Great Depression', *Economic and Social Review*, vol. 37, no. 2 (Summer/Autumn 2006), 215–243; Philip R. Lane, 'The Irish Crisis', IIIS Discussion Paper no. 356, February 2011, 2–3; IMF, *Country Report No. 12/264*, 5; Robert Skidelsky, *Keynes: The Return of the Master* (London, 2010), 65; and John Kenneth Galbraith, *The Great Crash 1929* (London, 2009), 186.

C. M. Casey, *Policy Failures and the Irish Economic Crisis*,
https://doi.org/10.1007/978-3-319-90182-4_2

While it is understandable that policymakers were keen to avoid adding to public panic during the crisis, the term 'recession' (representing two consecutive quarters of negative growth) seems decidedly euphemistic. At an immediate level, what we choose to term the event seems irrelevant. However, a striking feature of the boom period was the prevailing sense of separateness, that the world had changed, and that the economic tribulations of history were unlikely to be repeated and offered little insight into the present and future. In reality, the Irish experience had remarkably pertinent historical precedents, and a crucial step on the road to the crisis was the dismissal of the applicability of the lessons of the past.

This chapter will establish what happened to the Irish economy and put it in international context. It will examine some of the common features of asset bubbles and financial crises historically. It will also consider the psychological and behavioural influences that potentially contributed to the crash, before looking at some possible political and institutional factors. Finally, it will turn to evidence on the predictive capacities of experts and establish the parameters within which we can interrogate the interpretations of the Irish economy published during the boom.

1 What Happened to Ireland?

While the period from 1994 to 2000 was characterised by strong competitiveness and a rapid export-led convergence, the consensus is that the postmillennial period was defined by a credit explosion and the largest property bubble in the world. Two key phenomena enabled the rapid growth of Irish credit. Firstly, the adoption of the euro facilitated access by the Irish banks to external wholesale funding with no exchange rate risk premium. Secondly, the period was characterised by a global savings glut and low interest rates. Real interest rates in Ireland were actually negative during the period. Irish banks were also operating in a context of intensified market competition, encouraging them to rapidly expand lending to protect market share.[2]

[2] Donal Donovan and Antoin E. Murphy, *The Fall of the Celtic Tiger: Ireland and the Euro Debt Crisis* (Oxford, 2013), 2; Patrick Honohan, 'Resolving Ireland's Banking Crisis', UCD Economic Workshop Conference 'Responding to the Crisis', Dublin, 12 January 2009a, 3; Lane, 'The Irish Crisis' (2011), 3, 6; Morgan Kelly, 'The Irish Credit Bubble', UCD Centre for Economic Research Working Paper, WP 9, 32 (December 2009), 1, 6; and Klaus Regling and Max Watson, *A Preliminary Report on the Sources of Ireland's Banking Crisis* (2010), 22, 24.

The scale of the Irish credit boom was remarkable, with mortgage lending surging from €25 billion at the turn of the millennium to a peak of €127 billion in 2008. Suggestively, lending to the construction industry grew even more rapidly, to over €110 billion by 2008. The Honohan commission rightly identified these construction loans as the major weakness of the banks. The construction boom put additional pressure on existing bottlenecks, most notably the labour supply, driving wages across the economy to unsustainable levels. A poor understanding of the reversibility of booming construction and property-derived tax revenue encouraged policymakers to reduce the rates of more sustainable revenue sources, particularly income tax and VAT. This was accompanied by the highest increase in public spending in the OECD.[3]

When the crisis struck it manifested itself in four major aspects. Firstly, the crash of the construction and property sectors led to mass unemployment, widespread corporate bankruptcy, and a sharp fall in household wealth. Secondly, the instability of international financial markets led to a liquidity crisis for the Irish banks that precipitated the guarantee of their liabilities by the state. It was only later, when the extent of their potential losses on property and construction loans was properly appreciated, that they were recognised to be insolvent. The collapse of construction and property-derived revenue and the simultaneous surge in unemployment-related spending informed a remarkable fiscal reversal. The final aspect, and paradoxically one that was recognised by contemporaries but has garnered relatively little public attention since, was a cost and wage competitiveness crisis. From the beginning of the decade, Irish hourly manufacturing earnings had risen by 20% relative to those of the country's major trading partners. The construction boom had temporarily masked the effects, with its employment share doubling from the

[3]IMF, *Country Report No. 12/264* (2012), 4; Honohan, 'Resolving Ireland's Banking Crisis' (2009a), 4; Kelly, 'The Irish Credit Bubble' (2009), 1, 7, 8, 25; Nyberg Commission, *Misjudging Risk: Causes of the Systemic Banking Crisis in Ireland. Report of the Commission of Investigation into the Banking Sector in Ireland* (March 2011), 3; Mortgage Data courtesy of the Central Bank of Ireland; Karl Whelan, 'Ireland's Economic Crisis: The Good, The Bad and The Ugly', UCD Centre for Economic Research Working Paper, WP 13/6 (July 2013), 12; Honohan Commission, *The Irish Banking Crisis: Regulatory and Financial Stability Policy 2003–2008. A Report to the Minister of Finance by the Governor of the Central Bank* (2010), 6, 26, 29; and Klaus Regling and Max Watson (2010), *A Preliminary Report on the Sources of Ireland's Banking Crisis* (2010), 22, 24.

mid-1990s to 13.3%, the highest in the OECD. The GNP share of the sector had also doubled to almost 13% in the period.[4]

1.1 *The Credit Boom*

There is already an expansive literature on the Irish crisis, so to avoid needless repetition we will restrict ourselves to some of its more salient points. By contrast to international experience in the period, Irish credit expansion was not characterised by securitisation, but rather by 'plain vanilla property lending'. While banks in the USA, the UK and Europe lost money through financial innovation and exotic derivatives, the Irish method was decidedly 'old-fashioned'. Although much of the public ire in the wake of the crash has understandably been directed at the banks, it is important to stress that at €64 billion the gross cost of the bailout represents a minority of the total public debt accumulated during the crisis, and that the net cost will continue to fall. It is significantly exceeded by the cumulative debt incurred by the current fiscal deficits run in the meantime. Nonetheless, it is highly significant that the EU/IMF bailout of the state amounted to €67.5 billion, and there is a strong case to be made that without the bank liabilities it could have been avoided.[5]

Anglo Irish Bank has become synonymous with the more egregious behaviour of the period. Kelly has described it as 'a genuinely rogue bank' and has argued that its presence amplified the mismanagement of the other institutions. Anglo's rate of expansion was extraordinary, with its Irish loan book trebling in little over one year, and profits growing

[4]Donovan and Murphy, *The Fall of the Celtic Tiger* (2013), 8, 103; Kelly, 'The Irish Credit Bubble' (2009), 13–14, 22; Regling and Watson, *A Preliminary Report on the Sources of Ireland's Banking Crisis* (2010), 22; Whelan, 'Ireland's Economic Crisis' (2013), 7; and Patrick Honohan, 'What Went Wrong in Ireland?' Prepared for the World Bank (May 2009b), 6.

[5]Kelly, 'The Irish Credit Bubble' (2009), 13–14, 22, 23; Honohan, 'What Went Wrong in Ireland' (2009b), 7; Regling and Watson, *A Preliminary Report on the Sources of Ireland's Banking Crisis* (2010), 29, 40; Houses of the Oireachtas, *Report of the Joint Committee of Inquiry into the Banking Crisis*, vol. 1 (January 2016), 173; Donovan and Murphy, *The Fall of the Celtic Tiger* (2013), 106; and Philip R. Lane, 'International Financial Flows and the Irish Crisis', IIIS Discussion Paper no. 444 (March 2014), 8.

by 826% over the period. The bank expanded its market share from 3 to 18% in just over a decade, and by 2007 had become the country's joint second largest bank. Allied Irish Bank (AIB) responded by establishing 'Anglo win back teams' to try and recover developer customers. 'Chasing Anglo' became something of a mantra in the larger banks, and its aggression encouraged the relaxation of lending standards across the sector. While the boards of some banks explicitly decided to imitate Anglo, others increased growth targets with little appreciation of the corresponding risks. The insatiable demand for development finance ensured that these targets could be readily met. Between 2003 and 2008 the combined exposure of AIB, Anglo and Bank of Ireland (BOI) to construction and property firms grew almost fivefold to €157.8 billion. Anglo and Irish Nationwide Building Society (INBS) were particularly exposed, with construction and other commercial property loans representing over 70% of each of their total books.[6]

As competition increased in its core markets Anglo itself grew concerned about losing its big customers to foreign-owned subsidiaries like Bank of Scotland and Ulster Bank (owned by Royal Bank of Scotland). This further encouraged its risk appetite and crucially the heavier concentration of its lending to a small number of developers. By May 2008 the bank's exposure to its top twenty customers represented approximately half of its Irish loan book of €41.7 billion. The unrecognised vulnerability on the funding side was the growing reliance of the Irish banks on international wholesale markets. Prior to the late 1990s the banks had been essentially entirely deposit funded and the early years of the property boom had been financed without significant levels of foreign credit. This was to shift markedly from 2003. Both bankers and the regulatory authorities appear to have been largely oblivious to the risk that if the market soured this funding source could evaporate almost immediately. By 2008 the funding gap had reached €129 billion.[7]

[6]Kelly, 'The Irish Credit Bubble' (2009), 23; Donovan and Murphy, *The Fall of the Celtic Tiger* (2013), 68; Nyberg Commission, *Misjudging Risk* (2011), ii, iv, 13, 35; Tom Lyons and Brian Carey, *The Fitzpatrick Tapes* (Dublin, 2011), 46–47, 254–255, 257; Lane, 'The Irish Crisis' (2011), 27; Honohan Commission, *The Irish Banking Crisis* (2010), 27; and Regling and Watson, *A Preliminary Report on the Sources of Ireland's Banking Crisis* (2010), 32.

[7]Lyons and Carey, *The Fitzpatrick Tapes* (2011), 254–255; Nyberg Commission, *Misjudging Risk* (2011), 31, 34, 39; Regling and Watson, *A Preliminary Report on the Sources of Ireland's Banking Crisis* (2010), 31–33; Honohan, 'What Went Wrong in Ireland' (2009b), 7; and Kelly, 'The Irish Credit Bubble' (2009), 7.

There is ample evidence to suggest that the sector would have engaged in aggressive behaviour even without the presence of Anglo. The bank had virtually no involvement in the residential mortgage market, but there too intense competition with the entry of UK-owned subsidiaries encouraged the lowering of lending standards and the introduction of high-risk products. The combined mortgage loan books of AIB and BOI more than doubled to €97 billion from 2003 to 2008. In the three largest mortgage lenders high-risk trackers accounted for over half of all mortgage loans, again reflecting the assumption that funding would continue to be available at low cost in the long term.[8]

1.2 The Property and Construction Boom

Starting from a low base in the early 1990s, it was perfectly justifiable that property prices would rise in tandem with incomes and as interest rates fell. Even in retrospect, however, it is difficult to pinpoint exactly when increases became decoupled from these fundamental drivers. Between 1994 and 2006 real property prices increased threefold, far outpacing contemporary booms internationally. A key influence was Government policy. After the collapse of the dotcom bubble in 2001 Irish residential prices fell by an estimated 4.6%. Donovan and Murphy have argued that the subsequent withdrawal of policies that had been introduced to curtail price growth was attributable to pressure exerted by developer lobbyists. Price increases were thus intentionally resuscitated by the measures introduced in the 2002 Budget.[9]

Charles Kindleberger has contended that asset booms typically switch to busts once there is a pause in price increases. He argues that prices almost inevitably fall once they stop increasing, and that there is no middle ground. Insofar as expectations of capital appreciation are a key driver of demand this does seem an inescapable conclusion. The number and average size of residential mortgages approved in Ireland peaked in the autumn of 2006. On the basis of the data published to date it is

[8] Honohan Commission, *The Irish Banking Crisis* (2010), 8, 25; Lyons and Carey, *The Fitzpatrick Tapes* (2011), 67–68; and Nyberg Commission, *Misjudging Risk* (2011), 37.

[9] Honohan Commission, *The Irish Banking Crisis* (2010), 22; Kelly, 'The Irish Credit Bubble' (2009), 8, 10; Honohan, 'What Went Wrong in Ireland?' (2009b), 4; and Donovan and Murphy, *The Fall of the Celtic Tiger* (2013), 60–62, 79.

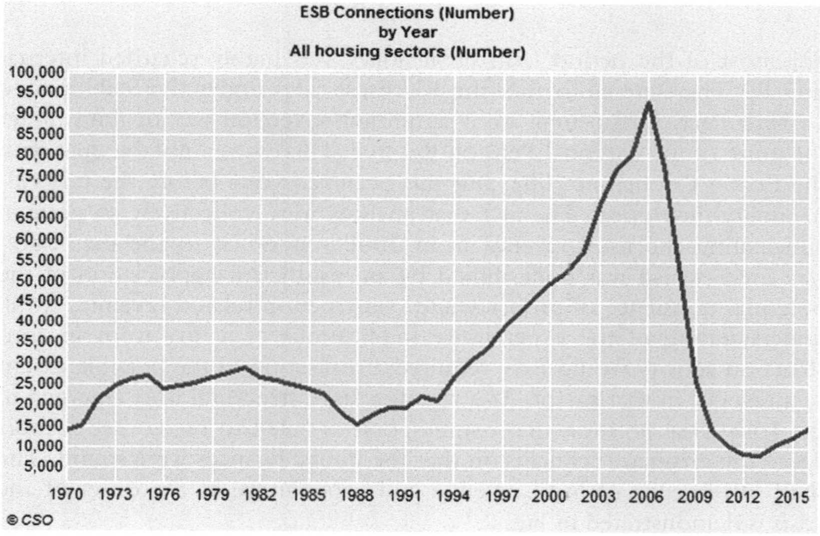

Fig. 1 Annual housing completions (*Source* Central Statistics Office)

clear that the losses that the banks suffered on construction and commercial real estate loans were a multiple of those incurred through residential mortgage lending. It is important then, that even if analysts recognised the precariousness of house prices during the boom that this did not necessarily equate to an insight into the vulnerability of the construction industry and thus of the banks, the Exchequer, or the real economy. The remarkable trajectory of Irish house completions is demonstrated in Fig. 1.[10]

[10]Charles P. Kindleberger and Robert Z. Aliber, *Manias, Panics and Crashes: A History of Financial Crises*, 5th ed. (Hampshire, 2005), 9–10; Kelly, 'The Irish Credit Bubble' (2009), 3; Lane, 'The Irish Crisis' (2011), 10; Graph data from www.cso.ie; Dirk Schoenmaker, 'Stabilising and Healing the Irish Banking System: Policy Lessons', 19 January 2015, 13–15. Available from https://www.imf.org/external/np/seminars/eng/2014/ireland/pdf/Schoenmaker_IrishBanking.pdf. Accessed 4 February 2016; Comptroller and Auditor General, *National Asset Management Agency: Progress Report 2010–2012*, Report No. 81 (Dublin, 2014), 21; and Central Bank of Ireland, *The Financial Measures Programme Report* (March 2011), 9.

1.3 *Fiscal Policy*

For most of the period Irish fiscal policy was highly regarded internationally. The state easily met the EU fiscal rules under the Stability and Growth Pact. It also built up a significant sovereign wealth fund under the guise of the National Pension Reserve. There was a notable spat with the Ecofin Council in 2001, but this occurred years before the real vulnerability developed. The fact that analysts were collectively so poor in anticipating the fiscal reversal from 2008 was down to the methodology used, which was undermined by an insufficient appreciation of the potential transience of property and construction-related revenue. A full understanding of the expenditure implications of a downturn in construction activity would have required a realisation of the possible extent of a reversal in that sector. As a result, a large structural hole emerged in the Irish fiscal position that contemporaries failed to recognise, encouraging the erroneous conclusion that the public finances were sound. The sharp divergence of fiscal revenue and expenditure at the onset of the crisis is demonstrated in Fig. 2.[11]

1.4 *Competitiveness*

The competitiveness crisis is particularly interesting insofar as it has had such a profound impact on Irish society vis-à-vis unemployment, but has been the subject of surprisingly little public discussion since the crash. Contemporary commentators, and in particular the international agencies, were highly mindful of rising wages and prices throughout the boom and repeatedly expressed concern. By 2007 Irish prices had reached the highest level in the Eurozone. Again however, a poor appreciation of the potential extent of the fall of construction activity was the crucial shortcoming. In the absence of this realisation, warnings about stagnant or declining employment in agriculture and industry predictably carried little weight with policymakers. When this transient construction

[11] Rob Wright et al., 'Strengthening the Capacity of the Department of Finance: Report of the Independent Review Panel' (December 2010), 4–6, 19; Regling and Watson, *A Preliminary Report on the Sources of Ireland's Banking Crisis* (2010), 25; European Commission, Directorate General for Economic and Financial Affairs, *European Economy: Public Finances in EMU—2001* (2001), 40, 141–144; Daniel Kanda, 'Asset Booms and Structural Fiscal Positions: The Case of Ireland', IMF Working Paper, WP/10/57 (March 2010), 3–7, 21; and Graph data from www.cso.ie.

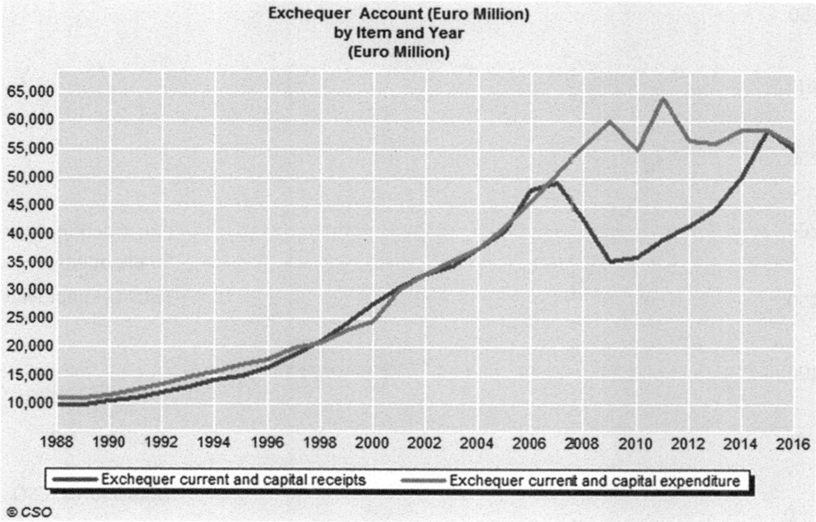

Fig. 2 Exchequer account (*Source* Central Statistics Office)

employment disappeared the repercussions were enormous, as shown in Fig. 3.[12]

2 International Context and EMU

Although the Irish crisis was one of the most dramatic internationally, it is important to properly contextualise it. The 'Great Recession' has proven to be the biggest global economic crisis since the Second World War. The losses involved are staggering: even relatively early estimates put the cost of global bank write-downs at $2.8 trillion, including $1.025 trillion in the USA, $814 billion in the euro area and $604 billion in the UK. The widespread consensus is that the seemingly benign macro-economic context of the period prior to the crash posed a severe test for policymakers, but Regling and Watson have argued that the Irish crisis

[12] Honohan Commission, *The Irish Banking Crisis* (2010), 24; Regling and Watson, *A Preliminary Report on the Sources of Ireland's Banking Crisis* (2010), 22; and Graph data from www.cso.ie.

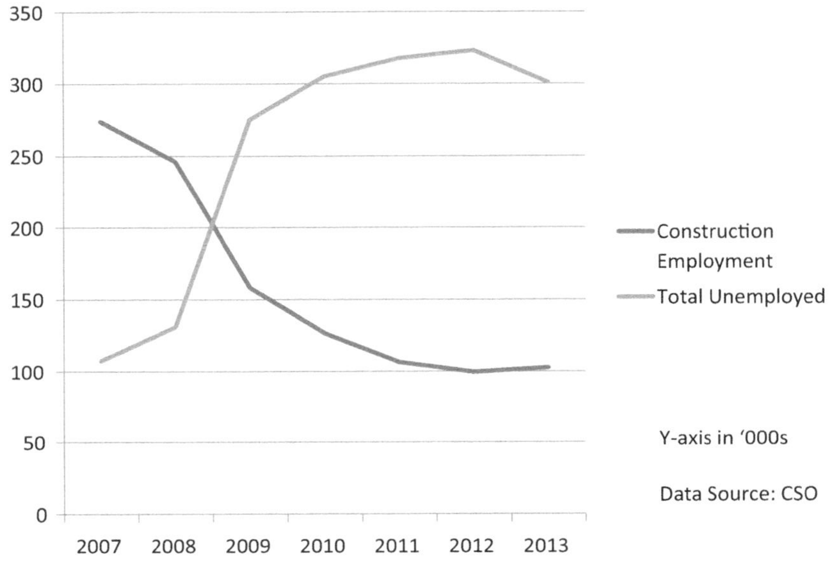

Fig. 3 Construction employment and total unemployment (*Data Source* Central Statistics Office)

was essentially 'home-made'. Perhaps the most convincing evidence that a crisis in 2008 was not inevitable is the Canadian example, where no banks even came under serious pressure, let alone needed to be bailed out.[13]

One key factor that led to the worldwide crisis was the shift away from rules-based and towards 'principles-based' regulation from the early 1990s, emanating from the UK and the USA. The principles-based approach encouraged national authorities to rely increasingly on the internal risk management systems of financial institutions, and to pay

[13] Skidelsky, *Keynes: The Return of the Master* (2010), ix, 7, 8, 15; Donovan and Murphy, *The Fall of the Celtic Tiger* (2013), 108; Regling and Watson, *A Preliminary Report on the Sources of Ireland's Banking Crisis* (2010), 5, 36; Nyberg Commission, *Misjudging Risk* (2011), ii; Honohan Commission, *The Irish Banking Crisis* (2010), 22; and Charles W. Calomiris and Stephen H. Haber, *Fragile by Design: The Political Origins of Banking Crises and Scarce Credit* (Princeton, 2014), 283.

attention to governance issues rather than arriving at their own independent assessments of risk. Underpinning the metamorphosis was a strong political and public belief in the benefits of largely unfettered financial markets. Among the key political leaders who drove this transition, Shiller and Akerlof predictably list Margaret Thatcher and Ronald Reagan, but also conspicuously Bertie Ahern. The widespread belief that modern financial markets were more stable than those of the past encouraged the erosion of many of the safeguards that had been introduced after the Great Depression. One oft-cited example was the gradual repeal of the Glass–Steagall Act in the USA, which had prohibited retail banks from trading in securities. To its critics the legislation was considered to be a relic from a bygone age, unnecessary in the context of sophisticated modern financial markets.[14]

This prevailing antipathy towards financial regulation had strong proponents in Ireland. Former Minister for Finance Charlie McCreevy was an explicit critic of the 'cost of regulation', and as European Commissioner attributed Ireland's success to 'economic freedom through low taxes, open borders, good corporate governance and light touch regulation'. Within the private sector, Sean Fitzpatrick as the chairman of Anglo likened state regulation to 'corporate McCarthyism', adding that 'in my humble opinion, our wealth creators should be rewarded and admired, not subjected to the levels of common scrutiny which known criminals would rightly find offensive'. While regulators internationally had some justification for struggling to recognise the risks inherent in new innovations like securitisation, the risks taken by financial institutions in Ireland were far more banal.[15]

The apparently benign global economic environment encouraged complacency on the part of many central banks in the face of rapid increases in credit supply and asset prices. On the fiscal front, most advanced economies ran pro-cyclical Budgets, including the USA, the UK and Japan. Another conspicuous factor in fuelling asset booms was

[14] Regling and Watson, *A Preliminary Report on the Sources of Ireland's Banking Crisis* (2010), 6, 17, 18; George A. Akerlof and Robert J. Shiller, *Animal Spirits* (Princeton, 2010), x–xi, xxv, 172; Skidelsky, *Keynes: The Return of the Master* (2010), ix, 7; and George Taylor, 'Risk and Financial Armageddon in Ireland: The Politics of the Galway Tent', *The Political Quarterly*, vol. 82, no. 4 (October–December 2011), 600.

[15] Lyons and Carey, *The Fitzpatrick Tapes* (2011), 129, 158–159 and Regling and Watson, *A Preliminary Report on the Sources of Ireland's Banking Crisis* (2010), 18.

the increased scale of capital flows across borders. Kindleberger points to the destabilising impact of these transnational flows in recent decades, in particular to the wave of money that 'sloshed' from Tokyo to Bangkok and other Southeast Asian countries after the Japanese crash in the early 1990s.[16]

Although the contention that the Irish crash was 'home-made' certainly has its merits, it is vital to recognise that it constituted one part of the much broader Eurozone crisis. In essence, this was caused by vast capital flows from the Eurozone's core to its periphery that were enabled by fundamental design flaws in the currency union, particularly the absence of a central financial regulator. The single currency facilitated the Irish banks in accessing an unprecedented volume of foreign credit at exceptionally low interest rates. In the millennial period there was minimal discussion of the scale of this overseas borrowing, the extent to which it had become the key driver of the Irish boom, or crucially the associated risks for financial stability. The treatments of the Irish crash have thus far focused on the failure of the domestic regulatory authorities to manage the new challenges that the currency union entailed. However, in this regard they were clearly far from alone, and the conceptual failings that underpinned the design of the Eurozone were perhaps the key ultimate cause of the Irish crisis. The stimulatory impact of the credit boom was exacerbated by the fact that the exchange rate set for the punt was likely too low given the strength of the Irish economy. Furthermore, the first three years of the union saw the euro depreciate sharply against the dollar, which gave a bigger competitiveness fillip to Ireland than other members given the extent of its trade with the USA and the UK.[17]

One obvious question is why Ireland succumbed more readily to the credit boom than other Eurozone countries. The temptation to attribute the discrepancy to greater moral or intellectual failings on the part

[16] Regling and Watson, *A Preliminary Report on the Sources of Ireland's Banking Crisis* (2010), 11, 13, 19 and Kindleberger and Aliber, *Manias, Panics and Crashes* (2005), 124, 244.

[17] Richard Baldwin et al., 'Rebooting the Eurozone: Step 1—Agreeing a Crisis Narrative', Centre for Economic Policy Research, Policy Insight no. 85 (November 2015), 1, 12, 13; Lane, 'The Irish Crisis' (2011), 26–28, 33; Regling and Watson, *A Preliminary Report on the Sources of Ireland's Banking Crisis* (2010), 5, 20; and Honohan Commission, *The Irish Banking Crisis* (2010), 22.

of bankers, politicians and regulators than those exhibited by their counterparts elsewhere is to succumb to a vein of Irish exceptionalism that is not particularly helpful. Analysts have already provided some plausible explanations. Morgan Kelly has pointed to the fact that the credit boom in Ireland followed a decade of genuinely exceptional performance. Commentators and policymakers had grown accustomed to high growth rates, and this helped to mask the extent of the problem. Pete Lunn has contended that Ireland's lack of relevant past experience may have encouraged flawed reasoning on the part of decision-makers. While recent Irish experience actually offered more guidance than is commonly recognised, many analysts in the period did exhibit distinctly limited historical perspectives. Another likely factor is that European monetary policy was particularly inappropriate for an economy that was already performing as strongly as Ireland.[18]

Commentators have been quick to point to an Irish predilection for homeownership as an explanatory factor. The evidence for this is actually somewhat mixed, and Conor McCabe has observed that 'it took decades to convince the urban working class that homeownership was one of their innate desires'. It is also important to recognise that the apparent virtues of residential property caught the imaginations of investors across many countries in the period. The USA in particular witnessed the biggest housing boom in its history, with prices almost doubling. As Akerlof and Shiller have suggested, it seems that people came to the strong intuitive feeling that residential prices everywhere were a one-way bet. This predictably informed the fear that waiting to buy carried the risk that prices would rise forever beyond one's means. In part, this mentality was informed by seemingly permanent lower interest rates and higher incomes, though factors like the tangibility and familiarity of housing were undoubtedly also at play.[19]

[18]Donovan and Murphy, *The Fall of the Celtic Tiger* (2013), 76; Regling and Watson, *A Preliminary Report on the Sources of Ireland's Banking Crisis* (2010), 22; Kelly, 'The Irish Credit Bubble' (2009), 24; and Pete Lunn, 'The Role of Decision-Making Biases in Ireland's Banking Crises', ESRI Working Paper no. 389 (May 2011), 1.

[19]Conor McCabe, *Sins of the Father: Tracing the Decisions That Shaped the Irish Economy* (Dublin, 2011), 53–56; Akerlof and Shiller, *Animal Spirits* (2010), 149–150, 169; and Regling and Watson, *A Preliminary Report on the Sources of Ireland's Banking Crisis* (2010), 15.

A final point worth making by way of providing a broader geographical context is that the international agencies had no more success in anticipating the global crisis than they did the Irish one. In May 2007 the Chief Economist of the OECD, Jean Philippe Cotis, observed that '...the current economic situation is in many ways better than what we have experienced in years'. The OECD's 'Economic Outlook' for 2008 predicted that contraction in the US housing market would drag down growth in the short term, but that it was 'unlikely to trigger a recession'. Inconveniently, the USA, Europe and Japan were actually already in recession at the time of publication. As Dirk Bezemer has argued, rather than predicting the future the prevailing economic models were struggling to assimilate what was already happening. The performance of the IMF was no better: even in mid-2009 the Fund was of the view that the worst was behind the USA and that it had escaped a hard landing.[20]

3 The Banking and Wright Reports

Among the most comprehensive accounts of the Irish crisis to date have been the official reports commissioned by the Irish Government and written by Irish and international experts. The 'Honohan', 'Nyberg' and 'Regling and Watson' reports all deal with the banking crisis, while the 'Wright' Report considers the performance of the Department of Finance. The credentials of the authors are conspicuous: Max Watson and Patrick Honohan both came with extensive experience from organisation like the IMF and the World Bank, Rob Wright is a former Canadian Deputy Minister of Finance, and Klaus Regling has since been appointed as Managing Director of the European Stability Mechanism (ESM).

It is worth briefly considering what the official reports were and what they were not. All four are unquestionably explanatory rather than retributive. Honohan and Nyberg considered a key objective to be the

[20] Steve Keen, *Debunking Economics: The Naked Emperor Dethroned* (London, 2011), 10; Dirk J. Bezemer, '"No One Saw This Coming": Understanding Financial Crisis Through Accounting Models', Munich Personal RePEc Archive Paper no. 15892 (June 2009), 19; Skidelsky, *Keynes: The Return of the Master* (2010), 13; and Independent Evaluation Office of the IMF (IEO), *IMF Performance in the Run-Up to the Financial and Economic Crisis: IMF Surveillance in 2004–2007* (Washington: IMF, 2011), 9.

identification of why so many got it wrong and missed the dangers. None of the four reports opted to explicitly allocate blame to named individuals within either the banks or regulatory authorities. The Nyberg Report justified this decision with a threefold explanation. Firstly, it argued that its terms of reference encouraged a focus on explaining systemic failures and that it would be easier to solicit information to this end if interviewees were not concerned about protecting their public images. Secondly, the Commission reported concern about prejudicing future criminal proceedings. Lastly, the authors believed that blame was implicitly allocated to the leaders of the named institutions by virtue of their positions.[21]

It is clear, however, that seeking to understand the mentalities and ideologies that informed poor decision-making in financial institutions and allocating blame are by no means mutually exclusive objectives. The Irish reports contrast strongly with the 'Valukas Report' into the collapse of Lehman Brothers, which considered key decisions taken within the bank by named individuals and freely published extracts from internal e-mails. One partial explanation is that the Valukas Report was an examiner's inquiry, while the Irish institutions were spared the intrusion of bankruptcy. Nonetheless, Nyberg's explanations seem to raise as many questions as they answer. The fact that the Commission's terms of reference discouraged the allocation of blame to individuals merely shifts the responsibility for the decision to politicians and senior civil servants, which is distinctly more worrying. Nyberg's concern about soliciting meaningful interviews would presumably have been far less pressing if the Commission had been granted the same level of access to internal files and correspondence as Valukas. The aversion to jeopardising potential criminal proceedings rings particularly hollow given that it erroneously conflates the aggressive lending decisions that destroyed the banks and the potentially criminal misdemeanours which played almost no direct role in this regard. At first sight, the last explanation that the decision-makers from named institutions are implicitly tarred anyway seems to be the most convincing of the three. However, this line of argument

[21] Honohan Commission, *The Irish Banking Crisis* (2010), 6 and Nyberg Commission, *Misjudging Risk* (2011), 5, 7.

also falls flat given that there would presumably be no reason to omit names if everybody knows who the culpable individuals are anyway.[22]

The fact that none of the four Irish reports sought to allocate blame to individuals does add weight to the widespread impression that those who were most responsible for the crisis have suffered little in the way of officially administered repercussion. Again we should challenge the assumption that Ireland is in any way unique in this respect, and American commentators have complained that Bernard Madoff was the only symbolic culprit of the US crisis and that he had virtually nothing to do with the crash itself. Insofar as the suspicion that Ireland is 'soft' on white-collar misconduct is true, the official reports can themselves be construed as having helped to perpetuate a culture of impunity. They will presumably do little to dissuade individuals in positions of power from engaging in high-risk behaviour in the future. Nyberg's contention that the Irish crisis involved 'a widespread lack of understanding and/or suspension of good judgement or critical discourse in large parts of society' is irrefutable. But the fact that bad judgement was commonplace goes only so far in excusing the actions of key decision-makers. It is certainly plausible that the decision to address only the systemic causes of the crisis may be the correct one, but the justifications that Nyberg gives for the decision are far from convincing. Regardless of the outcome, a more comprehensive and robust consideration of the benefits and costs associated with maintaining anonymity would have been helpful.[23]

George Taylor has argued that the Honohan report's attribution of the origins of the crisis to a failure on the part of the Financial Regulator to adequately supervise the banks is to miss the more fundamental issue. He contends that the intention behind regulatory reform in the period was to minimise the supervisory role of the state and to reallocate decisions about risk to shareholders and consumers. This mentality was informed by an attitude that it was misguided to attempt to regulate all risk and that efforts to do so would be counterproductive. In this sense, the failure of the Regulator to manage financial sector risks in Ireland can only be considered a proximate cause of the crash. According to Taylor,

[22] http://jenner.com/lehman/lehman/VOLUME%201.pdf, 102. Accessed 15 September 2014.

[23] James K. Galbraith, 'Foreword' in John Kenneth Galbraith, *The Great Crash 1929* (London, 2009), viii and Nyberg Commission, *Misjudging Risk* (2011), i, 5, 6.

the ultimate cause emanated from the international and national dynamics that shaped the Irish regulatory system.[24]

Taylor's train of thought certainly has its merits. Patrick Neary, first as Prudential Director of the fledgling Financial Regulator and subsequently as its CEO, has drawn much media criticism for his 'open and friendly' relationship with the leaders of financial institutions. It is important to recognise that Neary was almost certainly following the wishes of his political superiors and was in all likelihood appointed in part *because* he took a conciliatory attitude towards the banks. However, an attempt to pass the blame to the Government of the day is evidently vulnerable to the same attack. Presumably, the majority of those who voted for Fianna Fáil in the period were not under the illusion that the party would readily sacrifice the fruits of today to safeguard tomorrow. If Patrick Neary was an actor in a play written by others, then so too was Bertie Ahern. Taylor thus leads us down such a deterministic path that we are again brought to Nyberg's conclusion that the blame can be extended across much of society. Again however, conceding the premise that the appointment of negligent decision-makers had an air of inevitability in the period does not compel us to accept that those decision-makers had no personal discretion or free will. It is in fact to Honohan's credit that he does not use wider societal failings to let key decision-makers off the hook.[25]

4 Theoretical and Ideological Explanations

Taylor's 'international and national' dynamics essentially boil down to the drive to deregulate financial markets that had swept many developed countries in the decades prior to the crash. Commentators have pointed to the role of economic theory in underpinning this initiative, focusing on the impact of New Classical Macroeconomics and the Efficient Market Hypothesis (EMH) in encouraging the belief that unhampered financial markets would tend to be both efficient and stable and that almost any market development was intrinsically benign. New Classical Macroeconomics took the view that all risks were calculable, and that

[24] Taylor, 'Politics of the Galway Tent' (2011), 603, 606, 607.

[25] Financial Regulatory Authority of Ireland, *Annual Report: 2003/2004* (2005), 9 and George Stigler, 'The Theory of Economic Regulation', *Bell Journal of Economics and Management Science*, vol. 2, no. 1 (Spring 1971), 3–21.

market participants could correctly predict future events. The EMH extended this assumption to conclude that on average financial market participants price assets based on an accurate assessment that incorporates all available information about the future. The prevailing orthodoxies thus dismissed the roles of time and uncertainty, as well as the notion that markets are susceptible to bubbles. These assumptions informed the widespread belief that unregulated markets offered the best of all possible worlds and were used to legitimise much of the deregulation of the period. Large swathes of the economics profession thus sanctioned a model that minimised the supervisory role of the state. Assumptions about the stability of financial markets encouraged the adoption of principles-based regulation and in Ireland informed the unintrusive and deferential stance taken even in the face of governance breaches.[26]

Analysts certainly have a strong case in pointing to the role that theory played in convincing prominent American economists that financial markets were inherently efficient and stable. Ben Bernanke, who replaced Alan Greenspan as chairman of the US Federal Reserve, has come under significant criticism since the crash for his 2004 observation of a 'Great Moderation', a 'marked reduction in economic volatility, both in the United States and abroad'. Robert Lucas went even further, arguing in 2003 that the 'central problem of depression prevention has been solved, for all practical purposes'.[27]

However, for many economists, and even more so for non-economist policymakers and the general public, perceived recent experience also played a crucial role in informing their faith in the efficiency and stability of financial markets. The credence that people give to any hypothesis is heavily determined by whether its conclusions about the world resonate and are compatible with their own experiences. The Great Depression took economists by surprise because after a period of economic tranquillity they concluded that boom-bust cycles were passé. After the

[26] Skidelsky, *Keynes: The Return of the Master* (2010), xvi, 28, 44, 75, 84, 165–166; Nyberg Commission, *Misjudging Risk* (2011), ii, 29, 4, 59–62, 94; Donovan and Murphy, *The Fall of the Celtic Tiger* (2013), 83, 84; James K. Galbraith, 'Foreword' in John Kenneth Galbraith, *The Great Crash 1929* (2009), viii; Hyman P. Minsky, *Stabilising an Unstable Economy* (Yale, 2008), 4, 110–113; Akerlof and Shiller, *Animal Spirits* (2010), xiii; and Robert J. Shiller, *Irrational Exuberance* (Princeton, 2000), 171.

[27] Keen, *Debunking Economics* (2011), 10, 296 and Donovan and Murphy, *The Fall of the Celtic Tiger* (2013), 32, 46.

Depression people understandably abandoned the belief that markets were inherently stable. Galbraith has argued that the experience of the Wall Street Crash had such a profound impact on the consciousness of that generation that it never would have been induced to engage in speculation in the decades that followed.[28]

Akerlof and Shiller have contended that prior to the 1980s the purpose of financial regulation was well understood because of this collective memory of the Depression. From that juncture, they argue, the lessons learnt in the 1930s about how an economy really works were forgotten, and a depression again became possible. The generation that Galbraith termed the 'guardians of sound pessimism' was replaced by one that was encouraged by many years of sustained growth to conclude that the economic problem had been 'cracked'.[29]

The direct importance of historical experience is highly observable in the Irish case. Essentially nobody in academia or in the domestic or international agencies in the period explicitly appealed to theory in justifying their opinions about the vulnerability or robustness of the Irish economy. By contrast, analysts of all hues regularly invoked history in making the case for either caution or comfort about the future. As subsequent chapters will demonstrate, the IMF, the OECD, Caroline Gavin in the Central Bank of Ireland, *The Economist* newspaper, and several academics all drew on recent experiences from Ireland and abroad in substantiating their assessments of the Irish situation. The reasoning processes used by these analysts could thus be considered to have been much more inductive than those exhibited by more some of the more theoretically minded economists in the USA. As we will observe in the next section, however, many commentators and market participants arrived at conclusions that jarred considerably with recent international experience. In the Irish case this may be attributable in significant part to insularity and the primacy given to domestic experience. However, theory may have played a role here too, convincing observers that market failures elsewhere were largely aberrational. As we will observe in Chapter 7, several highly influential Irish politicians regularly extolled the benefits of unfettered markets, both for their efficacy and for their

[28]Bezemer, 'No One Saw This Coming' (2009), 186; Skidelsky, *Keynes: The Return of the Master* (2010), 65; and Galbraith, *The Great Crash 1929* (2009), vii, 11, 29, 35, 189.

[29]Akerlof and Shiller, *Animal Spirits* (2010), xi, xiii, xxi, Galbraith, *The Great Crash 1929* (2009), 205; and Skidelsky, *Keynes: The Return of the Master* (2010), xv.

contributions to individual freedom. The thrust of the arguments was decidedly similar of those that had been made by Friedrich Hayek and Milton Friedman decades earlier.[30]

5 The History of Asset Bubbles and Financial Crises

In a 2012 speech delivered at Georgetown University in Washington, former Taoiseach Brian Cowen referred to the 'unprecedented' turmoil and crisis in the Eurozone. The survival of the illusion that the European and Irish crises were in any way a break from the past is testimony to how completely the lessons of history had been forgotten or discarded. Far from being an aberration, the Irish property crash was a classic asset market collapse. The deep faith that people held in the stability of financial and asset markets is actually very difficult to explain given the number of crises experienced internationally in recent decades, which have been described as the most volatile in global monetary history. The twenty years from 1980 to 2000 were witness to more asset price bubbles than in any earlier period, with 112 financial crises in 93 countries. Nor were these episodes by any means the preserve of developing nations. Almost all of the financial institutions in Finland, Norway, Sweden and Japan went bankrupt or were nationalised in the early 1990s.[31]

Financial and asset market crises have been commonplace internationally for at least four hundred years, with the much-cited Dutch tulip bubble of 1636 and the Mississippi Company Crisis of 1720 as notable early examples. Proving definitively that intellectual capacity is at best a limited safeguard, Isaac Newton lost a fortune during the South Sea

[30] Lyons and Carey, *The Fitzpatrick Tapes* (2011), 23; Skidelsky, *Keynes: The Return of the Master* (2010), 27; F. A. Hayek, *The Road to Serfdom* (New York: Routledge, 2001); Milton Friedman, *Capitalism and Freedom*, Fortieth Anniversary Edition (Chicago, 2002); and Johan Christensen, *The Power of Economists Within the State* (Stanford: Stanford University Press, 2017), 92–93.

[31] Brian Cowen, 'The Euro: From Crisis to Resolution? Some Reflections from the Road Thus Far', at the BMW Centre of German and European Studies, Georgetown University, Washington (March 2012), 5; Calomiris and Haber, *Fragile by Design* (2014), ix; Donovan and Murphy, *The Fall of the Celtic Tiger* (2013), 5, 45; Kindleberger and Aliber, *Manias, Panics and Crashes* (2005), 1–3, 241, 243; Carmen M. Reinhardt and Kenneth S. Rogoff, *This Time Is Different: Eight Centuries of Financial Folly* (Princeton, 2011), 73; and IMF, *Country Report No. 12/264* (2012), 8.

Bubble. The 2000s did not even represent Ireland's first asset bubble in recent decades: agricultural land prices had exhibited a sizeable boom and bust cycle in the late 1970s and early 1980s. Unsurprisingly, one of the commonly shared characteristics of asset booms is their occurrence during periods of loose credit supply and robust economic expansion. Another striking association is between asset price bubbles and the construction of landmark buildings, such as the Empire State Building or Petronas Towers in Kuala Lumpur. The Irish boom followed precedent in both this respect and in the proliferation of trophy acquisitions such as the Savoy Hotel Group in London.[32]

Perhaps the most important characteristic of asset and financial bubbles is the propensity of those experiencing them to conclude that the world has somehow changed, that the economy has become more stable, and that the old rules of valuation are no longer relevant. Kindleberger has observed that during bubbles more confident analysts will proclaim no more recessions and the obsolescence of traditional business cycles. On the eve of the Wall Street Crash the economist Irving Fisher famously observed that 'stock prices have reached what looks like a permanently high plateau'. A contemporaneous article in the *New York Times* warned that it is 'a well-known characteristic of boom-times that the idea of their being terminated in the old, unpleasant way is rarely recognised as possible'. The propensity to ignore 'Cassandra-like' warnings is clearly also a key feature of asset bubbles. Shiller's work demonstrates that real estate prices exhibit virtually no increase over the long term, but go through a series of enormous bubbles as if people had never learnt from the past. In the Irish context, the Honohan Commission has suggested that a prolonged period of success lulled decision-makers into a false sense of invulnerability. As Dowd and Hutchinson observe, policymakers have often been blinkered limited historical and geographical horizons:

[32] Kindleberger and Aliber, *Manias, Panics and Crashes* (2005), 8–12, 31, 41, 97, 140, 239; Reinhardt and Rogoff, *This Time Is Different* (2011), xxvi–xxvii, xxxiv; Donovan and Murphy, *The Fall of the Celtic Tiger* (2013), 49–50; Akerlof and Shiller, *Animal Spirits* (2010), 13; and Maurice Roche and Kieran McQuinn, 'Testing for Speculation in Agricultural Land in Ireland', *European Review of Agricultural Economics*, vol. 28, no. 2 (2001), 112.

> If they learn from history at all, they learn from relatively recent crises, or from major events still close to living memory, but ignore lessons from foreign crises, while regarding those of a century and more ago as being too distant to be relevant.[33]

Reinhardt and Rogoff have argued that the tendency of many economists to draw conclusions from thirty years of data is inadequate given that financial crises have much longer cycles. The problem is often further exacerbated by the inclusion of a narrow range of countries. The criticism is clearly relevant to the assessments made in the run-up to the recent crash, both in Ireland and abroad. Ratings agencies calculated the expected default rate for subprime mortgage securities based on very recent data collected during a rising market. Likewise, the Irish banks operated on assumptions about a soft landing and the continued availability of funding based on recent trends specific to Ireland. Reinhardt and Rogoff's dataset, encompassing 66 countries over eight centuries, suggests that while many advanced economies have graduated from repeated sovereign debt defaults and bouts of runaway inflation, the myth that they had graduated from acute financial crises had little factual basis. Of the 66 countries sampled, only four had escaped banking crises between 1945 and 2007, three of which have been forced into funding enormous bank bailouts since.[34]

If crashes had been confined to emerging economies in the recent past, we could attribute the failure to learn from them in Europe and the USA to a belief that rich economies had progressed beyond such episodes. However, there were also clear pertinent examples within the OECD. The USA suffered an asset price collapse and ensuing recession in 2001. Paradoxically, the lesson taken from the bursting of the dot-com bubble seems to have been that it was wiser to invest in real estate

[33] Galbraith, *The Great Crash 1929* (2009), 95, 110, 116; Kindleberger and Aliber, *Manias, Panics and Crashes* (2005), 9; Minsky, *Stabilising an Unstable Economy* (2008), 237; Honohan Commission, *The Irish Banking Crisis* (2010), 7; Akerlof and Shiller, *Animal Spirits* (2010), 149; Robert J. Shiller, 'Long-Term Perspectives on the Current Boom in Home Prices', *Economist's Voice, The Berkeley Electronic Press* (2006), 1–2; and Kevin Dowd and Martin Hutchinson, *Alchemists of Loss: How Modern Finance and Government Intervention Collapsed the Financial System* (London, 2006), 33.

[34] Reinhardt and Rogoff, *This Time Is Different* (2011), xxvii–xxviii, 141–142, 171–172; Akerlof and Shiller, *Animal Spirits* (2010), 37; and Nyberg Commission, *Misjudging Risk* (2011), 22.

as an apparently safer asset class. Similarly, the financial and asset crises experienced in the Nordic countries, the UK and Japan in the 1980s and 1990s all clearly should have helped to dispel complacency. At the onset of the 2008 crash Paul Krugman observed that the Asian crises 'should have sent chills up the spine of anyone with a sense of history'.[35]

Perhaps past experience again helps us in this regard. Economic history suggests that asset and financial bubbles are so frequent and similar that they should be identifiable, but paradoxically that same frequency has been a function of the failure of many decision-makers and the wider public to learn from the past, across centuries and much of the globe. The propensity to mistake bubbles for a changed economic order is (quite logically) as salient a feature of economic history as the bubbles themselves. If the Irish asset bubble was nothing new, neither was the widespread failure to recognise its nature before it collapsed. The gusto with which the Central Bank of Ireland disregarded the applicability of the history of booms and busts on the basis that the world had changed strongly suggests that analysts were not mindful of the long tradition of those before them who had erroneously come to parallel conclusions on the basis of similarly short time horizons:

> In this literature, the majority of 'booms' and 'busts' in nominal and real house prices occurred prior to the 1990s. However, the incidences of 'booms' ending in absolute declines in real or nominal prices have fallen since the early-1990s. The reasons for the decline in the cyclicality of both nominal and real house prices are unclear but are likely to be linked to the so called 'Great Moderation' where volatility in a broad range of macroeconomic series have declined over a similar time period. Accordingly, there appears to be the important qualification that past international experience may not be an accurate guide to future developments in house prices because the international macroeconomic environment is now somewhat different.[36]

[35] Akerlof and Shiller, *Animal Spirits* (2010), 38 and Paul Krugman, *The Return of Depression Economics* (London, 2008), 4–5.

[36] Akerlof and Shiller, *Animal Spirits* (2010), 38; Kevin Dowd and Martin Hutchinson, *Alchemists of Loss: How Modern Finance and Government Intervention Collapsed the Financial System* (London, 2006), 33–34; and Central Bank and Financial Services Authority of Ireland, *Financial Stability Report* (2007), 30.

6 Behavioural Explanations

The primary achievement of behavioural economics over recent decades has been to empirically qualify assumptions about human rationality. The most celebrated proponent of the discipline is Daniel Kahneman, who was awarded the Nobel Prize in 2002. In this section we will turn to some of the biases or heuristics that have been scientifically demonstrated to influence decision-making, and consider how they might have been particularly relevant to the Irish situation. Pete Lunn has already published a paper considering the Irish crisis from a behavioural perspective (one of the best on the subject to date), which offers a strong starting point. Some of Shiller's insights into behavioural influences will also be examined.[37]

One bias that seems to have played an enormous role in influencing the judgement of those assessing the Irish economy in the period is exaggerated emotional coherence, or the halo effect. The effect describes the tendency to be wholly positive or wholly negative about a person, object or development. Closely related is confirmation bias, the readiness to accept information that is consistent with prior beliefs and to dismiss new information that contradicts or challenges them. Given that Ireland had enjoyed years of stellar growth on the basis of competitiveness and export performance many commentators understandably had a very positive view of the economy. Concerns about vulnerabilities like the potential flight of the multinationals were largely assuaged by Ireland's resilience in the wake of the dotcom crash. As will be argued in Chapter 3, the international organisations in particular celebrated Ireland as an example of how a country could thrive by adopting the 'correct' policies. The IMF went so far as to take partial credit for the boom.[38]

An associated bias is the affect heuristic, which describes the tendency of people to make assessments emotionally, often without being consciously aware that they are doing so. It seems to have had an impact on commentators and market participants in the period in a number of ways. It undoubtedly would have been very unpleasant for observers of the Irish economy to conclude that it was in a precarious position, in

[37] Pete Lunn, 'The Role of Decision-Making Biases in Ireland's Banking Crisis', ESRI Working Paper no. 389 (2011).

[38] Daniel Kahneman (2011), *Thinking Fast and Slow* (London, 2011), 82, 83, 199 and Lunn, 'The Role of Decision-Making Biases in Ireland's Banking Crisis' (2011), 6.

terms of both the personal anxiety and the reactions in others that such a position could evoke. Domestic commentators understandably took satisfaction from seeing the economy thrive after a long history of stagnation, which presumably made an objective radical reappraisal of the boom as it evolved very difficult. It is likely that the affect heuristic also played a role in fuelling property booms across many countries in the period, inasmuch as it informed the widespread intuitive belief that residential prices everywhere could only increase.[39]

One of the conspicuous features of the discourse on the Irish economy in the period is that so many notionally autonomous analysts arrived at similarly sanguine conclusions. In situations where individuals show poor judgement the aggregated assessment of a large number of observers is often far superior because the extremes cancel each other out. However, the principle of independent judgements holds that this is only true if the individuals involved have not influenced each other and their errors are uncorrelated. If the observers share a bias, then the aggregation of their judgements will not reduce it. Later chapters will make it clear that analysts influenced each other enormously throughout the period. The international agencies relied heavily in their assessments of the property market on the 'Bacon Reports' for example. Furthermore, the Irish authorities in turn were bolstered in their view by the positive results of the IMF's 2006 assessment of the Irish banks. This kind of cross-contamination was almost inevitable given that analysts inevitably rely on existing research. However, it does help to explain how large swathes of observers can be either correct or incorrect in unison. The impact can clearly be compounded by the effect of behavioural convergence, which describes the tendency to copy the decisions and conform to the views of the majority.[40]

Extrapolation bias played a vital role in the Irish context. It is described as the tendency of people to pay excessive heed to more recent events in predicting the future at the expense of earlier experience. The radical changes to the economy also made it more difficult to tell the wood from the trees in recognising what was temporary or unjustifiable. Rising incomes and falling interest rates were used to rationalise the

[39] Kahneman (2011), *Thinking Fast and Slow*, 139 and Akerlof and Shiller (2010), *Animal Spirits*, 150.

[40] Kahneman, *Thinking Fast and Slow* (2011), 84–85 and Lunn, 'The Role of Decision-Making Biases in Ireland's Banking Crisis' (2011), 6.

abandonment of long-standing methods for housing valuation, often with little accompanying effort to arrive at new ones. Many in Ireland and abroad concluded that real house prices had risen to a permanently higher plateau on the basis of data over recent decades. While this view did have some justification based on semi-permanently lower interest rates, it did not preclude future volatility or crashes. Suggestively, Shiller presents data pertaining to Amsterdam from 1628 to 1973, the USA from 1890 to 2005 and Norway from 1819 to 1989, which suggest that real home prices in those territories have not increased significantly over the very long term, but rather go through a series of long boom and bust cycles. Extrapolation bias presumably plays some role in driving the booms and busts captured in the data, since it encourages market participants and actors to dismiss the long-term trends on the assumption that there has been a permanent break from the past.[41]

Hindsight bias is recognised to have a particularly powerful influence, and is relevant to the boom period as well as an important reminder that the crash was less predictable than it appears in retrospect. Trials have demonstrated that people exaggerate the probability that they assigned to the likelihood of an event if it occurs and underestimate the probability that they assigned it if it does not. This is important in a number of ways. Firstly, it makes it imperative for us to rely on the material that people published in the period and to be cautious of subsequent interpretations of the warnings issued. Secondly, it helps to explain the apparent disinclination of many policymakers to learn from history. Hindsight bias perhaps encouraged decision-makers during the boom to assume that the fiscal choices made in the late 1970s were easily recognisable as being imprudent at the time, and that they themselves were unlikely to make similar errors. As Kahneman has suggested, 'The core of the illusion is that we believe we understand the past, which implies that the future also should be knowable, but in fact we understand the past less than we believe we do'. Lastly, an awareness of the impact of hindsight bias should make us very wary of lambasting analysts who declined to predict the future. The 2008 crisis seems to have been so obvious in

[41] Lunn, 'The Role of Decision-Making Biases in Ireland's Banking Crisis' (2011), 6 and Shiller, 'Long-Term Perspectives on the Current Boom in Home Prices' (2006), 1–2.

retrospect precisely because it definitively proved that such deep recessions can still happen to advanced economies in the modern world.[42]

Shiller also has some interesting observations about the potential role of behavioural influences. There is no definitive way of calculating what the fundamental value of residential property should be, and many market participants spend little time thinking about whether prices are justifiable. In such ambiguous situations the evidence is that buyers will instead reach for whatever anchor is available, generally the most recently remembered price. The role of narrative-based decision-making is crucial, and buyers will often determine that prices are justifiable on the basis of a plausible story rather than a quantitative assessment. The Irish discourse of the period is replete with examples of this, with commentators regularly pointing to demographic influences without actually calculating the impact that one would expect these to have in quantitative terms. As Shiller argues, 'the likelihood of any event affecting market prices is enhanced if there is a good, vivid, tellable story about the event'. To this end the radical transformation of the Irish economy and society over the preceding decade offered a wonderful, emotionally charged story.[43]

7 Political and Institutional Explanations

In keeping with their terms of reference, the banking and Wright reports focused heavily on the institutional shortcomings of the Financial Regulator, the Central Bank and the Department of Finance. However, fiscal policy, bank regulation and the banking system were also clearly heavily influenced by political forces. The absence to date of an officially commissioned investigation into the role of politics in informing flawed policy during the boom has been conspicuous, the parliamentary Banking Inquiry notwithstanding. This section will consider the regulatory environment in which the banks operated, the institutional incentives that they faced and the political and broader societal factors that shaped both.

[42] Kahneman, *Thinking Fast and Slow* (2011), 201–203 and Lunn, 'The Role of Decision-Making Biases in Ireland's Banking Crisis' (2011), 10.

[43] Shiller, *Irrational Exuberance* (2000), 135, 137–140, 161 and For examples see 156, 270.

7.1 *Banking and Bank Regulation*

The banking reports focused significantly on the resource limitations and the lack of professional scepticism that hindered the efficacy of the Financial Regulator. There is a marked difference of opinion between Honohan and Regling and Watson over which was the fatal weakness, with the former report suggesting that the regulator could not have been effective with its level of staffing and the latter contending that it was a question of insight rather than bodies. In a similar vein, Rob Wright has pointed to the marked skills shortfall that existed in the Department of Finance, with just 39 economists trained to postgraduate level out of 542 staff (7%), compared to 40% in Holland or 60% in Canada. However, efforts to explain the analytical shortcomings of the Irish authorities by reference to their particular staffing and skills deficiencies go only so far given that the IMF and international ratings agencies also deemed the Irish banks to be robust. Furthermore, no external economists or agencies raised concern about the reliance of the Irish banks on wholesale funding prior to Patrick Honohan in 2006, despite the fact that the extent of their aggregate exposure had been published in the Central Bank's FSRs (Financial Stability Reports) from 2004. A number of countries with large teams of highly trained economists showed comparable complacency at the same time. If the Irish authorities were impeded by limited insight and scepticism, they were far from alone. In this case the reports do seem to have missed the central point: the skills and staffing deficiencies of the Irish authorities can go some way towards explaining why the Irish crisis was worse than those experienced elsewhere, but the fact that it was in the context of a widespread regulatory failure across Europe and the USA suggests that the core problem was more universal, and emanated from prevalent fundamental misconceptions about asset and financial markets.[44]

The genesis of the Financial Regulator had a pronounced impact on its institutional design. Calls for a regulatory body emanated from financial scandals like overcharging customers or assisting clients in tax

[44] Honohan Commission, *The Irish Banking Crisis* (2010), 66; Regling and Watson, *A Preliminary Report on the Sources of Ireland's Banking Crisis* (2010), 6, 38; Nyberg Commission, *Misjudging Risk* (2011), 63; Rob Wright et al., *Strengthening the Capacity of the Department of Finance: Report of the Independent Review Panel* (2010), 44; Independent Evaluation Office of the IMF (IEO), *IMF Performance in the Run-Up to the Financial and Economic Crisis* (2011), 21; and For the IMF's FSAP.

evasion, rather than stability concerns. Once established in 2003, the authority reflected these priorities, doing relatively little about prudential risk but acting energetically on consumer issues. Tellingly, just 15% of the authority's resources were allocated to prudential banking supervision. While the McDowell Commission had recommended the establishment of an independent regulator, officials within the Central Bank and the Department of Finance were concerned that this would diminish the authority of the Bank. The Regulator was thus the product of political compromise, a 'sister organisation' of the Central Bank with its own board, but located within the offices of the Bank and unable to act on stability concerns without the permission of its Governor.[45]

The worldview and priorities of political decision-makers evidently influenced the behaviour of the regulatory authorities. Honohan has observed that the popularity of senior Anglo staff in political circles was not lost on management within the Financial Regulator. In turn, he has also suggested that line staff within the Regulator would have been cognisant of the fact that intrusive demands could be set aside on the basis of appeals by bankers to senior officials within their own ranks. The diffidence that was exhibited in the face of regulatory breaches is striking, and no sanction was imposed on any institution prior to the crisis. Also significant is the availability of powerful instruments that the Regulator had at its disposal to curb the rate of credit expansion and concentration. Perhaps most inexplicable was its failure to address the fact that four of the six major institutions had exceeded the regulatory limits dictating the proportion of their loans that could go to property and construction. Remarkably, the enforcement of these limits alone would have reduced the risk-weighted exposure of the banks to Irish property by €62 billion.[46]

Nyberg rightly asserts that the losses incurred by each financial institution in proportion to its size reflect the level of prudence with which it engaged during the boom. By this measure Bank of Ireland conducted itself much more carefully than its competitors. While the public

[45] Donovan and Murphy, *The Fall of the Celtic Tiger* (2013), 82; Nyberg Commission, *Misjudging Risk* (2011), viii; Taylor, 'Politics of the Galway Tent' (2011), 601–602; and Honohan Commission, *The Irish Banking Crisis* (2010), 37, 63–64.

[46] Honohan Commission, *The Irish Banking Crisis* (2010), 9, 12, 17, 54, 105–111; Nyberg Commission, *Misjudging Risk* (2011), iv, 54, 64; and Lyons and Carey, *The Fitzpatrick Tapes* (2011), 193–194, 258.

discourse has focused on the impact of greed on the part of bankers, another key influence was the fear of predatory takeover by competitors, both domestic and foreign. Both AIB and Bank of Ireland viewed Anglo as a major threat to market share. Crucially then, in the pillar banks the adoption of more aggressive strategies partially stemmed from a drive to conserve and safeguard what they already had. This goes some way towards explaining why such traditionally conservative banks acted so uncharacteristically. The exposure of Anglo staff and directors to the bank's equities suggests that there was minimal internal appreciation of the nature or extent of the risks involved for even that institution.[47]

In a similar vein to Taylor, Calomiris and Haber argue that to blame the failings of individuals within financial institutions or regulatory authorities for the shortcomings of the banking system is to miss the point, and that the ultimate causes are the institutional rules under which banks operate. These institutions themselves are the predictable products of implicit and explicit political bargains, and determine whether the banking system is designed to optimise either market outcomes or the outcomes for special interests. If financial crises were random events, or primarily attributable to the shortcomings of individuals rather than institutions, one would expect them to be relatively evenly distributed across different countries. This is clearly far from the case. Some countries, such as the USA, suffer routine banking crises while others essentially avoid them entirely, notably Canada. In the past 180 years the USA has suffered 14 major banking crises while Canada has suffered only two minor liquidity crises, both in the 1830s. At the other extreme, Argentina has suffered four crises since 1970. The balance for the state is to ensure both a plentiful supply of credit *and* a stable banking system. Just 6 of 117 countries sampled were considered to have achieved both criteria.[48]

Calomiris and Haber attribute the political choices made that shape national banking systems to a society's historical evolution. Again

[47]Nyberg Commission, *Misjudging Risk* (2011), v, 11, 21–24, 27, 35; Honohan, 'Resolving Ireland's Banking Crisis' (2009a), 2, 3, 5; and Lyons and Carey, *The Fitzpatrick Tapes* (2011), 42–43.

[48]Calomiris and Haber, *Fragile by Design* (2014), x, 3–6, 9–10, 13–20, 38 and Charles W. Calomiris and Stephen H. Haber, 'Why Banking Systems Succeed—And Fail: The Politics Behind Financial Institutions', *Foreign Affairs*, November/December 2013. Available from www.foreignaffairs.com. Accessed 24 September 2014.

however, no matter how strong the influence of history was on Irish decision-makers, including voters, they retained at least some capacity to transcend its impact. The Honohan Commission has suggested that there would have been a consumer backlash against regulatory action which restricted the mortgage products that the banks could offer, and that a 'reluctance to swim against the tide of public opinion' played a significant part in discouraging intervention. In this respect, much of broader society played a critical role, both as market participants and as voters in terms of the demands made of the regulatory system that betrayed a marked lack of concern for financial stability. There is a balance to be struck between recognising the influence of historical and ideological forces on banking regulation and ensuring that we do not absolve individuals of all responsibility.[49]

7.2 Politics and Fiscal Policy

One of the conspicuous conclusions of the Wright Report was that the budgetary process during the boom was 'completely overwhelmed' by successive Programmes for Government and the Social Partnership Process. The proposals made by the Department of Finance in the June Memoranda were often significantly amended in order to incorporate political objectives. Informing the strong political commitment to both agenda was the belief of successive Governments that the buoyant revenue from the construction and property boom should be distributed across the population, a commitment that was at least partially informed by electoral considerations. The boom placed the Ahern administrations in the unusual position of being able to please most of the electorate most of the time. The key problem, of course, was the use of unsustainable revenue to fund permanent increases in current expenditure outflows.[50]

Measures to reduce income tax and increase social spending were in keeping with what many Governments do during a boom. However, these efforts to benefit the broader population were accompanied by

[49] Calomiris and Haber, *Fragile by Design* (2014), x; Calomiris and Haber (2013), 'Why Banking Systems Succeed—And Fail'; and Honohan Commission, *The Irish Banking Crisis* (2010), 107.

[50] Wright et al., 'Strengthening the Capacity of the Department of Finance' (2010), 5 and Donovan and Murphy, *The Fall of the Celtic Tiger* (2013), 112, 114, 136.

much more targeted initiatives, a function of the readiness of politicians to meet the demands of interest groups. The bias in the tax system in favour of homeownership was essentially unparalleled in the OECD and benefitted one section of the population at the cost of another. Remarkably, by 2005 the cost to the Exchequer of tax reliefs and exemptions had grown to exceed the total amount of income tax actually collected. Such exemptions amounted to over three times the EU average, and their often ad hoc and opaque introduction betrayed significant lobbyist influence.[51]

8 Prediction

In this brief final section, we will consider the predictive capacities of economists and other experts. There is considerable evidence to suggest that in several crucial spheres predicting the future is far more difficult than is generally believed. Philip Tetlock collected thousands of predictions from 284 experts across 58 countries over fourteen years. The participants were drawn from a wide array of institutions, including academia, research institutes, Government service and international agencies. They were asked to forecast political, economic and national security outcomes between 1988 and 2003. The accuracy of the expert forecasters was found to be remarkably poor by comparison with that of formal statistical models. Tetlock takes discernible pleasure in comparing it to the predictive performance of a dart-throwing chimp. The predictive capacity of participants was similar across disciplines, with economists, political scientists and historians all demonstrating equally poor results. Even more unsettlingly, experts were no better at making accurate forecasts in their areas of specialisation than well-informed amateurs. Nor was there any correlation between performance and years of experience. While this line of argument could be interpreted as an attempt to absolve experts of responsibility for failing to anticipate the crash, it is a double-edged sword in that it should serve to severely undermine the credence given to the predictions made by expert economists in the future.[52]

[51] Donovan and Murphy, *The Fall of the Celtic Tiger* (2013), 120–123, 141.

[52] Philip E. Tetlock, *Expert Political Judgement: How Good Is It? How Can We Know?* (Princeton, 2005), 20, 44–46, 51, 54–55, 68, 118.

In view of the inherent difficulty in forecasting economic events, we should take a sympathetic view of commentators who declined to predict how the Irish boom would end. That almost nobody successfully anticipated the nature and scale of the crash is likely in keeping with what we should expect. Correspondingly, however, this line of argument tends to make the position of those who confidently made unduly sanguine predictions doubly uncomfortable. Galbraith concluded that one of the pregnant lessons of 1929 'is that very specific and personal misfortune awaits those who presume to believe that the future is revealed to them'.[53]

9 Conclusion

The core vulnerabilities of the Irish economy in the period were the reliance on construction and property activity for tax revenue and employment, and the exposure of the banks to the fortunes of these sectors. It is important to reemphasise that an appreciation on the part of some analysts of the unsustainability of house prices did therefore not equate to predicting a deep recession. The international and national agencies were quite prescient in pointing out the potential for residential property price falls, and there was an enormous amount written on the subject. By contrast, there was far less consideration given to the prospects of the construction sector and the potential ramifications for the macroeconomy. When the formal organisations did incorporate falls in construction activity into their models, their 'worst-case' scenarios were unjustifiably benign. The key to recognising the threat that faced the Irish economy was an understanding of the fact that construction output could fall to or below its historical level, and an appreciation of the attendant implications for the banks, the Exchequer and employment.

However, the evidence presented in this chapter should provide a significant caveat against the assumption that predicting the future was easy. The history of asset bubbles suggests that a widespread correct anticipation of how the boom would end was far from to be expected. Correspondingly, to critique the analysis of the Irish economy in the period on the basis that commentators were unable to accurately predict

[53] Kahneman, *Thinking Fast and Slow* (2011), 240; Skidelsky, *Keynes: The Return of the Master* (2010), 90; and Galbraith, *The Great Crash 1929* (2009), 205.

the future is to set the bar unreasonably high. Much of the focus of our analysis in subsequent chapters will be to determine whether commentators were accurately observing what was happening to the economy and whether their reasoning was coherent. Illogical or unsubstantiated arguments are open to criticism irrespective of time and even if their proponents arrived at the right conclusions.

This shifts the goalposts less than one might imagine. Recognising bubbles for what they are is on the evidence a tall order in itself, even without attempting to predict when or how they will end. By its nature an asset boom requires widespread societal exuberance insofar as price increases depend on buyer confidence. The fact that economic history is replete with examples of bubbles therefore suggests that it is equally characterised by populations who failed to recognise them and policy-makers who failed to act. We should thus be inclined to give at least some leeway to contemporary analysts. However, as discussed above, those who confidently anticipated a benign future seem to stand at the intersection point of two firing squads.

The widespread tendency to blame classical theories for encouraging the mistakes of the period has its justifications, but in the Irish case we must be careful. People like Alan Greenspan or Ben Bernanke held enormous power over the US economy and were deeply committed to free market ideologies. Classical theory encouraged Greenspan to keep interest rates low in the face of enormous asset price and credit growth. It also informed his support for the financial deregulation drive over several decades. By contrast, it seems likely that in Ireland the advocates of financial deregulation who held positions of power were by and large not directly influenced by the works of free market theorists and formative intellectual relationships with libertarian ideologues. Claims about the way that markets and economies worked were routinely substantiated with appeals to recent Irish experience, or rather how it was perceived. This clearly does not mean that the internationally prevailing theories played no role, since Irish commentators could have assimilated the accepted wisdoms from abroad without being explicit advocates of the formal theories from which they emanated. As discussed, theories gain traction only if they resonate with the world as people have witnessed it. Conversely, the propensity of people to accept or reject the lessons of historical episodes is heavily determined by their ideological biases and assumptions. These can be embraced even by those who are not explicitly convinced by the theories from which they first emanated, through what Keynes termed 'the gradual encroachment of ideas'.[54]

Much of the material written by economic theorists and historians suggests that the assumption that the world has changed does not arrive without any substantiation, but will come after a period of prolonged stability. What is striking about the recent boom is that the international evidence was so clearly stacked against the contention that asset and financial markets had graduated to a more benign plateau. Irish and international commentators and populations showed a decided disinclination to learn from the mistakes of others, even in neighbouring countries. Personal experience of a perceived long period of unabated rising property prices evidently carried much more weight in informing intuitive conclusions.

However, even recent Irish history carried ample evidence that property prices could fall. The 27% fall in real house prices in the 1980s and the five consecutive months of falls after the bursting of the dotcom bubble were both episodes which should have helped to soften the popular conviction that property was one-way bet. That these falls were so largely brushed over and quickly forgotten in the national discourse is telling of its own accord. There seems to be little memory of them even today. Similarly, the fact that policymakers had first-hand memory of a bank bailout and a fiscal crisis did little to encourage caution because the 1980s was considered to have been something of a bygone age. The extent to which Irish policymakers and the public succumbed to the boom was therefore a function not only of limited relevant past experience, but also of a tendency to dismiss or forget the instructive experience that they did have. More precisely then, the key determinant in informing complacency was not historical experience but how it was perceived and remembered. Irish policymakers have the unenviable record of steering the economy into two depressions within a generation. The need to pursue more prudent fiscal policy is a conspicuous lesson from both episodes. Another striking lesson from the recent crash is that rather than reactively dismissing criticism and the relevance of the past, decision-makers should be eager to consider all of the warnings they can get. It is equally critical to pay due heed to the experiences of other countries since there is no reason to assume that the next crisis will resemble the last one.

[54]John Maynard Keynes, *The General Theory of Employment, Interest and Money* (BN Publishing, 2008), 239.

CHAPTER 3

International Organisations

If you are out of trouble, watch for danger.
Sophocles, *Philoctetes*

1 Introduction

The IMF has suggested that the primary purpose of its surveillance was arguably to warn member countries about domestic vulnerabilities and threats to the international economy. It seems reasonable to assume that this was also a core function of the surveillance by the OECD (Organisation for Economic Cooperation and Development) and the European Commission (EC), and to evaluate their performance on this basis. The formal international agencies were highly-influential contributors to the discourse on the Irish economy, and were regularly invoked by proponents of prevailing policy. Bertie Ahern went so far as to claim that he was more concerned about the opinion of the IMF than with 'all the criticisms of Opposition finance spokespersons'. It is therefore clear that unduly benign analyses by the international organisations were likely to be harmful rather than useless. A sanguine forecast for the Irish economy from an esteemed international agency could bolster the conviction

C. M. Casey, *Policy Failures and the Irish Economic Crisis*,
https://doi.org/10.1007/978-3-319-90182-4_3

of key policymakers, while also providing them with a powerful rebuttal to dissenting voices.[1]

For our purposes, the most important regular publications by the international agencies were the IMF's 'Staff Country Reports' (generally referred to as the 'Article IV Consultations'), their accompanying 'Selected Issues Papers', and the OECD's 'Economic Surveys'. The process in both cases was that agency analysts would travel to Ireland and meet with key officials before compiling their reports. The IMF's Article IV Consultations were sometimes quite frank about disagreements between Irish officials and agency staff, which gives them a rather unique dimension and adds some welcome colour. Significantly, the Fund also published two analyses of the stability of the Irish financial system under its 'Financial Sector Assessment Programme' (FSAP), in 2000 and 2006. The EC published far less than the other two organisations. This was most likely in keeping with its mandate, but as a result we will focus primarily on the IMF and OECD. This chapter is based on all of the relevant reports on the Irish economy by the three organisations from 2000 to 2006, which are outlined in Table 1.[2]

The comparative expertise of international analysts vis-à-vis domestic authorities was clearly important, and the Fund has observed that its missions were often slow to challenge the consensus held by large numbers of highly-qualified economists in large, advanced economies. This was presumably less of a factor in Ireland, and Michael Breen has suggested that the Department of Finance was beset by skill-set shortages relative to the Fund. Nonetheless, IMF analysts surveyed after the international crash maintained that the incentives facing them had not encouraged harsh criticism of national policies, particularly since they could not

[1]This chapter is derived, in part, from an article published in the Economic and Social Review. See Ciarán Michael Casey, 'Averting Crisis? Commentary from the International Institutions on the Irish Property Sector in the Years Before the Crash', in *Economic and Social Review* vol. 45, no. 4 (Winter 2014), 537–557. Independent Evaluation Office of the IMF, *IMF Performance in the Run-Up to the Financial and Economic Crisis: IMF Surveillance in 2004–2007* (Washington: IMF, 2011), vii; *Dáil Eireann Debate 2002*, vol. 554, no. 5: Private Members' Business—Public Finances: Motion, Charlie McCreevy, 9 October 2002; *Dáil Eireann Debate 2003*, vol. 576, no. 3: Financial Resolutions 2003—Financial Resolution No. 5: General (Resumed), Bertie Ahern, 4 December 2003; and *Dáil Eireann Debate 2006*, vol. 620, no. 101: Priority Questions—House Prices, Brian Cowen, 23 May 2006.

[2]The IMF has been unable to provide the 2000 FSAP Report. Key findings are summarised in the Staff Country Reports and in the 2006 Report.

Table 1 International organisations—Key publications

Key publications by the IMF, OECD and European Commission									
Title	*1999*	*2000*	*2001*	*2002*	*2003*	*2004*	*2005*	*2006*	*Total*
OECD									
Economic Surveys	1		1		1			1	4
Economic Outlooks		2	2	2	2	2	2	2	14
Working Papers								1	1
IMF									
Staff Country Reports		1	1	1	1	1	1	1	7
Selected Issues		1		1		1	1		4
FSAP Reports (FSSA)								1	1
European Commission									
Public Finances in the EMU		1	1	1	1	1	1	1	7
Economic Forecasts		2	2	2	2	2	2	2	14
EcFin Country Focus						1		1	2

rely on the support of their own executive board. Less than half of staff reported that they considered that their opinions had been listened to by national authorities.[3]

The single biggest obstruction to frank analysis in the publications by the formal international organisations was paradoxically a result of the widespread esteem they enjoyed. It was feared that warnings of an imminent crash by any of the big agencies could have been self-fulfilling, and the IMF has observed that analysts had to walk a very fine line. For the same reason the Irish authorities exercised significant editorial control over what could be published. Tom O'Connell, as former Chief Economist at the Central Bank, has recounted parsing through the OECD's reports line-by-line to tone down any negative conclusions. A memorandum leaked to *The Irish Times* in 2005 documented that OECD analysts privately warned Central Bank officials that Irish house prices were overvalued by 15%. The predictable reaction from the Irish officials was to insist that such findings should only be published 'with extreme caution to avoid destabilising the market'. The incident helps to

[3]Michael Breen, 'IMF Surveillance of Ireland During the Celtic Tiger', *Irish Political Studies*, vol. 27, no. 3 (2012), 434 and IMF, *IMF Performance in the Run-Up to the Financial and Economic Crisis* (2011), 17, 35.

explain the rather ungainly conclusion in the OECD's 2006 Economic Survey, that 80–90% of price increases had been justified by the fundamentals, with the remainder memorably described as 'speculative froth'.[4]

The key benefit of the commentary from the IMF and OECD was that their analysts had international experience that could help inform their interpretations of the Irish economy. This clearly had a positive impact, particularly in terms of the international precedents for the Irish housing and construction booms. While the external organisations could also bring a fresh perspective to the discourse on the Irish economy this had its limits. Although it is perfectly understandable, it is quite clear from the contemporary reports that the international agencies relied heavily on research conducted by Irish analysts, and were thus exposed to their assumptions and misconceptions. One also would have expected the international analysts to be at a greater emotional remove from the Irish situation, and thus to be more dispassionate in their commentary. However, the international agencies were clearly heavily-invested in the Irish success story, and the IMF explicitly lauded Ireland as an example of what a country could do if it followed policies in keeping with the Fund's advice.[5]

There is a final important point to consider before turning to an analysis of the publications themselves. Joe Lee has argued that international reports on the Irish economy cannot offer a cut-price substitute for home-grown analysis. This view is corroborated by the analysis provided by the international agencies in the millennial period, and these contributions certainly should have been treated as complementary to domestic analysis. Since international economists were only assigned to studying the Irish economy for part of the year, they were inevitably unable to devote the same level of intellectual energy to interrogating prevailing assumptions about its trajectory. This was further exacerbated by the fact that the personnel comprising the IMF missions changed from

[4]IMF, 'IMF Performance in the Run-Up to the Financial and Economic Crisis' (2011), 35; Houses of the Oireachtas, *Joint Committee of Inquiry into the Banking Crisis*, vol. 2, no. 26, Tom O'Connell, 10 June 2015, 84; Houses of the Oireachtas, *Joint Committee of Inquiry into the Banking Crisis*, vol. 2, no. 33, John McCarthy, 24 June 2015, 6–7, 9–10; Emmet Oliver, 'OECD Believes Irish Property Market Over-Valued by 15%', *The Irish Times*, 7 November 2005, 1; and OECD, *Economic Surveys: Ireland, 2006* (2006), 123.

[5]IMF, *Ireland: Staff Report for the 2005 Article IV Consultation (IMF Staff Country Report No. 5/369)* (Washington: IMF, 2005), 3, 7, 8, 11.

year to year. Crucially, there was also the risk that analysts could apply a standardised model or stress-test that was inappropriate to Irish circumstances, with very far-reaching consequences.[6]

2 Competitiveness

Ireland was feted as the model of an economic success story by all three organisations from the late 1990s. The OECD described it as astonishing 'that a nation could have moved all the way from the back of the pack to a leading position within such a short period'. The genesis of the boom was attributed to a combination of good choices and structural advantages, including the decision to the join the European Union, the atypical baby boom of the 1970s, and above all the success in attracting investment from US multinationals. The IMF also rightly appreciated the role played by a certain degree of luck. Somewhat unsurprisingly, the EC tended to focus on the importance of factors like the disciplining effect of EU membership, increased inward investment within the single market, EU structural funds, and lower interest rates secured through monetary union.[7]

The international organisations were quite cognisant of Ireland's deteriorating cost competitiveness and the problems posed by high inflation. The OECD returned to this again and again, pointing to excessive wage increases that were unjustified by productivity improvements, particularly in sheltered sectors like construction. It also blamed the 'poorly timed fiscal expansion' at the start of the decade for exacerbating the collapse in export growth. By 2005 the IMF observed that the damage had been done, and that Ireland's cost base had risen to levels above those of its main trading partners. To compound the problem, the Fund was also markedly sceptical of the apparently enormous productivity gains attributed to Irish labour, arguing that these were in large part the effect of

[6] J.J. Lee, *Ireland: 1912–1985, Politics and Society* (Cambridge, 1989), 624.

[7] OECD, *Economic Surveys: Ireland* (OECD, 1999), 10–12; IMF, *Ireland: Staff Report for the 2000 Article IV Consultation (IMF Staff Country Report No. 0/97)* (Washington: IMF, 2000), 5–7, 13, 22; IMF, *Ireland: Staff Report for the 2002 Article IV Consultation (IMF Staff Country Report No. 2/170)* (Washington: IMF, 2002), 3, 9, 10, 12, 24; and Zdeněk Čech and John Macdonald, 'The 'Celtic Tiger' Learns to Purr', *EcFin Country Focus*, vol. 1, no. 18 (European Commission, 2004), 1–2.

multinational investment in research, product development and advertising. Nonetheless, both organisations were also notably inconsistent in their warnings. In 2004 the Fund discounted falling competitiveness as a major risk since Ireland's industrial export share had apparently stabilised. In 2006 the OECD partially backtracked on its warnings about wage increases, suggesting that they were somewhat justified by productivity gains, as evidenced by a falling wage share.[8]

The warnings issued about Ireland's competitiveness losses were also tempered by the fact that both organisations believed the Irish economy to be fundamentally strong throughout the period. The IMF considered Ireland's performance in the wake of the global downturn in 2001 to be indicative of the inherent robustness of its economy and the flexibility of its workforce, and crucially to vindicate its policy approach. In 2005 the Fund went so far as to take partial credit for the country's continued success, arguing that 'Ireland's impressive economic performance since the early 1990s reflects in significant measure the implementation of sound policies consistent with Fund advice'. This propensity to treat the Irish success story as a vindication of the Fund's worldview was crucial. If economic progress emanated 'in significant measure' from the pursuit of IMF-approved policies then analysts were presumably less likely to admonish Ireland's approach so long as it continued to implement the same policies, even if the economic context had fundamentally changed.[9]

The OECD similarly perceived the Irish economy as being fundamentally robust throughout the period, observing in 2006 that 'Ireland has continued its exemplary economic performance'. Remarkably, the

[8]OECD, *Economic Surveys: Ireland, 2006* (2006), 8, 10, 20, 23, 46; OECD, *Economic Surveys: Ireland, 1999* (1999), 5; OECD, *OECD Economic Outlook, Volume 2003, Issue 1* (OECD, 2003), 81–84; OECD, *OECD Economic Outlook, Volume 2002, Issue 2* (OECD, 2002), 83, 84; IMF, *Ireland: Staff Report for the 2005 Article IV Consultation (IMF Staff Country Report No 5/369)* (Washington: IMF, 2005), 3, 7, 8, 11; IMF, *Staff Country Report, 2004* (2004), 1, 2, 6, 7, 10, 25; and IMF, *Ireland: Staff Report for the 2001 Article IV Consultation (IMF Staff Country Report No 1/139)* (Washington: IMF, 2001), 4, 10, 18, 31.

[9]IMF, *Selected Issues (IMF Staff Country Report No. 2/171)* (Washington: IMF, 2002), 7–10; IMF, *Ireland: Staff Report for the 2004 Article IV Consultation (IMF Staff Country Report No 4/348)* (Washington: IMF, 2004), 1, 2, 6, 7, 10, 25; IMF, *Staff Country Report, 2003* (2003), 4, 9, 12, 13, 25; and IMF, *Ireland: Staff Report for the 2005 Article IV Consultation (IMF Staff Country Report No 5/369)* (Washington: IMF, 2005), 3, 7, 8, 11.

organisation maintained the position that Irish economic fundamentals were strong right into 2008. Like the IMF, it attributed Ireland's apparent resilience in the face of the global slowdown to what it considered a sensible policy regime, including a business-friendly regulatory environment, moderate tax rates, and sound fiscal policy. Somewhat fatefully it also observed that 'a well-timed construction boom helped plug the gap nicely'.[10]

Summary
The IMF and the OECD approached the Irish economy with the assumption that its continued success reflected an intrinsic resilience and perhaps even an integral merit. This can be attributed in significant part to the fact that the Irish boom seemed to vindicate the economic philosophies of the two organisations, and they were keen to emphasise its low tax, pro-business, and open trade policies. Like many commentators, the two agencies recognised that inflation was making Ireland less competitive, but did not fundamentally re-evaluate their views of the nature of the economy. This was in part because many of the core indicators were still so positive, and under such circumstances it was easier for analysts to evolve their beliefs rather than radically change them. The two organisations therefore maintained a core positive concept of the Irish economy to which they tacked their reservations, rather than revising the concept itself on the basis of those misgivings. The economy was presented as being robust and booming, with marginal risks, rather than inherently vulnerable because of its high cost base.

3 Property and Construction

By far the most compelling contributions by the international organisations were their studies of the precedents for the Irish residential property and construction booms. In 2000 the IMF presented Irish policymakers with a study of almost forty housing booms over the preceding two decades. Though the Fund acknowledged that several European and US property booms of the 1990s were still underway or had been followed by soft landings, it suggested that the rate of increase in Ireland made it much more akin to the booms of the 1980s, nearly all of which

[10]OECD, *Economic Surveys: Ireland* (OECD, 2003), 9, 10, 21–4; OECD, *Economic Surveys: Ireland, 2006* (2006), 8, 10, 20, 46; and OECD, *Economic Surveys: Ireland, 2008* (2008), 8.

had ended badly. The authors likened the Irish experience to those of Hong Kong and Singapore, where prices had more than trebled over the course of a decade and were followed by very significant falls, suggesting that this 'may not necessarily be a source of comfort regarding the prospects for a soft landing in the Irish housing market'. The Fund observed that 'if property prices in Ireland were to level off without a significant fall, it would be an event unprecedented in the last 20 years. Of the nearly 40 episodes of high property price inflation examined here, there has not been a single experience of price inflation on the scale of Ireland's which did not end in prices falling'.[11]

At this juncture the Fund was clearly highly concerned about the prospects for the Irish housing market. While analysts did concede that that a price fall was not inevitable, this study of international precedent and the manner in which the conclusions were presented should probably be taken as the most explicit warning that they were able to issue in the public domain. Ireland was considered to have witnessed one of the highest rates of house-price inflation of the recent international episodes. The following extract should thus have resonated particularly with Irish policymakers:

> Comparing house price inflation during the boom with subsequent growth, it is clear that most high inflation episodes have been followed by price declines. There is a pronounced tendency for these declines to be larger the higher the growth during the boom. This is particularly true when ranking episodes by annual growth rates. Countries and regions experiencing booms comparable to Ireland's have all suffered sizable price declines; the most extreme case was Finland, where prices declined by 46 per cent in four years, but even excluding Finland, episodes characterised by real house price inflation of 14 per cent or more suffered on average a loss in the next four years of over 40 per cent of the cumulative price increase during the boom.[12]

[11] IMF, *Selected Issues and Statistical Appendix 2000* (2000), 23–27 and IMF, *Staff Country Report on Ireland, 2000* (2000), 16.

[12] IMF, *Selected Issues and Statistical Appendix 2000* (2000), 19, 27; IMF, 'IMF Performance in the Run-Up to the Financial and Economic Crisis' (2011), 35; and Houses of the Oireachtas, *Joint Committee of Inquiry into the Banking Crisis*, vol. 2, no. 26, Tom O'Connell, 10 June 2015, 84.

In its 2006 Economic Survey the OECD published a study of residential construction booms, tellingly entitled 'Has residential construction ever had a soft landing?'. The authors found that between 1960 and 2004 there had been 49 house building booms in 23 countries for which data were available. The ensuing downturns were usually very rapid, with an average of 40% of the trough to peak increase in residential investment lost in the first year, and another 40% lost in the second. In a remarkable paragraph the report asked:

> How common are soft landings? If a soft landing is defined as a relatively small reduction in the investment rate, they are not especially common. There have only been four cases where the decline in per capita investment has been smaller than one-third of the increase that occurred during the boom years (these are the Netherlands after 1978, Belgium after 1990, the United Kingdom after 1998 and Finland after 2000). Soft landings are more common if they are defined as gradual declines, i.e. where it takes at least three years to hit the trough. There have been around 20 examples of these. But all of these were comparatively deep declines. If a soft landing is defined as something that is both mild and gradual, there has not been a single case out of the 49 boom-bust cycles.[13]

The implications of this finding were critically important for Ireland. At this juncture residential construction accounted for some 13% of GNP compared to 4–6% prior to 1997, a level in keeping with other industrial countries. Historical precedent clearly suggested that a reversion to more typical levels was highly likely and could happen very rapidly. In a remarkable display of cognitive dissonance however, the worst-case scenario proposed by the same OECD Report for Ireland was that residential construction would fall by a third and cause a direct decline in GNP of 2 or 3% if it was accompanied by fiscal tightening. Furthermore, analysts suggested that a gradual fall-back rather than a decline of even that magnitude was the most likely outcome. The reason for the disparity is clear. Analysts estimated underlying demand for housing in Ireland to be 50–60,000 units per annum, and then treated this as the likely floor that output would fall to (representing a decline in the region of 40%). This of course completely flew in the face of the organisation's own study of how construction booms had ended in the past, with the most probable

[13]OECD, *Economic Surveys: Ireland, 2006* (2006), 37–38, 128.

scenario that investment in residential construction would fall close to its pre-boom level, when average output was approximately 23,000 units. Two possible explanations are either that the OECD shied away from making an overly-negative forecast for political reasons, or that the publication was a pronounced example of design by committee. There is no evidence that other commentators on the Irish economy recognised that the implication of the historical study was that a construction collapse was highly likely and would have a very significant impact on GNP within a short timeframe. Similarly, the OECD continued to predict a 'soft landing' for the Irish housing market, missing the lessons of the analysis conducted on house price booms by the IMF, just as it failed to apply the lessons of its own analysis on the recent history of construction booms.[14]

The IMF and OECD were very vocal in their recommendations on housing policy throughout the period, and were quite prepared to criticise Government decisions. This is another example of where their international perspectives proved useful, and the two organisations were well-placed to appreciate how unusual Irish housing policy actually was. The Irish tax regime for owner-occupied housing was considered unique in the OECD, since it allowed households to deduct mortgage interest against income tax, while simultaneously not taxing property values, capital gains, or imputed rent. Analysts were evidently concerned about the role played by these advantages in driving up prices, and urged policymakers to expose homeowners to higher costs by phasing out 'the strong bias towards housing that is embedded in the tax system'. In particular, the policy of not taxing capital gains on owner-occupied homes was singled out as a possible 'catalyst for the upward spiral'.[15]

The OECD was cognisant of the fact that the house price boom was a zero-sum game, benefitting current homeowners at the expense of first-time buyers. Analysts also pointed to the large capital gains achieved by some landowners as a result of rezoning and of major infrastructural investment by the state, arguing that part of these windfalls should have

[14] Government of Ireland, *2006 Annual Housing Statistics Bulletin* (Dublin, 2007), 36; Kelly, 'The Irish Credit Bubble (2009)', 13; OECD, *Economic Surveys: Ireland, 2006* (2006), 8, 16–17, 36–38, 43; and Housing completions data from www.cso.ie. Accessed 5 November 2015.

[15] OECD, *Economic Surveys: Ireland, 1999* (1999), 19 and OECD, *Economic Surveys: Ireland, 2006* (2006), 119, 121, 126, 129, 131.

been taxed in order to help fund the infrastructure that had created the gains in the first place.[16]

Both organisations were highly critical of erratic policy choices that they blamed for distorting the market and fuelling price increases, with the IMF particularly unreserved in this regard. The Fund argued that price increases had decelerated sharply after 1998, with the introduction of market-calming measures recommended by the 'Bacon Reports'. Analysts believed that a soft landing had been achieved in the market, and pointed to five months of consecutive falls from September 2001. The Fund then explicitly blamed the 2002 decision to reverse the Bacon measures for inciting the resurgence in prices. Crucially, it added that any measures introduced to postpone the adjustment of prices would increase the risk of a sharper decrease down the line. Highly unusually, and in an indication of the ire provoked by the reversal of the Bacon measures, analysts even quoted Charlie McCreevy's speech introducing the 1998 changes, presumably with a view to highlighting the inconsistency:

> ... the package of measures announced last Thursday will help restore balance to the housing market. It will also help to remove another significant factor that has been fuelling price escalation, namely the expectation or- depending on one's perspective- fear of further price increases.[17]

A particularly relevant divergence of opinion between the IMF and the Irish authorities was the Fund's view that the propensity of the public to buy property was a strong argument against the state subsidising housing through a favourable tax regime. In a quote that perhaps explains much of the basis of Irish housing policy in the period, the mission reported that 'the authorities noted the political, likely insurmountable, difficulties of removing interest-deductibility of mortgages or introducing taxation on property given the electorate's long history of strong attachment to, and preference for owning, property'. The result of this rather perverse

[16]OECD, *Economic Surveys: Ireland, 2006* (2006), 126, 129, 131.

[17]IMF, *Staff Country Report, 2003* (2003), 16; IMF, *Ireland: Public Information Notice on the Executive Board Discussion for the 2002 Article IV Consultation (IMF Public Information Notice 2/83)* (Washington: IMF, 2002), 2; IMF, *Selected Issues, 2004* (2004), 32, 33; OECD, *Economic Surveys: Ireland, 2001* (2001), 11, 12; and OECD, *Economic Surveys: Ireland, 2006* (2006), 119, 121.

logic was that a favourable tax regime for homeowners was maintained *because* of high demand for housing, with policymakers exacerbating the problem and expressly rejecting the IMF advice because it would have been politically unpopular.[18]

We have already touched on the dependence of the international organisations on analysis conducted by Irish commentators. Although this was unavoidable, it did dilute the detachment of IMF and OECD analysts from the domestic discourse. A prominent example was the OECD's heavy reliance on the first Bacon Report on housing, which was commissioned by the Irish Government in 1998. In particular, Bacon's emphasis on the need to increase supply and reduce investor demand framed much of the discussion. Nonetheless, the international agencies clearly recognised some of the limitations of Bacon's approach, and both expressly regretted the fact that structurally-transformative items like a property tax or water and sewage charges had been left off the policy agenda.[19]

The two organisations did consider two key issues that should have alerted them to the precariousness of the Irish housing market, namely rents and vacancy rates, but did not extrapolate anything like the extent of the problem. By the end of the period both agencies took the view that a soft landing was the most likely outcome, even if they did acknowledge the possibility of a more deleterious scenario. The IMF's changed position in this regard is highly significant, and a point we will return to. The Fund was concerned that rental yields were falling in tandem with increasing house prices and construction output. The OECD subsequently contended that the number of vacant dwellings had risen by 80,000 units between 2000 and 2003, which it suggested represented half of all the new units built in the period. While the numbers here should be treated with a degree of scepticism, the phenomena of falling rental yields and increasing vacancy levels were clearly interlinked, and should have prompted a radical re-evaluation of the Irish housing boom. The clear implication was that a very significant proportion of the demand for houses was not underpinned by any fundamental demographic need. Factors like natural population growth, falling household

[18]IMF, *Staff Country Report, 2004* (2004), 19, 20, 26 and IMF, *Staff Country Report, 2006* (2006), 3, 11–13.

[19]OECD, *Economic Surveys: Ireland, 1999* (1999), 76–77, 103–106 and IMF, *Staff Country Report on Ireland, 2000* (2000), 31.

sizes, and immigration alone could not explain what was happening. Both organisations did point to speculative demand as a factor, but should have been far more cognisant of its significance, and consequentially the extent to which prices could fall.[20]

In terms of their estimates of the extent to which house prices were overvalued the IMF clearly outperformed the OECD. As we have seen, the latter's estimate was in the region of 10–20%. However, *The Economist* pointed to a critical problem with the applicability of a key OECD model to the Irish market. Ireland presented an unusual case because it enjoyed very low interest rates and a very high proportion of variable mortgages. The OECD assessed whether prices were appropriate on the basis of affordability, but because of these features a small interest rate change could have an enormous impact. Remarkably, a rate increase of just one percentage point could increase the estimated overvaluation of Irish prices to 50%. This was patently a major caveat to the model, and one that the OECD should have been far more proactive about establishing in its publications on Ireland. The IMF was clearly much more concerned, and crucially warned that the overvaluation could be as much as 50% from 2003. The finding received significant attention from other commentators, though conspicuously was published in an annex to the main report. While the Fund did recognise that an abrupt unwinding of the housing market constituted a risk to the broader economy, analysts were clearly curtailed in how they could address the issue. In what could be perceived as an implied dig at other commentators, staff also suggested that it was far easier to justify Irish house price increases qualitatively rather than quantitatively.[21]

The Irish authorities were perceptibly defensive about the housing market, pointing to Ireland's low number of dwellings per capita, as well the fact that some commentators were justifying price levels by reference to supply-side factors like land and building costs. In a perfect example

[20]OECD, *Economic Surveys: Ireland, 2006* (2006), 126; IMF, *Staff Country Report on Ireland, 2000* (2000), 16, 23, 26, 31; IMF, *Selected Issues, 2004* (2004), 18–32; IMF, *Staff Country Report, 2005* (2005), 3, 11; and IMF, *Ireland: Financial System Stability Assessment Update (IMF Country Report No. 6/292)* (Washington: IMF, 2006), 13.

[21]OECD, *Economic Surveys: Ireland, 2006* (2006), 123–126; IMF, *Staff Country Report, 2003* (2003), 14, 28; IMF, *Selected Issues (IMF Staff Country Report No. 4/171)* (Washington: IMF, 2004), 16, 25–28; and IMF, *Staff Country Report on Ireland, 2000* (2000), 3, 11, 23.

of a qualitative rationalisation of prices, the authorities also pointed to the Irish predilection for homeownership. Unsurprisingly, IMF staff were unconvinced, particularly in view of the rapidly increasing levels of supply. The 2006 report was unusually frank in detailing the divergence of opinion between the IMF mission and the Irish authorities. Staff from the Fund considered prices to be overvalued, Central Bank staff considered them to be becoming somewhat overvalued, and Department of Finance officials deemed them to be in line with fundamentals. What all parties could agree on was that by this juncture construction activity rather than house prices posed the key risk. The Fund had been openly concerned about the size of the sector since 2004, warning that it represented some 12% of GNP compared to 5% in the US and 3% in the UK. While the Irish authorities were evidently encouraged by the perceived flexibility of the labour force after the 2001 global downturn, the Fund declared its staff to be more 'agnostic' about the likelihood of a smooth redeployment of labour.[22]

Summary

The performance of the IMF and OECD in analysing the Irish property and construction booms was decidedly mixed. The organisations conducted remarkably pertinent and commendable studies of the relevant international precedents. The OECD's examination showed that when residential construction booms ended investment tended to revert to close to pre-boom levels over a very short period. The implications of such an eventuality for Ireland would clearly be enormous. However, the worst-case scenario that analysts proposed for the Irish residential construction sector was far more benign. No explanation was provided for the incongruity, and the upshot was that the OECD clearly presented the lessons of international experience but failed to properly apply them. Similarly, when the IMF investigated the recent history of house price booms it evidently prompted significant concern about the Irish market within the Fund. The observation that a benign outcome would be unprecedented was almost certainly as close to an explicit warning of a housing crash that analysts were able to publish. The agency's 2003 finding that house prices could be 50% over their fundamental values was also highly significant. In a remarkable turn-around however, the Fund

[22] IMF, *Staff Country Report, 2004* (2004), 3, 4, 7, 18–21, 26; IMF, *Staff Country Report, 2005* (2005), 11; IMF, *Staff Country Report, 2006* (2006), 4, 8, 9.

proposed in 2005 that a soft landing was the most likely outcome for the housing market. The disparity with its 2000 analysis was never justified, and at an institutional level the IMF had evidently forgotten or disregarded the lessons of its own study. The fact that there was no personnel-overlap between the two missions was almost certainly a key determining factor.[23]

The two organisations were very strong on the need to moderate demand by increasing the ongoing costs of homeownership. However, the OECD's methodology for assessing house price affordability and fundamental values evidently had limited applicability to the Irish context. If even a very modest increase in interest rates could completely change the results, then policymakers should have derived little comfort from the analysis. Conspicuously, the OECD did not pay adequate attention to this major caveat in its Irish publications, and likely encouraged undue complacency. Both organisations paid markedly little attention to the history of booms in commercial real estate prices, which represented a significant gap in their analyses.

4 The Financial Sector

The IMF and OECD were much less thorough in substantiating their views on the stability of the Irish banking system than they were in respect of the property market. The IMF has since suggested that its staff had less access to micro-level data than national authorities, but as the next chapter will demonstrate, analysts should have been cognisant of the extent of the risks to the Irish financial system on the basis of the aggregated data. As was so often the case in the period, commentators recognised many of the key risks without appreciating anything like the scale of the problem. The OECD was particularly brief in its treatment of the financial sector, and analysts did little more than reiterate the findings of the Central Bank's own stress tests. There is a strong argument to be made that the agency should either have committed to a thorough independent analysis of the financial system or else qualified its

[23] IMF, *Staff Country Report, 2000* (2000), 1 and IMF, *Staff Country Report, 2005* (2005), 1, 3, 11.

macroeconomic analyses on the basis that they relied on the accuracy of the financial sector assessments of other organisations.[24]

The IMF's regular publications certainly paid more attention to the financial sector than the OECD, and qualitatively recognised many of the worrying trends. These included a disproportionate concentration of lending to residential and commercial property and rapidly expanding credit to households. However, little further analysis was conducted in this regard, and the reports were too light on specifics to provoke a major clampdown by policymakers or spark much wider debate. The Fund only examined the Irish financial sector in any real depth in the reports published under its FSAP. As such, the 2006 FSAP report should be considered the key analysis of the Irish financial system published by the formal international organisations in the period. Crucially, the FSAP concluded that the sector would be well-placed to weather a potential economic downturn or a fall in house prices. Analysts also suggested that the liquidity risks to the sector seemed manageable, despite the fact that the Irish banks had the highest loan-to-deposit ratio in Western Europe and were correspondingly exposed to wholesale funding markets. The Honohan Report has suggested that such positive conclusions were sufficient to assuage internal concerns, which seems quite likely given that questions about Ireland's regulatory system had been rebutted on the basis of the positive conclusions of the previous FSAP report.[25]

The Fund's overly-sanguine view of the Irish banking system was primarily attributable to the questionable design of its stress tests. On the funding side analysts recognised that the sector's reliance on wholesale funding posed a liquidity risk, since wholesale markets represented a less stable funding source than deposits. However, the test applied was a 10% reduction in the amount that banks could raise by selling assets like debt securities or Government bonds. It is hardly surprising that the banks were found to have sufficient liquidity for such an event, and the

[24] Independent Evaluation Office of the IMF, *IMF Performance in the Run-Up to the Financial and Economic Crisis* (2011), 17 and OECD, *Economic Surveys: Ireland, 2006* (2006), 127.

[25] IMF, *Ireland: Financial System Stability Assessment Update (IMF Country Report No. 6/292)* (Washington: IMF, 2006), 1, 5, 16–17, 20–12; Patrick Honohan, *The Irish Banking Crisis: Regulatory and Financial Stability Policy 2003–2008. A Report to the Minister for Finance by the Governor of the Central Bank* (2010), 10, 91–92; and *Dáil Eireann Debate 2002*, vol. 553, no. 3, Central Bank and Financial Services Authority of Ireland Bill, 2002: Second Stage (Resumed), Charlie McCreevy, 19 June 2002.

test clearly set far too low a bar. Analysts should have paid much more attention to the effects of past fluctuations in the wholesale markets and designed the test explicitly on that basis. Such an approach would have made their assessment significantly more authoritative.[26]

In conjunction with the Irish Central Bank the IMF tested the financial sector for very significant house price falls. Crucially, it suggested that the system could potentially weather falls of 55% and a 10% default rate, figures strikingly close to what came to pass. Analysis by Karl Whelan has since suggested that the Fund's conclusion was correct, and that the banks could indeed have survived house price falls on this scale. The critical factor that analysts ignored was the exposure of the banks to the construction industry, which was of comparable magnitude to the exposure to housing by the time the crisis hit. The Fund's failure to consider the risks emanating from this concentration was likely attributable to the fact that analysts applied a standardised set of tests for typical risks, such as house prices and interest or exchange rate movements, rather than critically appraising the key exposures of the Irish banks and then designing the tests accordingly. Given that the FSAP team was only in Dublin for a fortnight the reasons for this are quite comprehensible, further corroborating the contention that external surveillance was no substitute for home-grown analysis. The Fund's finding that good progress had been made in strengthening the regulatory system on the back of the 2000 recommendations and that the financial system and regulatory framework were generally robust is highly significant. The logical implication is that Irish regulatory policy was largely in keeping with advice from the IMF, which must consequently bear a proportion of the blame for its evident failure.[27]

[26] IMF, *Ireland: Financial System Stability Assessment Update* (2006), 11, 16, 20–21, 42.

[27] IMF, *Ireland: Financial System Stability Assessment Update* (2006), 1, 5, 6, 19, 42–43; Karl Whelan, 'Policy Lessons from Ireland's Latest Depression', *Economic and Social Review*, vol. 41, no. 2 (Summer 2010), 243; and Karl Whelan, 'Ireland's Economic Crisis: The Good, The Bad and The Ugly', UCD Centre for Economic Research Working Paper no. WP/13/6 (July 2013), 11.

5 Fiscal Policy

The international agencies issued what was essentially standard mainstream advice to the Irish Government throughout the period, namely to run balanced Budgets or small surpluses. Of course the crash that followed was to prove this approach to be totally inadequate. While analysts were disapproving of the rate of spending growth on the public wage bill, it was evidently because they considered such dramatic increases irresponsible for their own sake rather than because they appreciated anything like the precariousness of Government revenues. The failure of the international organisations to recognise the extent of Ireland's fiscal vulnerabilities was essentially down to the methodology used. The IMF and the OECD took a similar approach in calculating Ireland's structural balance. While they did account for some cyclical revenues and expenditures, conspicuously the two agencies did not subtract cyclical income attributable to asset booms or sectoral shifts. Given the size of the Irish property and construction booms this proved a critical mistake.[28]

Since it was mandated to supervise the fiscal positions of its members, the EC was considerably more vocal about Ireland's budgetary policy than other areas. In the early years of the decade the general consensus from the three organisations was that Ireland's persistence in pursuing an expansionary fiscal policy during a boom was inappropriate. The international agencies grew markedly more approving of Irish fiscal policy in the middle of the period. Broadly, 2003 and 2004 were characterised by general approval from the OECD and particularly the IMF, with conspicuously little comment from the Commission. 2005 and 2006 were notable in that the international agencies were perceptibly more concerned about general threats to the fiscal position, even if they completely missed the scale of the problem.

The OECD was quite frank about Ireland's historically poor approach to fiscal policy, suggesting that it 'has been seen mainly as an instrument for building consensus and strengthening the economy's supply side rather than to manage aggregate demand'. However, the agency was simultaneously cognisant of the political demands on decision-makers, and recognised that they were trying to address social and infrastructural shortcomings. Analysts were also mindful of the difficulty involved

[28] Daniel Kanda, 'Asset Booms and Structural Fiscal Positions: The Case of Ireland', IMF Working Paper no. WP/10/57 (March 2010), 1–6, 21.

in convincing the population of the merits of continued high levels of public saving after the dramatic turnaround in the fiscal position achieved from the mid-1980s. The agency was patently reassured by what it considered to be Ireland's moderate level of public expenditure, as well as its low level of public debt.[29]

In 2005 and 2006 the OECD warned that the Exchequer was reliant on the continued health of the construction sector for stamp duty, capital gains, and corporate tax receipts, and that these were susceptible to a sharp fall. It thus advised the Government to leave room to manoeuvre in the event that such a shock materialised. However, the fact that analysts recommended running a balanced Budget or small surpluses clearly suggests that they were unprepared for the extent to which revenue could decline. Despite its various misgivings, the agency still considered the Irish budgetary position to be fundamentally healthy.[30]

In their discussions with the IMF the Irish authorities suggested that the demand effect of fiscal policy was less pronounced in Ireland because the economy was so open, and that they would have to run unreasonably high surpluses to have any meaningful impact on inflation and competitiveness. As will be demonstrated in Chapter 7, Charlie McCreevy was strongly of this view during his tenure at Finance. The IMF mission countered that because EMU membership effectively removed Irish control over interest rate and exchange rate movements, fiscal policy would have more of an impact than in the past. In particular, staff suggested that it would affect the relative prices of non-tradables like labour and property. Given that both house prices and wages were increasing at unsustainable rates Irish policymakers undoubtedly should have paid more attention to the Fund on this issue.[31]

While the IMF had opposed the expansionary fiscal stance adopted from 2000 to 2002, the 2003 and 2004 Budgets were considered to have made welcome moves towards fiscal consolidation. Analysts were also more sympathetic towards Irish policymakers at this point because

[29] OECD, *Economic Surveys: Ireland, 1999* (1999), 84; OECD, *Economic Surveys: Ireland, 2001* (2001), 40; OECD, *Economic Surveys: Ireland, 2003, 12* (2003), 36, 41–42; and OECD, *OECD Economic Outlook, Volume 2003, Issue 1* (OECD, 2003), 81–84.

[30] OECD, *OECD Economic Outlook, Volume 2005, Issue 2* (OECD, 2005), 90 and OECD, *Economic Surveys: Ireland, 2006* (2006), 8, 17, 140, 143–145, 148.

[31] IMF, *Selected Issues and Statistical Appendix 2000* (2000), 41, 46; IMF, *Staff Country Report on Ireland, 2001* (2001), 19, 20, 21, 27, 33.

they believed that fiscal policy had helped to ameliorate the impact of the global downturn, and the Fund considered the Irish fiscal position to be sustainable and resilient to shocks. However, the IMF's position changed again in 2005 and 2006, and analysts recommended fiscal tightening so as to dampen demand and to build a cushion to prepare for a potential downturn. Nevertheless, the Fund believed Irish fiscal policy to have been prudent in recent years, and most of its directors considered the Exchequer to be in a sound position.[32]

The EC also warned of overheating at the turn of the decade, and suggested that the challenge for the Irish Government was to achieve a soft landing without control over monetary policy. Interestingly, the Commission acknowledged that monetary conditions in the euro area were probably inappropriate for Ireland at that point of its economic cycle. Given the increased importance of fiscal policy, analysts suggested that it might have been more appropriate to have deferred recent tax cuts. Like the OECD however, the Commission was mindful of the political pressures facing policymakers. Of course, the most significant exchange between Ireland and Europe in the early part of the decade was the so-called 'Brussels-Dublin Controversy', when the Ecofin Council censured the 2001 Budget for being inappropriately expansionary during a boom. While the ensuing spat generated significant discussion in the Irish newspapers, events intervened and it was quickly superseded by the global slowdown. McCreevy was particularly incensed by the reprimand, and was memorably glib about Europe's Broad Economic Policy Guidelines (BEPGs), 'because, as their name suggests, they are broad and they are guidelines'.[33]

[32] IMF, *PIN 2003*, 3; IMF, *Ireland: Staff Report for the 2003 Article IV Consultation (IMF Staff Country Report No. 3/242)* (Washington: IMF, 2003), 4, 9, 12, 13, 22, 25, 27, 44; IMF, *Staff Country Report, 2004*, 13, 22, 23, 35; IMF, *Staff Country Report, 2005* (2005), 3, 7, 8, 13–16; IMF, *Staff Country Report, 2006* (2006), 3, 11–13; and IMF, *PIN on Staff Country Report, 2006* (2006), 3.

[33] European Commission, Directorate General for Economic and Financial Affairs, *European Economy: Public Finances in EMU—2000* (2000), 109–110; European Commission, Directorate General for Economic and Financial Affairs, *European Economy: Public Finances in EMU—2001* (2001), 141–144; European Commission, Directorate General for Economic and Financial Affairs, *European Economy: Public Finances in EMU—2002* (2002), 191–194, 205; Denis Staunton, 'McCreevy Eschews EU Guidelines', *The Irish Times*, 7 November 2001; and European Commission, Directorate General for Economic and Financial Affairs, *European Economy: Public Finances in EMU—2001* (2001), 141–144.

The Commission found the 2002 Budget to be broadly neutral and in compliance with its recommendations, though warned the Government to remain vigilant. The 2003 and 2004 reports were distinctly muted, notably coinciding with the years in which the other agencies considered fiscal policy to have been more prudent. In 2005 analysts concluded that the efforts made to improve the management of public expenditure control had been successful and commended efforts to systematically analyse the impact of expenditure. In 2006 the Commission forecast that public finances would remain strong throughout the following year, while cautioning that overall risks were mounting. Analysts warned that in the event of a sharp downturn in construction activity, property-related taxes would be particular vulnerable in the Irish system compared to countries with an annual residential property tax, since in Ireland tax revenue was affected by both the level of house prices and housing output. Although the Commission recognised that the Exchequer was accordingly vulnerable to developments in the housing sector, as well as changes in the global economy, it was totally unprepared for the scale of what followed.[34]

Summary

The international agencies did recognise the nature of the threat to the Exchequer on several occasions, though clearly never its extent. In 2005 and 2006 the OECD warned of the precariousness of stamp duty, capital gains, and corporate tax revenue flows. Discussions between the IMF and the Irish authorities in 2005 suggested that both parties were similarly mindful of the threat to property-based tax revenues, though certainly not of the potential scale of the falls should they arise. The Commission also recognised the threat to property-related taxes, as well as the inherent weakness imbedded in a system that relied on transactional rather than annual charges. However, the general consensus was clearly that the fiscal position was fundamentally sound, and the

[34]European Commission, Directorate General for Economic and Financial Affairs, *European Economy: Public Finances in EMU—2002* (2002), 191–194, 205; European Commission, Directorate General for Economic and Financial Affairs, *European Economy: Public Finances in EMU—2005* (2005), 261–263; European Commission, Directorate General for Economic and Financial Affairs, *European Economy: Public Finances in EMU—2006* (2006), 269–271; and Zdeněk Čech, *Ireland: No Place Like (My Own) Home, EcFin Country Focus*, vol. 3, no. 13 (European Commission, 2006), 3–5.

accompanying recommendations to run small surpluses, suggests a complete misapprehension of the degree of the risk.

The advice on keeping spending increases under control was entirely warranted, and unsustainable spending commitments were a key factor in the ensuing malaise of the Exchequer. However, recommendations from the international agencies about redistributive issues like optimal social welfare levels or tax rates arguably constituted an encroachment from notionally objective economic analysis and advice into subjective opinion about preferred political-economic approaches. The advice that the international agencies issued in this respect was based on strikingly little empirical evidence or research, and it marked a discernible shift into the realm of ideology and conjecture. While more external analysis of the choices that Irish policymakers made in dividing the fruits of booming tax revenue would have been very welcome, it is debatable if analysts from these organisations stayed within the confines of their remits and expertise, and whether such discussions should have been interspersed into these reports.

6 Conclusion

The IMF's 2012 and 2015 Article IV reports on Ireland included a standard risk assessment matrix, rating both the likelihood and the potential impact of the primary threats to the Irish economy as low, medium, or high. The tool would have been useful in the years prior to the crash, since it would have required analysts to quantify both the probability and the potential scale of the risks that they identified. Although the international agencies recognised the nature of many of the vulnerabilities of the Irish economy, their misreading of the degree of the risks was crucial. Analysts continued to perceive the Irish economy as fundamentally strong and sustainable, and the risks that they identified did not prompt a significant reappraisal. This was in fact totally incompatible with the historical lessons evident from the studies produced by the IMF and the OECD themselves. If the lessons of these studies had been properly applied, analysts would have anticipated that at least 40% of the house price increases and 80% of the construction investment increases observed during the boom were likely to be reversed. These realisations would have alerted the international organisations to the precariousness of construction employment, and thus the real extent of the implications of the cost competitiveness losses of the boom years. It would have been similarly apparent that running small Budget surpluses was entirely inadequate.

The fact that the OECD estimated that housing demand was 50–60,000 units and used this as the basis for its forecast for the construction sector is important for two reasons. Firstly, the estimate itself was highly dubious, since it was predicated on high levels of demand stemming from inward migration and the continued proliferation of second homes. These sources were clearly inflated, and their continued contribution to demand was contingent on the boom itself. The OECD thus implicitly made the assumption that the cycle of high housing demand generating economic activity that in turn generated further demand was sustainable into the medium-term. Secondly, the OECD's study of the recent history of construction booms had demonstrated that construction investment tended to revert towards its pre-boom level. Predicting that after the boom peaked output would fall to estimated demand levels was therefore to miss the crucial point, since there was no equivalent evidence to suggest that this was likely.

For the IMF's part, analysts evidently recognised the likelihood of a very significant price crash in 2000 but were presumably unable to say so in the report. There is no evidence to date of stronger warnings that were issued in private, but this may well emerge in the future. However, the incident does raise a broader issue: if the formal organisations were unable to issue frank warnings should they even have published these reports in the first place? While the question may seem dramatic, its basis is very concrete. Irish policymakers were bolstered in their conviction by the sanguine conclusions in the international reports, and correspondingly less receptive to dissenting voices. Since Bertie Ahern claimed to treat the IMF's view with greater import than the combined views of the Opposition Finance spokespeople, and since the IMF was never liable to warn of an imminent crash, there was unlikely to ever be a scenario whereby he was convinced by his political opponents that the economy was unsound. In the event that policymakers needed to be convinced of the likelihood of a crash the formal domestic and international organisations were always likely to be part of the problem. One possible way that this bias could be addressed is for the formal organisations to acknowledge the limits of what they can publish at the start of all their reports, which would make it harder for policymakers to use the analysis to dismiss dissenting opinion. A second option would be for the formal organisations to issue policymakers with a more forthright confidential memo, which would be published after the identified dangers had passed. It would presumably encourage politicians to act if they knew that their subsequent political careers could be jeopardised if they were found to have made the wrong decisions despite having received better advice.

The IMF's suggestion in 2005 that the Irish housing market was most likely headed for a soft landing was totally incompatible with the findings of its study of recent international housing booms in 2000. This further adds to the contention that the constraint against warning of catastrophe created a problematic bias, since the Fund faced no such impediment when its forecasts were benign. From an analytical point of view, the 2005 conclusion was also highly questionable. By way of evidence the IMF pointed to lower price increases and survey data suggesting reduced consumer expectations. However, the Fund's 2000 study had demonstrated that for Ireland to experience a boom of such magnitude without a subsequent fall would have been unprecedented in its sample of almost forty incidents, and that the scale of the price increases during a boom was closely linked to the scale of the subsequent falls. There was no comparable evidence to suggest that falls could be averted because prices had recently stabilised or expectations had lowered, and in fact such developments could equally have been considered the early signs of an impending crash. Similarly, debates over whether prices were justified by fundamentals seem to have missed the vital point in view of the ubiquity of housing boom/bust cycles in modern economic history. A fall was highly likely on the basis of the boom alone. Both organisations thus came to the brink, but shied away from making the conclusions that their highly-commendable studies of historical precedent demanded. We cannot definitively know the reasons for this, but political and market sensitivities were potentially just as important as analytical failures.[35]

Another bias emanated from the fact that the international organisations were evidently keen to present Ireland as a poster child of what could be achieved through the implementation of what they considered to be 'good' policies. That the IMF went so far as to claim some of the credit for the Irish success story was remarkable. Like domestic analysts, international commentators approached the Irish economy with a positive partiality that coloured their conclusions, often in spite of the evidence that they produced. While one would expect international

[35] IMF, *Ireland: Staff Report for the 2005 Article IV Consultation* (2005), 11.

observers to have considered the Irish economy from a greater emotional remove, this was further compromised by their extensive use of the research conducted by Irish analysts, including academics, consultants, research institutes, economists in private companies, and the Central Bank. Although such dependencies were unavoidable, it did ensure a significant degree of cross-contamination. This was also apparent with respect to other international analysts, and significantly the 2006 FSAP report observed that the Irish banks had been given good rankings by the international ratings agencies. Like all other commentators, international analysts were working within something of a self-reinforcing feedback loop that perpetuated a positive view of the Irish economy.[36]

The IMF's suggestion that Irish authorities recognised that a residential property tax was desirable but rejected it on the basis that it would have been politically unpopular is of enormous significance. The fact that such statements were made so unguardedly to a third party and allowed to be published is indicative of how inured Irish officials were to policy choices that they knew to be economically flawed but politically advantageous. The choice for Government lay in balancing the conflict between its duty to minimise the risk to the economy, and the presumably strong motivation to ensure continued public support. It is very difficult to avoid the conclusion that in this respect economic stability was potentially jeopardised for political gain. It is also worth considering the contention made by the authorities that the political opposition to a property tax or removal of stamp-duty relief would likely have been 'insurmountable' given the electorate's drive for homeownership. This raises the key question of whether the electorate had installed a Government whose support was contingent on making the politically palatable choices, but that it did not trust to make unpopular decisions on the basis of what it determined to be the national good. In this regard, one could argue that there was a sense of determinism about the outcome of the boom, given the apparently highly-restrictive mandate given to successive Ahern administrations.[37]

It is possible then, to propose a convincing explanation for why the IMF and OECD failed to recognise the precariousness of the Irish economy despite their cognisance of the nature of the various threats. The

[36] IMF, *Ireland: Financial System Stability Assessment Update* (2006), 5.

[37] IMF, *Staff Country Report, 2004* (2004), 20.

agencies were concerned about Ireland's eroding cost-competitiveness, but because the OECD underestimated the possible fall-off in construction output in its worst-case scenario it expected the sector to continue as a major employer and revenue source. Since by the end of the period the two organisations anticipated a soft-landing for the housing market they were both similarly unprepared for the extent to which associated tax revenue could fall. Though neither organisation ruled out a sharper fall for house prices, they did not demonstrate any appreciation of the potential extent to which construction output could fall. Even their worst-case scenarios were therefore far too optimistic in terms of their implications for employment and the Exchequer. The IMF's 2006 FSAP report did test the financial sector for very dramatic house price falls, but conspicuously its test on the funding side was far less rigorous. There is no evidence that it applied any test for a major shock to the construction sector, an oversight that proved pivotal. Therefore, the failure of the international organisations to appreciate the extent of the risks facing employment and economic activity, financial stability, and the Exchequer all emanated from an overly-benign forecast for property, and especially construction. This in turn was attributable to the failure to properly apply the lessons of recent international history.

These shortcomings only partially absolve policymakers. Just because analysts did not appreciate the scale of the problem or anticipate how the boom would end does not mean that their advice was all inappropriate. If Irish decision-makers had followed the recommendations made by the international agencies they would not have presided over such remarkable increases in current spending in tandem with income tax cuts, particularly in the early years of the decade. This would have quite possibly have eased inflationary pressures and even more importantly reduced the exposure of the Exchequer when the crash hit. As we will see in Chapter 7, a more prudent approach to fiscal policy would have had a remarkable impact from a fiscal stability perspective, since current spending increases were compounded year-on-year. Furthermore, if they had followed the advice issued by the international organisations the authorities would have pursued a less favourable housing policy, easing demand from potential owner-occupants and especially from investors. By taxing windfall gains on development land, decision-makers would have removed much of its speculative demand, thus helping to stabilise prices. The Irish crash was indisputably attributable to a failure on the part of decision-makers as well as a failure of analysis.

CHAPTER 4

Domestic Organisations

There is nothing new in the story. It is as old as the Sibylline Books. It falls into that long, dismal catalogue of the fruitlessness of experience and the confirmed unteachability of mankind. Want of foresight, unwillingness to act when action would be simple and effective, lack of clear thinking, confusion of counsel until the emergency comes, until self-preservation strikes its jarring gong- these are the features which constitute the endless repetition of history.

Winston Churchill, *House of Commons*, 1935[1]

1 Introduction

For the most part we can only know the public positions taken by the organisations who commented on the Irish economy, and have far less insight into internal debates or disagreements. This is less of a problem than one might expect, since in terms of the public discourse it was the official lines that organisations took that really mattered. However, the Central Bank and Financial Services Authority of Ireland (CBFSAI) was different to the other formal institutions examined in two major respects. Firstly, the Governor as the head of the authority regularly voiced his opinions about the economy in the public domain. Secondly, unlike the international organisations or a research institute, the CBFSAI was a key policymaker in its own right. If there was a discrepancy between policy

[1] http://www.winstonchurchill.org/resources/speeches/90-air-parity-lost. Accessed 29 May 2015.

C. M. Casey, *Policy Failures and the Irish Economic Crisis*,
https://doi.org/10.1007/978-3-319-90182-4_4

and the analysis in the Bank's formal publications one could attribute this to an internal disagreement between research economists and key decision-makers. However, any disconnect between the Governor's pronouncements and the actions of the Bank would clearly be far more significant.

Before delving into the Central Bank publications, it is therefore important to briefly consider the noteworthy public statements made by the two Governors. As early as 1999, Maurice O'Connell wrote to the banks and warned of excessive mortgage lending and its impact on house prices. His successor, John Hurley, similarly expressed concern about the rate of personal credit growth. In 2004 Hurley identified house price increases as a major threat to the economy. These warnings garnered significant attention and were routinely transmitted in the newspapers. Hurley also warned about eroding competitiveness and declining exports, calling for 'every effort' to be made to tackle inflation. While the Governor considered a 'soft landing' to be the most likely outcome for the housing market, he warned against complacency about price increases and mortgage borrowing.[2]

Such concerns were entirely at odds with the marked inaction of the CBFSAI in the period. The Honohan report outlines the significant powers that were available to the authority to curtail lending, including banning high loan-to-value mortgages, imposing sectoral lending limits and increasing provisioning or liquid reserve requirements. If these measures proved ineffective the joint authority was even empowered to place a ceiling on the rate at which institutions could expand lending. As Honohan argues, this would have halted the credit boom in its tracks and would have been justifiable under the circumstances. The reader will also remember Nyberg's point that the joint authority could have reduced lending to the property sector enormously by just enforcing existing sectoral lending limits. There was similarly a striking lack of external pressure on the CBFSAI to act and little evidence that

[2] http://www.rte.ie/news/1999/0430/1505-mortgage/. Accessed 29 October 2015; Pat Boyle, 'Housing Costs Big Threat to Economy, Warns Banker', *The Irish Independent*, 21 April 2004; Brendan Keenan, 'Rising Debt Could Push Mortgage Rate to 6pc, Warns Bank', *The Irish Independent*, 2 November 2005; Marc Coleman, 'Malignant Political System Robs Economy Blind', *The Irish Times*, 16 September 2006; 'Era of Strong Growth at an End, Says Central Bank', *The Irish Times*, 15 September 2006; and Una McCaffrey, 'Hurley Stresses Need to Remain Competitive', *The Irish Times*, 29 January 2005.

commentators were even cognisant of the powers it enjoyed. This was a key shortcoming of the contemporary discourse, particularly since the authority's relevant powers were outlined in an *Irish Times* article written by a former Central Bank official.[3]

The fact that commentators paid far more attention to fiscal measures than credit restrictions as the potential means to tackle inflation is particularly conspicuous given that the headline data suggest that credit was a far greater driver of demand in the period than fiscal policy. If public expenditure had been maintained at the 2000 level throughout the period to 2006, cumulative state spending would have been some €85 billion lower. By contrast, in the same period private-sector debt increased by a remarkable €224 billion, or by 340%. Tighter restrictions on credit growth would have had a greater impact than fiscal measures as long as any meaningful curtailments were imposed. The discourse on inflation in the period thus missed the key issue insofar as analysts pressed almost exclusively for fiscal solutions when the primary driver was rapidly growing indebtedness.[4]

This chapter will examine the relevant publications by the CBFSAI and the ESRI. The most important contributions were the Bank's annual Financial Stability Reports (FSRs) and the ESRI's Medium-Term Reviews, which were published biennially. The primary material used in the chapter is detailed in Table 1. The publications by the National Economic and Social Council (NESC) from the period were also examined, but added little in the way of new analysis or prediction about how the boom would end.

[3] Central Bank of Ireland, *Annual Report: 2006* (2007), 64; Central Bank Act, 1998, Section 5, article 6-(1). Accessed 2 November 2015, at http://www.irishstatutebook.ie/eli/1998/act/2/section/5/enacted/en/html; Central Bank Act, 1971, Section 23. Accessed 2 November 2015, at http://www.irishstatutebook.ie/eli/1971/act/24/section/23/enacted/en/html#sec23; Michael Casey, 'Watchdog Sanguine on Property Boom', *The Irish Times* (2005), 14 October; Honohan Commission, *The Irish Banking Crisis* (2010), 105–106; Nyberg Commission (2011), *Misjudging Risk*, 64; Houses of the Oireachtas, *Joint Committee of Inquiry into the Banking Crisis*, vol. 2, no. 19, John Hurley, 21 May 2015, 3–10. https://inquiries.oireachtas.ie/banking/. See Honohan's follow-up letter to Ciarán Lynch and John Hurley's clarification of statement. Accessed 29 October 2015; and On Nyberg see Chapter 2.

[4] Fiscal data from http://www.per.gov.ie/. Accessed 29 October 2015. Credit data courtesy of the Central Bank.

Table 1 Domestic organisations—Key publications

Key publications by the Central Bank, the Financial Regulator and the ESRI

Title	*1999*	*2000*	*2001*	*2002*	*2003*	*2004*	*2005*	*2006*	*Total*
Central Bank and Financial Regulator									
Quarterly Bulletins		4	4	4	4	3	4	4	27
Financial Stability Reports						1	1	1	3
Central Bank Annual Reports[a]	1	1	1	1	1	1	1		6
Financial Regulator Annual Reports						1	1		2
Technical Papers				1		2			3
CBFSAI[b] Strategic Plans						1			1
The ESRI									
Quarterly Economic Commentaries		4	4	4	4	4	4	4	28
Medium-Term Reviews			1		1		1		3
External Publications			1		1	1	1		4

[a]Since the annual reports for a given year are published in the subsequent year, the Central Bank's 1999 report is included while the 2006 reports are not
[b]Central Bank and Financial Services Authority of Ireland: Used to denote the combined Central Bank and Financial Regulator

2 Property and Construction

The domestic organisations understandably paid a great deal of attention to the residential property sector and the risk it posed to the broader economy throughout the boom. However, economists were overly sanguine in two fundamental respects. Firstly, their predictions about the most likely outcome for the property boom and the broader economy were far too optimistic. Any form of a smooth transition was improbable given the international precedent of boom/bust cycles, the extent of recent house price growth and the exposure of the macroeconomy to property and construction activity. However, the Central Bank was clearly in a conflicted position, since warnings of a likely market collapse undoubtedly risked 'spooking the horses'. The organisation was certainly too quick to bolster the consensus view about the likely outcome for the boom even within these parameters, but even had they been more concerned analysts within the Bank were not especially well-placed to take up the vanguard in challenging it. By contrast, there was no comparable tension for analysts in considering worst-case scenarios. Both organisations could publicly contemplate very undesirable futures as long as they clarified that they considered these to be unlikely. Much more significant then, is the fact that analysts evidently believed that a recession on the scale of what materialised was so improbable that they never seriously raised it as a possibility. From a purely intellectual perspective this is the key point of interest, and we will thus focus on the outer limits of the shock scenarios that analysts explicitly considered plausible enough to justify examination.[5]

Despite the general perception that the core failure of economists was to anticipate the house price crash, the two organisations were in fact quite prepared to consider the possibility that prices could fall precipitously. Central Bank economists conducted stress tests on the Irish banks for house price falls of up to 55%, while the ESRI's shock scenario in its 2005 Medium-Term Review modelled price falls of a third. What is notable about the ESRI's shock scenario is that its other predictions for such an event were far more benign than what actually took place. Anticipated unemployment of 11% was reasonably prescient but the model forecast a much more benign trajectory for GNP, with growth falling to a low of 1% in 2007 and rebounding to 5% by 2010.[6]

Given that analysts were quite clearly willing to consider the impact of major house price falls, the key question is why they were so unprepared for the broader economic consequences of such an event. One might intuitively point to the banking collapse as having been key, but as we saw in the previous chapter the financial system probably would have withstood a fall in house prices alone. Of course, the global financial crisis clearly played a key role in exacerbating the Irish crash, but even notwithstanding the international context the domestic organisations significantly underestimated the internal risks. The decisive domestic vulnerability that analysts underappreciated was the potential for construction activity to come to a near standstill. The worst-case scenario considered

[5] Houses of the Oireachtas, *Joint Committee of Inquiry into the Banking Crisis*, vol. 2, no. 26, Tom O'Connell, 10 June 2015, 83.

[6] CBFSAI, *Financial Stability Report* (2004), 31–32; Allan Kearns, Maurice McGuire, Anne Marie McKiernan, and Diarmaid Smyth, 'Bottom-Up Testing: The Key Results' in CBFSAI, *Financial Stability Report* (2006), 121; ESRI, *Medium-Term Review*: 2005–*2012* (2005), 91; and ESRI, *Quarterly Economic Commentary: Winter 2004* (2004), 20–21.

by the Central Bank was a fall in construction output from 76,954 units in 2004 to 50,000 units per annum over a two-year period, a decline of 35%. The ESRI's shock scenario allowed for a 48% fall to 40,000 units from the same baseline. In reality output grew to a peak of 93,419 units in 2006 and then fell dramatically to a trough of 8301 in 2013, constituting a remarkable drop of 91%. This had predictably large consequences for construction employment. While the ESRI shock scenario predicted a fall-off in building and construction employment of 15% or 40,000 jobs, it actually fell by 64%, representing 174,000 lost jobs.[7]

A crucial question is therefore whether the parameters of what Central Bank and ESRI analysts considered viable for a decline in construction activity in a shock scenario were justifiable. One key statistic that should have been considered was annual Irish housing output in the decades prior to the boom. The mean from 1970 to 1994 was 22,899 units per annum, and although the population had increased significantly in the interim this should have been considered a good starting point. Significantly, the ESRI's estimate of the underlying demographic demand for housing in 2004 was 30,000 units, allowing for both population growth and declining household sizes. Analysts should have at least considered the possibility of output falling to this level in the event of a shock. Construction output of forty or fifty thousand units per annum would still have represented a significant multiple of the per capita output of neighbouring European countries. At UK levels, construction output would have been closer to 12,000 units. Of course, one could point to an exceptionally low existing stock of dwellings in Ireland, but in the event of a severe shock this would have been unlikely to matter much.[8]

[7]CBFSAI, *Financial Stability Report* (2005), 159; ESRI, *Medium-Term Review: 2005–2012* (2005), 91–92; ESRI, *Quarterly Economic Commentary: Winter 2004* (2004), 20–21; and Construction employment data from www.cso.ie. Accessed 5 November 2015.

[8]ESRI, *Quarterly Economic Commentary: Winter 2004* (2004), 20; Tony Fahey, 'The Housing Boom in Ireland: Causes, Effects on Affordability and Policy Responses', *Housing Finance International*, vol. 18, no. 4 (London, 2004), 11; Anthony Murphy, *Housing and National Competitiveness: A Report for the National Competitiveness Council* (Unpublished, 2004), 12, 18; Ministry of Infrastructure of the Italian Republic, *Housing Statistics in the European Union 2005/6*, 74. Available from http://www.bluomelette.net/bluomelette/wp-content/uploads/hs_annual2006.pdf. Accessed 5 November 2015; and Housing completions data from www.cso.ie. Accessed 5 November 2015.

While the history of property price collapses was well documented, there is still a surprising dearth of cross-country analysis about what happens to construction activity in such an event. We therefore cannot expect that analysts should necessarily have appreciated that output could fall by over 90%. Nonetheless, the Bank and the ESRI should have arrived at much more pessimistic worst-case scenarios on the basis of historical and regional comparisons, as well as the institute's own underlying demand estimates. Analysts also should have allowed for the strong possibility that falls would overshoot in the event of a major shock. Figure 1 demonstrates the trajectory of housing output, the pre-boom average, the ESRI's underlying demand estimate for 2004 and the worst-case scenarios envisaged by the two organisations.[9]

We should resist the temptation to treat the decline in construction output and employment as the lynchpin of the crisis. In fact, the fiscal, banking, property price and construction industry crises were mutually reinforcing, and the Irish crash is best understood as an escalating spiral of these interlinking elements. However, the fall-off in construction activity does seem to have been the critical factor that the domestic organisations underappreciated in their analyses. In the worst-case scenarios that they posited, the financial system would have fared much better because the default rate among developers would have been significantly lower. Similarly, construction would have continued as a major source of employment and tax revenue.

One particular point of interest is the manner in which Central Bank analysts responded to the lessons from elsewhere. There are two incidents in direct contrast, which serve as a useful reminder of the differing mentalities of staff within the formal organisations. As we saw in the last chapter, the IMF and the OECD conducted studies of the outcomes of international housing and construction booms. However, they made no comparable examinations of commercial real estate. This shortcoming was addressed to a significant extent by Caroline Gavin in the Central Bank, in what was certainly one of the most impressive contributions of the period. In response to the IMF study, Gavin examined the international precedents for the surge in Irish commercial property prices. She observed that commercial property booms in Sweden, Japan, Thailand and the USA had all coincided with financial liberalisation and had been

[9] Output data from www.cso.ie.

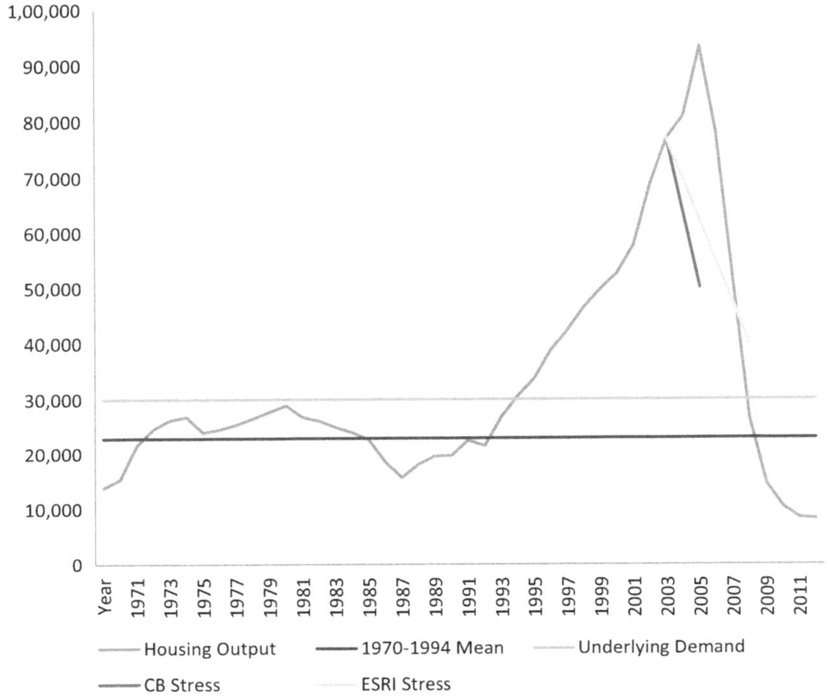

Fig. 1 Irish housing output vs. forecasts

followed by substantial price falls. Several of the downswings examined had precipitated financial-sector instability, and Gavin noted that the experience of these countries demonstrated the need to ensure that institutions did not over-extend their exposures to property in the face of increased competition in the banking sector.[10]

Gavin argued that the commercial property sector warranted particular attention, since in Ireland it had historically proven to be more volatile than residential property and tended to exaggerate swings in the business cycle. She warned that it was unlikely that the extent of Irish

[10]Caroline Gavin, 'Swings in Property Prices: A Global Perspective', in Central Bank of Ireland, *Quarterly Bulletin: Winter 2000* (2000), 73–86.

property price increases was fully justified, and remarkably even suggested that on the basis of past experience 'a significant fall in commercial property prices' was *likely* if the economy slowed. Gavin observed that falls in commercial property prices had generally resulted in greater losses to the financial system than residential price falls during a downswing, and thus argued that in the event of a significant setback that commercial property price falls were more likely than to have 'a severe impact on the real economy and jeopardise the financial stability of the economy'. The recent history of commercial property booms was clearly highly relevant to Ireland, and Gavin's analysis should have prompted significant discussion and further investigation on the part of the Bank. Instead, the paper generated essentially no public debate and represented an important lost opportunity to change the discourse on the Irish boom.

The Bank's 2004 Financial Stability Report represented a far less favourable reaction to the IMF study. The FSR acknowledged that the IMF had found that no country in its sample had experienced house price increases comparable to those in Ireland without subsequent falls. Rather than welcoming the warning however, analysts challenged its applicability, arguing that the IMF study pertained particularly to reversals in the 1980s and that growth episodes in the 1990s had proven more stable. This was highly misleading given that the IMF had specified that the scale of the price increases made the Irish boom more akin to those of the 1980s than the 1990s. The obvious question is how Bank analysts arrived at the conclusion that the world had fundamentally changed and that asset booms were somehow less precarious than they had been in the recent past. One likely explanation was offered in the 2007 FSR, which rather opportunistically pointed to Ben Bernanke's observance of a 'Great Moderation' and contended that 'past international experience may not be an accurate guide to future developments in house prices because the international macroeconomic environment is now somewhat different'. While Gavin embraced and built on the IMF's study with further analysis, the 2004 FSR rejected it with the paltriest of arguments, presumably because its conclusions were so unpalatable.[11]

[11]CBFSAI, *Financial Stability Report* (2004), 10, 54, 71 and CBFSAI, *Financial Stability Report* (2007), 30.

A notable distinction between the international and the domestic organisations is that the former were far more vocal about the need to introduce recurring property taxes and charges. The likely explanation is that domestic analysts were just more cognisant of the Irish political realities. The ESRI's John Fitzgerald observed that while there was a good economic argument for a property tax, it had proved unacceptable to the public. Instead, he proposed tax a tax on second or vacant houses as a more agreeable alternative. Bertie Ahern as Taoiseach flatly rejected even that much, questioning the objection to people owning second homes where they could go 'with their children for long weekends and summer holidays'. Fitzgerald rightly pointed to the fact that the proliferation of second homes was adding significantly to demand and pushing up prices in rural areas. He also argued that the state was actively encouraging the purchase of second homes both through tax incentives and crucially by failing to pass on the costs of infrastructural investment or ongoing services to their owners.[12]

The Central Bank's relative silence on the issue of a residential property tax was conspicuous, particular since analysts explicitly acknowledged that recent tax and subsidy decisions were overwhelmingly in favour of homeownership. The user cost of housing represents the net cost of homeownership, allowing for interest rates, taxes, and price expectations. It is a key concept in housing economics and has a fundamental impact on prices. It was particularly low in the millennial period because of historic declines in real mortgage interest rates and high rates of capital appreciation. However, Bank analysts recognised that even in the absence of these factors the Irish user cost had been negative for most of the period from the mid-1970s, in significant part because of the favourable tax regime and the absence of recurring charges. Of particular benefit was the non-taxation of capital gains, which gave housing a unique advantage over other assets. Analysts were also evidently cognisant of the significant impact that policy changes could have on housing demand and prices. Even allowing for the unfavourable political

[12] John Fitzgerald, 'The Irish Housing Stock: Growth in Number of Vacant Dwellings', in ESRI, *Quarterly Economic Commentary: Spring 2005* (2005), 1–2, 15–19 and *Dáil Eireann Debate 2005*, vol. 605, no. 4: Questions–Social Partnership Agreement, Bertie Ahern, 29 June 2005.

environment, the Bank should thus have pushed much more energetically for a property tax and the abolition of key incentives.[13]

There are two final points of interest about the analysis of the housing market that the domestic organisations conducted in the period. Like the IMF, the Bank was aware that rents were falling in both nominal and real terms from late 2002 to early 2005. However, analysts still attempted to explain house price increases by reference to factors like population increase, falling household size, the small existing stock of houses, income tax reductions and wage growth. Clearly, if these factors were the core drivers of price growth one would expect to see a comparable increase in rents. Analysts thus paid too little attention to the clear contradiction between falling rents and the factors they used to explain the price boom.[14]

The position that the Central Bank took on the housing market in its 2004 FSR was largely informed by a model developed by Bank analyst Kieran McQuinn. The approach taken was deeply problematic because of the inclusion of two key explanatory variables. On the demand side the model pointed to the impact of larger mortgages in driving up prices. Of course, this should have immediately raised questions about whether the prevailing credit criteria and level of mortgage lending were sustainable into the medium term. If not, then prices were being buoyed by a transitory credit bubble. On the supply side the model incorporated increased land prices as an explanatory variable. Even if one accepts the questionable premise that house prices were not fuelling land price increases, the model just shifted the problem to whether or not there was a bubble in land prices. Policymakers should have derived little comfort from the distinction, and justifying high house prices on the basis of inflated land

[13]CBFSAI, *Financial Stability Report* (2004), 11, 61, 65, 89, 92, 95, 97; CBFSAI, *Financial Stability Report* (2005), 66; Anthony Murphy, *Housing and National Competitiveness: A Report for the National Competitiveness Council* (Unpublished, 2004), 1–4, 6–7; and David Duffy, 'User Cost and Irish House Prices', in ESRI, *Quarterly Economic Commentary* (Autumn 2011), 2.

[14]Central Bank of Ireland, *Quarterly Bulletin: Spring 2004* (2004), 8; Central Bank of Ireland, *Quarterly Bulletin: Number 2* (2005), 59; Central Bank of Ireland, *Quarterly Bulletin: Number 4* (2005), 60; CBFSAI, *Financial Stability Report* (2005), 29, 30–32; and Morgan Kelly, 'On the Likely Extent of Falls in Irish House Prices'. UCD Centre For Economic Research, Working Paper 7/1 (2007), 10.

prices or a possible credit bubble was to miss the fundamental purpose of the exercise.[15]

Summary

The domestic organisations were certainly overly optimistic in their predictions about the most likely outcome for the housing market. They did show a good appreciation of the extent to which prices could fall in a worst-case scenario, but they critically underestimated the impact that such falls would have on GNP, construction employment, the Exchequer and the banks. The key factor was that they had unduly favourable expectations for the construction sector in the event of a housing market collapse. Even after the most pessimistic falls considered by the Bank and the ESRI, housing output would still have been a multiple of the per capita levels in neighbouring countries. This was a critical mistake, and one that significantly undermined the extent to which they appreciated the key associated threats to the economy.[16]

Caroline Gavin's reaction to the IMF's study of housing boom/bust cycles was in marked contrast to the Bank's response in its Financial Stability Report four years later. While the FSR dismissed the applicability of the lessons from abroad, Gavin added significantly to the discourse. The fact that her analysis did not influence the Bank's position does not reflect particularly well on senior decision-makers. While the ESRI and the Bank had to pick their battles, they should have been more outspoken about the arguments in favour of an annual residential property tax. Although a more explicit stance would have been unlikely to achieve direct results, omitting appropriate advice on the basis that it was unlikely to be followed was a questionable tactic. By highlighting the gulf between policy and best practice, the domestic organisations could have strengthened their hands in pushing for the withdrawal of property-based

[15]Anthony Murphy, *Housing and National Competitiveness: A Report for the National Competitiveness Council* (Unpublished, 2004), 35–38; Kieran McQuinn, 'A Model of the Irish Housing Sector', Research Paper 1/RT/4 (2004), Central Bank and Financial Services Authority of Ireland (2004), 13; Maurice J. Roche, 'Will There Be a Crash in Irish House Prices?' in ESRI, *Quarterly Economic Commentary, Winter 2003* (2003), 1–12; and Jim O'Leary, 'Single-Digit House Price Inflation May Be at Hand', *The Irish Times*, 9 January 2004, 5.

[16]For house building comparisons see 'The Hague: Ministry of the Interior and Kingdom Relations', *Housing Statistics in the European Union 2010*, 74. Available from http://www.bmwfw.gv.at/Wirtschaftspolitik/Wohnungspolitik/Documents/housing_statistics_in_the_european_union_2010.pdf. Accessed 23 March 2016.

tax incentives. Analysts should have been far more sceptical about economic and demographic explanations for house price increases in the context of falling rents. Similarly, a key model underpinning the Bank's understanding of the market was fundamentally problematic.

3 Fiscal Policy

Although fiscal policy was clearly the jurisdiction of the Department of Finance, the Central Bank was mandated to influence other policymakers through its commentary and analysis. Bank analysts considered fiscal policy to be the key tool for managing domestic demand, since Irish policymakers no longer had control over interest or exchange rates. The situation was made even more pressing by the fact that high inflation meant that wholesale interest rates were negative in real terms. The Bank was also cognisant that the Exchequer had benefited significantly from the strength of the property and construction sectors and would have to cope with reduced revenue from these sources in the future. Crucially however, the concern was explicitly that the housing market would 'revert to more normal levels of activity', and the notion that construction activity could come to a near standstill was never even considered. The Bank advocated what it considered to be prudent fiscal policy throughout the period, raising concerns about pro-cyclical Budgets and the stability of the public finances. However, analysts considered neutral Budgets to be sufficiently restrictive and to offer adequate protection against potential shocks, and they showed no appreciation of the extent to which the state was running structural deficits.[17]

[17] CBFSAI, *2004–2006 Strategic Plan of the Central Bank and Financial Services Authority of Ireland: (2006)* (2004), 14; Central Bank of Ireland, *Quarterly Bulletin: Winter 2000* (2000), 6–7, 42; Central Bank of Ireland, *Quarterly Bulletin: Autumn 2001* (2001), 8–9; Central Bank of Ireland, *Annual Report: 2000* (2001), 12; Central Bank of Ireland, *Quarterly Bulletin: Autumn 2002* (2002), 7; Central Bank of Ireland, *Quarterly Bulletin: Winter 2002* (2002), 6–7; Central Bank of Ireland. *Quarterly Bulletin: Autumn 2003* (2003), 6; Central Bank of Ireland, *Quarterly Bulletin: Autumn 2004* (2004), 6–7; Central Bank of Ireland, *Quarterly Bulletin: Number 2* (2005), 7–8; Central Bank of Ireland, *Quarterly Bulletin: Number 4* (2005), 9; Central Bank of Ireland, *Annual Report: 2005* (2006), 16; Central Bank of Ireland, *Quarterly Bulletin: Number 1* (2006), 8; Central Bank of Ireland, *Quarterly Bulletin: Number 2* (2006), 9; and Central Bank of Ireland, *Quarterly Bulletin: Number 4* (2006), 9.

The ESRI was somewhat less consistent than the Bank or the international agencies in its stance on fiscal policy. Analysts were broadly supportive of what they viewed as the mildly expansionary stance of the 2005 Budget, pointing to the downside risks stemming from the US economy and the reliance of the Irish economy on housing construction. The rationale for advocating a fiscal stance that would further undermine export competitiveness and increase housing demand in order to address concerns about an excessive dependence on construction is difficult to fathom. The institute did draw attention to the fiscal dependence on construction activity somewhat earlier than the Bank, contending that the contribution of the sector could not be expected to continue and that it was 'very vulnerable to a shock'. Analysts urged policymakers to stop using policy to boost construction activity and to leave scope to partially offset the consequences of a collapse in the sector. As we have seen however, the ESRI's definition of what constituted a collapse in construction output was also far too optimistic. By 2006 the institute was distinctly more critical, admonishing the Government decision not to plan for an Exchequer surplus and pointing to the need to control demand and to build up reserves that could be used to tackle a potential slowdown. It also advocated that policymakers play a role in smoothing the transition to more normal levels of construction activity by pursuing a counter-cyclical strategy. Like the Bank however, the ESRI did not convey anything like the potential scale of the risk to the Exchequer.[18]

Summary

The Central Bank and the ESRI irrefutably recognised many of the key threats to the Exchequer during the period. However, the decisive shortcoming was the failure to recognise the extent of those threats, and the two organisations were unwavering throughout in their confidence that the public finances were fundamentally sound. It is striking that the most sober fiscal advice given by analysts, to run neutral Budgets so as

[18] ESRI, *Quarterly Economic Commentary: Autumn 2004* (2004), 1; ESRI, *Quarterly Economic Commentary: Winter 2004* (2004), 1, 39; ESRI, *Quarterly Economic Commentary: Spring 2005* (2005), 35, 39; ESRI, *Medium-Term Review: 2005–2012* (2005), 96–99; ESRI, *Quarterly Economic Commentary: Autumn 2005* (2005), 28; ESRI, *Quarterly Economic Commentary: Winter 2005* (2005), 14–15; ESRI, *Quarterly Economic Commentary: Spring 2006* (2006), 1, 36; ESRI, *Quarterly Economic Commentary: Summer 2006* (2006), 14–15, 34; and ESRI, *Quarterly Economic Commentary: Winter 2006* (2006), 16.

to secure breathing space in the event of a potential shock, was to prove totally inadequate. It is also pertinent that in more normal circumstances such advice would have been perfectly sufficient and that analysts had no experience of considering the Irish fiscal position in the context of a major asset bubble.

Underpinning the collective failure to anticipate the potential scale of a drop in revenue was the fact that both organisations critically underappreciated the potential scale of a 'collapse' in construction output. The Bank's warning that a shock would precipitate a return to normal levels of activity, and the worst-case scenario envisaged by the ESRI, proved to be highly optimistic. Without a proper appreciation of the extent to which construction-related revenue could evaporate, analysts were never likely to appreciate the scale of the Exchequer's exposure. Furthermore, while the domestic organisations recognised the possibility of very significant falls in residential property prices, there is no indication that they anticipated how dramatically the number of transactions could decline, with attendant impacts on receipts from taxes such as VAT and stamp duty.

4 Competitiveness

The Central Bank routinely voiced concerns about inflation and cost competitiveness from the outset the decade. Analysts rightly recognised that external factors like oil prices and currency fluctuations could explain only part of the problem, and at over 6% the Irish inflation rate was more than double Eurozone average. On the domestic front wage inflation was identified as the key driver, fuelled by widespread labour shortages across the economy. While very significant headline productivity increases were used to justify wage increases, the Bank expressed concern that the aggregated productivity figures masked very stark sectoral discrepancies. The rapid wage growth that was warranted in the booming high-tech industries was found to be unduly generalised across the economy, stimulating inflation in the more sheltered sectors, particularly services.[19]

[19] Central Bank of Ireland, *Quarterly Bulletin: Spring 2000* (2000), 6–8, 13–14, 35–36, 42–45; Central Bank of Ireland, *Quarterly Bulletin: Summer 2000* (2000), 7, 27, 30, 57–60; and Central Bank of Ireland, *Quarterly Bulletin: Autumn 2000* (2000), 5–7, 23, 31, 33–34.

In the wake of the 2001 global downturn Bank analysts observed the contrast between moderating inflation in the manufacturing sector, which was exposed to competitive pressures, and the continued rapid growth of prices in sheltered services like education, health care and transport. They pointed to the very high inflation rate in the construction sector as being particularly problematic, describing housing as the archetypal non-tradable. While the headline inflation rate did moderate significantly in 2004 and 2005, the Bank observed that by that point Ireland had overtaken Finland as the most expensive country in the Eurozone, with consumer prices at 16% above the area average.[20]

The ESRI echoed the Central Bank's concerns about inflation routinely, again focusing on non-tradable goods and services like housing, legal services and taxis. Rapid price growth in the non-traded sectors prompted repeated calls for regulatory reform to enhance competition in these areas. Like the Bank, the institute largely attributed upward pressure on wages to a rising vacancy rate in firms across the economy. In stark contrast to Charlie McCreevy as Minister for Finance, analysts warned that the vulnerability of the economy to exogenous inflationary pressures made the need to address those factors that were under domestic influence all the more important.[21]

The focus by the Central Bank on the sub-sectoral discrepancies within Irish manufacturing demonstrated a robust understanding of the limits of the structural changes of the late 1990s. Enormous productivity increases in the high-tech multinationals contrasted sharply with very modest gains achieved in the traditional, largely indigenous sectors. While the headline manufacturing output growth rate was 8.2% at the

[20] Central Bank of Ireland, *Quarterly Bulletin: Summer 2002* (2002), 35, 38–39; Central Bank of Ireland, *Quarterly Bulletin: Autumn 2003* (2003), 41; Central Bank of Ireland, *Quarterly Bulletin: Winter 2003* (2003), 6; Central Bank of Ireland, *Quarterly Bulletin: Autumn 2004* (2004), 42; Central Bank of Ireland, *Quarterly Bulletin: Number 2, 2005* (2005), 7, 45; Central Bank of Ireland, *Quarterly Bulletin: Number 3, 2005* (2005), 35, 47, 51–52; and Central Bank and Financial Services Authority of Ireland, Financial Stability Report (2005), 18–19.

[21] ESRI, *Quarterly Economic Commentary, March 2000* (2000), 27, 28, 31, 33; ESRI, *Quarterly Economic Commentary, September 2000* (2000), 37, 40; ESRI, *Quarterly Economic Commentary, December 2000* (2000), 5, 32, 34, 37–39; ESRI, *Quarterly Economic Commentary, Summer 2002* (2002), 1; and ESRI, *Quarterly Economic Commentary, Autumn 2002* (2002), 34.

turn of the millennium, this masked increases of 11.1% in the high-tech sector and just 0.5% in traditional manufacturing. The ICT and chemicals sectors were found to have contributed a remarkable 90% of total industrial output and employment growth from 1995 to 2000, dwarfing the improvements in traditional sectors such as food processing. The recognition that the very strong productivity gains of the 1990s were confined to a small number of sectors had significant implications for how analysts understood the fundamental nature of the Irish economy. Furthermore, Bank analysts also appreciated that because of transfer pricing at least some of the very high output credited to workers in the high-tech sector was really attributable to research and development or marketing activities conducted abroad.[22]

The two domestic organisations were also quick to realise the negative impact of inflation on Ireland's export performance. Although the strong export growth of the late 1990s continued into the first year of the new decade, the effects of the global slowdown were evident by mid-2001, and the Bank reported declining exports as a number of US technology firms downsized their Irish operations. The primary factors were initially considered to be weak global demand, as well as sector-specific difficulties experienced in ICT and tourism. However, as world trade recovered it became apparent to both the Bank and the ESRI that the laggardly Irish export performance increasingly reflected domestic factors rather than the external environment. Total goods and services export growth, at just 2% in 2004, was less than a third of the growth in world trade, signifying a declining export share that was the inevitable consequence of deteriorating price competitiveness. In 2005 the ESRI warned that Ireland's share of world exports had fallen over the preceding three years and that this increased its reliance on domestic demand. The trend was

[22] Central Bank of Ireland, *Quarterly Bulletin, Spring 2000* (2000), 20, 21; Central Bank of Ireland, *Quarterly Bulletin, Winter 2000* (2000), 57–59; Central Bank of Ireland, *Quarterly Bulletin, Spring 2002* (2002), 17, 19, 21, 36, 43, 44; Central Bank of Ireland, *Quarterly Bulletin, Autumn 2002* (2002), 22; Geraldine Slevin, 'Is There a "New Economy" in Ireland?' (*Technical Paper 3/RT/02*) (2002), 2; Central Bank of Ireland, *Quarterly Bulletin, Winter 2002* (2002), 7, 44; Central Bank of Ireland, *Quarterly Bulletin, Spring 2003* (2003), 52; Central Bank of Ireland, *Quarterly Bulletin, Autumn 2003* (2003), 7; and Central Bank of Ireland, *Quarterly Bulletin, No. 4* (2006), 58.

in marked contrast to the period from 1990 to 2003, when the Irish share had essentially doubled.[23]

One recurring theme in the Central Bank publications is the comfort that analysts derived from the 'resilience' exhibited by the Irish economy in the face of the global downturn in 2001. From a post-2008 vantage point it is difficult to appreciate how sizeable the slump was considered to be at the time, but crucially the Bank described it as the 'sharpest downturn in global economic activity in two decades'. The reaction gives a good insight into what commentators considered to be a serious economic event, and presumably encouraged confidence in the ability of the Irish economy to weather other shocks in the future.[24]

Like most commentators the ESRI tended to treat the post-millennial boom as a continuation of the exceptional economic performance of the 1990s rather than as something fundamentally different. The five years preceding 2001 were considered to have 'finally convinced doubters that the process of accelerated economic convergence is not a mirage and that the Irish economy has come of age', and analysts described the period as 'this golden age for the Irish economy'. Like the Bank, the institute also repeatedly observed how 'remarkably resilient' the Irish economy had proved in the wake of the international slowdown. Such sentiments almost certainly made the task of those unconvinced about the fundamental nature of the Irish boom all the more difficult. By 2003 the narrative on the Irish performance had become decidedly effusive, with the Medium-Term Review of that year contending that:

[23]Central Bank of Ireland, *Quarterly Bulletin: Spring 2001* (2001), 10, 14–17; Central Bank of Ireland, *Quarterly Bulletin: Autumn 2001* (2001), 5–7; Central Bank of Ireland, *Quarterly Bulletin: Summer 2002* (2002), 12; Central Bank of Ireland, *Quarterly Bulletin: Spring 2003* (2003), 6; Central Bank of Ireland, *Quarterly Bulletin: Number 3* (2005), 6–7; Central Bank of Ireland, *Annual Report* (2005), 14; CBFSAI, *Financial Stability Report* (2005), 17; Central Bank of Ireland, *Quarterly Bulletin: Number 1* (2006), 7–8, 14, 19; Mark Cassidy and Derry O'Brien, 'Export Performance and Competitiveness of the Irish Economy', in Central Bank of Ireland, *Quarterly Bulletin: Number 3* (2005), 75, 77–78, 93–94; ESRI, *Quarterly Economic Commentary: Autumn 2005* (2005), 13; ESRI, *Quarterly Economic Commentary: Winter 2005* (2005), 17; and ESRI, *Quarterly Economic Commentary: Spring 2006* (2006), 30.

[24]Central Bank of Ireland, *Quarterly Bulletin: Winter 2003* (2003), 5 and Central Bank of Ireland, *Quarterly Bulletin: Winter 2001* (2001), 5, 6, 9.

> In the mid-1990s, when Ireland's period of exceptional growth began, there were some who feared that it was a mirage and that, as the dust settled, Ireland would wake up and find that the growth in output had never happened. However, as successive years of growth built into a boom, such fears were seen to be groundless.[25]

Summary

Both the Central Bank and the ESRI appreciated that the remarkable productivity performance of Irish manufacturing was in reality confined to the multinational ICT and chemicals sectors. Both expressed concern that what they considered to be unjustified wage increases in traditional manufacturing and services were leading to rising unit wage costs across many sectors and that deteriorating cost competitiveness was creating fundamental problems for the Irish economy. The organisations also recognised that stagnant manufacturing export growth increased the dependence on domestic consumption and that the booming construction sector offered only a temporary buffer against falling manufacturing employment. Again however, the assumption that construction would continue to provide significant employment after the property boom ended was vital and ensured that analysts critically misjudged the potential scale of the ramifications of deteriorating competitiveness and declining manufacturing employment for the Irish economy.

5 The Financial Sector

While organisations like the ESRI had less access to micro-level data than the Irish banks or regulatory authorities, the mounting risks to financial stability should have been evident from the headline figures. In March 2006 *The Irish Times* reported that outstanding mortgage debt was growing at almost 29% and had doubled to €100 billion in just three years. The same article reported that total private-sector credit was growing at a rate of 28.8% and had exceeded €262 billion. This is just one example, and the aggregated data on total mortgage and private-sector

[25] ESRI, *Quarterly Economic Commentary: September 2000* (2000), 35; ESRI, *Quarterly Economic Commentary: December 2000* (2000), 33, 36; ESRI, *Quarterly Economic Commentary: Winter 2002* (2002), 30; ESRI, *Quarterly Economic Commentary: Winter 2003* (2003), 35; ESRI, *Medium-Term Review*: 2001–*2007* (2001), vii; and ESRI, *Medium-Term Review*: 2003–*2010* (2003), vii.

credit and their respective growth rates were frequently published in the newspapers throughout the boom years. For an analyst who knew how exceptional these growth rates were, they should have sparked immediate alarm. Patrick Honohan has since suggested that a very simple warning about financial stability is if an institution's balance sheet grows by over 20% per annum. The fact that the entire Irish sector was exceeding this threshold by a considerable margin was therefore highly significant. In June 2006 the *Irish Independent* reported the European Central Bank's unease about credit growth of 11% across the Eurozone. As Davy stockbrokers observed at the time, one could only imagine what it made of the Irish situation.[26]

One question then, is why analysts outside of the Central Bank underreacted to this level of credit growth. Donovan and Murphy have argued that the ESRI suffered from something of a skills gap in macro-finance after Patrick Honohan left the institute in 1998. Honohan was at the World Bank until 2007, and there was no comparable financial expert working in Ireland in the period. Even if economists with different specialities were concerned about the level of credit growth, they would presumably have been more cautious about confronting policymakers than someone with the relevant core expertise.[27]

The other key risks to the financial system should have been evident from the headline data provided within the Central Bank's publications. The 2006 FSR observed that property-related loans accounted for 84% of all lending growth to the non-financial corporate sector and now accounted for 61.5% of the total owed. This of course represented an enormous exposure, compounded by the fact that construction and property lending was heavily concentrated among a small number of firms. An even greater proportion of personal lending was for housing,

[26] Marc Coleman, 'Home lending Rises 29% as ECB Worries Over Rapid Lending Growth', *The Irish Times*, 1 March 2006, 18; Patrick Honohan, 'Resolving Ireland's Banking Crisis', UCD Economic Workshop Conference 'Responding to the Crisis', 'Dublin, 12 January 2009 (2009a), 7; and Brendan Keenan, '"Rampant" Growth in Private Debt as Borrowing Up 30pc', *Irish Independent*, 1 June 2006.

[27] Donovan and Murphy, *The Fall of the Celtic Tiger* (2013), 154 and Alan Barret and Brian Lucey, 'An Analysis of the Journal Output of Irish-Based Economists, 1970–2001', *Economic and Social Review*, vol. 34, no. 2 (Summer/Autumn 2003). http://www.centralbank.ie/about-us/pages/ourseniorteam.aspx/. Accessed 11 November 2015.

and property-related loans thus represented just under two-thirds of all outstanding private-sector debt. This of course raises the question of why the remarkable exposure of the banking system to the broad property sector did not prompt more alarm within the CBFSAI itself. Analysts were cognisant of the possibility that commercial and residential property prices could fall in tandem in the event of a serious downturn. Although they were clearly aware of how precipitously house prices could fall in a worst-case scenario, however, there is no evidence that they were comparably alert to the risks posed by construction and commercial real estate lending.[28]

The extent of the exposure on the funding side was also evident in the data provided in the Central Bank's core publications. From 2004 onwards successive FSRs noted the vulnerability posed by the declining deposits-to-loans ratio of the Irish financial sector. This increased the funding gap, which needed to be filled by interbank borrowing and by issuing debt securities. By 2006 the funding gap of the Irish institutions had risen to 46%, up from just 7% a decade earlier. The Bank was cognisant that this represented the highest level in the Eurozone and that it constituted a vulnerability, since international funding had evaporated 'many times in the past following a shock to the global economy'. However, analysts showed a marked lack of imagination about the potential consequences of such an eventuality, pointing to possible difficulties for first-time buyers accessing mortgages and a reduction in discretionary income for existing homeowners. A cross-country historical study of how countries with large financial-sector funding gaps had fared in the event of a liquidity shock would clearly have been very welcome and might have better attuned the Bank to the degree of the risk.[29]

Like the IMF, the Central Bank concluded that the Irish banks could withstand a very significant fall in house prices, with John Hurley suggesting a figure of 40%. The Bank economists who conducted the relevant stress tests added significant caveats to their analyses, which we will come to presently. What is immediately striking however, is Hurley's

[28]CBFSAI, *Financial Stability Report*, 12, 39, 130; CBFSAI, *Financial Stability Report* (2004), 23, 26; Central Bank of Ireland, *Quarterly Bulletin: Number 3* (2006), 30; and CBFSAI, *Financial Stability Report* (2005), 9.

[29]CBFSAI, *Financial Stability Report* (2004), 27–29, 34; CBFSAI, *Financial Stability Report* (2005), 41–42, 71, 91; and CBFSAI, *Financial Stability Report* (2006), 46.

contention that a residential property price fall and an increased default rate by mortgage holders constituted the biggest risk to the banking system. Similarly, the Bank's FSRs considered mortgage debt in enormous detail and paid remarkably little attention to the exposure of the banks to the construction sector or to commercial real estate. This is a major discrepancy, since as we have seen the Bank's own publications recognised the enormous concentration of corporate lending to a small number of very big property and construction firms. It should thus have been relatively straightforward for analysts within the Bank to deduce that this constituted at least a comparable exposure to residential property.[30]

The most likely explanation for the Bank's disproportionate focus on mortgage lending rather than the exposure to property and construction firms is that in a more typical scenario corporate lending would be far better diversified and mortgages would constitute the key risk. In evaluating financial stability economists would thus automatically examine the housing market as a basic consideration. Even in the Irish case at this juncture residential mortgages still represented 64% of all property-related lending, with construction and commercial real estate constituting 26 and 10%, respectively. But the headline figures were only a partial indication of the relative risks attached to each sector, since developers were much more likely to default than homeowners in the event of a crisis, and the assets underpinning their loans had the potential to fall far more precipitously in value. A second possible explanation is again that the standard studies of financial crises provide conspicuously little examination of what happens to construction activity in the event of a house price crash. It would have been considerably more difficult for analysts to find useful precedents for the scale of the Irish construction boom than for the house price boom. Even if these examples had been presented to senior decision-makers within the Bank, there is no guarantee that they would have fundamentally changed their views on the stability of the Irish financial system. As we have seen, officials were not above dismissing the applicability of inconvenient historical lessons.[31]

[30] Pat Boyle, 'Banks "Could Cope with 40pc House Price Fall"', *Irish Independent*, 22 September 2004 and CBFSAI, *Financial Stability Report* (2004), 31–32.

[31] For example, see Charles Poor Kindleberger and Robert Aliber, *Manias, Panics and Crashes: A History of Financial Crises* (2005); Robert Shiller, *Irrational Exuberance* (2003); and CBFSAI, *Financial Stability Report* (2006), 134.

Even notwithstanding the various shortfalls of the analysis conducted by the Central Bank, the response of the Financial Regulator in the face of key risks was clearly unjustifiable. The authority displayed remarkable tolerance in the face of serious governance transgressions by individual banks, as well as the wholesale flouting of sectoral concentration limits. Perhaps most remarkable of all was the recent acknowledgement by the Regulator's former CEO, Liam O'Reilly, that the authority never compiled data on the cross-exposures of different banks to the same large developers. Nor were these key loans particularly discreet. The various shortcomings of the Regulator have been examined in detail elsewhere, but it is important to stress that identifying the analytical shortfalls of the Central Bank's publications in no way absolves the inaction of senior decision-makers in either institution.[32]

The last major point of interest regarding the analysis of the financial sector is the stress testing that was conducted by the Central Bank. Stress testing by its nature is highly quantitative and rather complex, which presumably made the Banks' analyses rather inscrutable for its non-specialist senior decision-makers. However, stress tests are also fundamentally subjective and are only as good as the parameters of the shocks that are modelled. Furthermore, their predictive value becomes increasingly diluted as the scale of the shock increases. The subjectivity arises from the fact that analysts consider the potential impact of shocks based on past scenarios or what they consider to be plausible future ones. The decisive factor therefore becomes the historical perspective of the analyst selecting the scenarios. Given that the 2001 slowdown was considered to be the sharpest global downturn in two decades, an analyst with a short-term historical perspective could quite conceivably have considered it the worst shock that was likely enough to justify consideration. If one subscribed to the notion of a 'Great Moderation', as the Bank subsequently professed to, shocks in the more distant past could even be dismissed as being largely irrelevant.[33]

[32] Nyberg Commission, *Misjudging Risk* (2011), i, ii, iv, vii, 27–28, 32, 44, 46, 49, 59, 62, 94; Honohan Commission, *The Irish Banking Crisis* (2010), 8, 47, 55, 58–59, 109; and Houses of the Oireachtas, *Joint Committee of Inquiry into the Banking Crisis*, vol. 2, no. 27, Liam O'Reilly, 11 June 2015, 15.

[33] Houses of the Oireachtas, *Joint Committee of Inquiry into the Banking Crisis*, vol. 2, no. 26, Tom O'Connell, 10 June 2015, 80 and Andrew Mawdsley, Maurice McGuire, and Nuala O'Donnell, 'The Stress Testing of Irish Credit Institutions', in CBFSAI, *Financial Stability Report* (2004), 103, 104.

The second major limitation was one that the analysts within the Bank highlighted repeatedly in the FSRs. Their stress tests only modelled the first-round effects of shocks to the banking system. In reality, almost any conceivable shock to the banks would also affect other aspects of the economy, which in turn would further impact the banks. This was particularly limiting in the context of the crash that followed given that the multiple facets of the crisis were so mutually reinforcing. A closely related problem was that the results assumed that the relationship between the size of a shock and its impact would be linear rather than exponential. The Bank's stress tests were thus far better-suited to predicting the effects of a typical shock rather than the disproportionate impact of an extreme outlier.[34]

Summary

The key exposures of the broader financial system were in plain sight and should have been evident from the Central Bank's core publications and even the newspapers. Rather than micro-level data, the additional information that would have best-equipped an analyst to recognise the extent of the systemic risk was a good knowledge of the history of financial crises and the thresholds beyond which financial systems had run into trouble in the past. Significantly, when Morgan Kelly first argued that the Irish banks were vulnerable he compared the proportion of lending to construction and real estate to the Japanese level immediately prior to the 1989 crash. By contrast, while analysts within the Central Bank recognised where the key exposures lay, they made remarkably little use of international precedent to determine the degree of the risk.[35]

The same pattern was repeated on the funding side, and while Bank analysts noted that the Irish funding gap was unusually large, they paid little attention to episodes where this had undermined financial stability elsewhere. It seems quite possible from the contemporary reports that analysts within the Central Bank were discouraged from 'looking for trouble' or being overly alarmist. Insofar as this was the case the responsibility of course rests with the senior decision-makers within the CBFSAI. So too does a marked reluctance to act in the face of mounting risks, a

[34] CBFSAI, *Financial Stability Report* (2004), 9, 31–32, 36–37, 105, 109; CBFSAI, *Financial Stability Report* (2006), 13; and Allan Kearns, 'Top-Down Stress Testing: The Key Results', in CBFSAI, *Financial Stability Report* (2006), 110.

[35] CBFSAI, *Financial Stability Report* (2006), 135 and Morgan Kelly, 'Banking on Very Shaky Foundations', *The Irish Times*, 7 September 2007.

disinclination that was evident even in the contemporary publications. The CBFSAI was often remarkably receptive to tentative indications that house price increases were moderating, and was clearly prepared to wait patiently for a market correction to avoid decisive intervention.[36]

6 Conclusion

The domestic organisations clearly appreciated the nature of many of the key vulnerabilities of the Irish economy in the period. Analysts repeatedly issued warnings about the excessive reliance on property-related tax revenue, inflationary fiscal policy, eroding competitiveness, excessive house price growth, excessive credit growth and the exposure of the financial sector. However, the domestic organisations were still far too sanguine about the future and about the probability and potential scale of a crisis. As we have seen, this was clearly not because they failed to contemplate the possibility of a dramatic fall in house prices. The critical shortcoming in both cases was that analysts never considered the possibility that construction activity could fall by over 90%. This proved decisive, ensuring that they significantly underestimated the potential scale of the risks to employment and domestic demand, to the Exchequer and to the banks. This in turn informed an overly positive reading of the fundamental health of the macroeconomy and of the financial system.

The worst-case scenarios proposed for the construction sector were particularly myopic given that forty or fifty thousand units would still have been well in excess of the ESRI's underlying demographic demand estimate, and a multiple of the per capita output in comparison countries. Analysts clearly had trouble envisaging the near total collapse of a seemingly vibrant sector. Many commentators, both in Ireland and internationally, have pointed to the influence of ideology in encouraging analysts to place excessive faith in markets in the run-up to the crash. While formal economic ideology may have played a role, it is important not to overstress its importance in this case. The fact that the domestic organisations considered the prospect of very large house price falls disproves any contention that they were unwilling to countenance the possibility of significant market failures.

[36] Houses of the Oireachtas, *Joint Committee of Inquiry into the Banking Crisis*, vol. 2, no. 26, Tom O'Connell, 10 June 2015.

By contrast, recent Irish economic history and the first-hand experience of the analysts writing the reports had a very substantial influence on the analysis. The domestic organisations repeatedly warned of the risks posed by runaway inflation, an oil crisis, fiscal improvidence and the potential knock-on effect of a recession in the USA. The fact that all of these events had played a deleterious role within living memory is highly significant. Irish analysts had no collective first-hand experience of asset bubbles or systemic financial crises, and the fact that no senior officials in the CBFSAI or Department of Finance had worked overseas must have exacerbated the primacy given to Irish experience. Although analysts gave some consideration to the experiences of other countries, they did so in a decidedly limited manner. Given the extent to which the macroeconomy was exposed to the construction sector, there was far too little investigation of how construction activity had fared in the event of house price crashes elsewhere. Similarly, the potential consequences considered in the event that interbank funding dried up were implausibly optimistic and not underpinned by any explicit examination of relevant precedent.[37]

The Central Bank's explicit dismissal of the IMF's study of the recent history of boom/bust cycles in international property markets was a manifestation of the subsequently expressed mentality that the past served as a poor predictor of the future. As extensive analysis by Reinhardt and Rogoff has since demonstrated, such beliefs had remarkably little factual basis. Many of the conceptual problems with the Central Bank's model of the housing sector and stress tests of the banking system were recognised at the time and should have encouraged analysts to rely far more heavily on the lessons of international history. Even if one could devise a seemingly robust model rationalising house price increases, it should have provided little comfort if such increases had invariably preceded falls across dozens of countries in the recent past.[38]

Analysts struggled to explain what was happening in the real economy, and were evidently tempted to shape their analyses to fit the world around them. Shortly after suggesting that the underlying demographic demand in the Irish economy was for 30,000 housing units a year, the ESRI anticipated that demand would be for 71,900 units annually from 2007 to 2011. Remarkably, under a quarter of this demand was forecast

[37] Donovan and Murphy, *The Fall of the Celtic Tiger* (2013), 289.

[38] Reinhardt and Rogoff, *This Time Is Different* (2011), xxvii–xxviii, 141–142, 171–172.

on the basis of natural population growth, with the rest attributed to second homes, inward migration, obsolescence and falling household sizes. Such forecasts should have been considered highly dubious and ultimately relied on circular dependencies: the atypical importance of two of the four factors was a consequence of the boom, itself increasingly a function of property and construction activity.[39]

The regular references made by analysts to the 'resilience' of the Irish economy and financial sector in the wake of the international slowdown in 2001 are of enormous importance. The downturn shaped much of the discourse on the Irish economy until well into 2004, and from a post-2008 vantage point it is hard to appreciate how significant an event it was considered to be at the time. The smooth redeployment of labour and the apparent robustness of the banks in the face of the 'sharpest downturn in global economic activity in two decades' played a significant role in confirming the view that the Irish economy was built on strong fundamentals and could weather a potential shock. Similarly, analysts within the ESRI were clearly deeply invested in the Irish success story. While this was quite understandable, it presumably made it all the more difficult to sustain a watchful scepticism.

There was unquestionably a tension between the regular warnings issued by analysts within the CBFSAI about inflation, rising house prices and loosening credit criteria and the marked inaction of senior officials to address these concerns. A suggestive contention in the 2005 FSR was that regulators could not attempt to supersede the judgements of banks on specific loans, since lenders made these judgements routinely and the authorities were too far removed from individual cases. This belief was probably indicative of a broader deference to the judgement of senior decision-makers within the private banks. While the bad lending practices underpinning the Irish financial crash were fundamentally different to those that precipitated the US subprime mortgage crisis, the mentalities of the respective regulatory authorities were evidently quite similar. The cognitive dissonance between the warnings issued by the analysts within the Central Bank and the reluctance to 'stop the party' is somewhat more comprehensible in this light.[40]

[39] ESRI, *Medium-Term Review*: 2005–*2012* (2005), 74.

[40] Central Bank of Ireland, *Financial Stability Report* (2005), 64.

The warnings issued to lenders by the CBFSAI from the outset of the period right up until 2006 clearly had minimal effect. The benign summary conclusions of the FSRs contributed to the core problem significantly, since they helped to bolster the confidence of both the authorities and those working within the private financial institutions. It is quite possible that senior officials within the CBFSAI would have acted more assertively if analysts within the Bank or elsewhere had been more accurate in recognising that construction and real estate activity could fall so precipitously, and warned of the attendant implications for the banks, the economy and the Exchequer. However, there was plenty of justification for decisive action given the analysis that was available. Since the fiscal, employment and financial stability implications of a potential downturn were generally perceived to be manageable, decision-makers may well have either consciously or subconsciously concluded that decisive intervention was not worth the inevitable political fallout and public disapprobation, especially since almost nobody was calling for it.[41]

The contrasting responses from Caroline Gavin and the 2004 FSR to the IMF study of housing boom/bust cycles represented two fundamentally differing mindsets. The dismissal of the IMF warning in the FSR, added to the fact that Gavin's study generated minimal discussion in subsequent Bank publications, strongly suggests that there was little incentive for an analyst within the Bank to concentrate on undesirable possible futures. Given the evident mentality that the past offered a poor guide to the future, it seems likely that examining the lessons of international experience was not considered the core business of the research department. This insularity and sense of exceptionalism were all the more limiting given the relative narrowness of recent Irish economic experience. Neither policymakers nor commentators were particularly well-prepared for the challenges that came with economic success.[42]

Analysts were largely surprised by scale of the boom and undoubtedly failed to anticipate the depth of the crash. In part, this may be attributed to the assumption that Ireland's recent economic performance was a good indicator of future performance. It is perhaps unsurprising that institutional predictions were skewed towards what would widely

[41] Nyberg Commission, *Misjudging Risk* (2011), 67.

[42] Houses of the Oireachtas, *Joint Committee of Inquiry into the Banking Crisis*, vol. 2, no. 26, Tom O'Connell, 10 June 2015, 113.

be considered 'reasonable' based on recent experience. While this bias may help to reduce the likelihood that predictions will be significantly wide of the mark most of the time, the excessive weight given to recent experience also significantly reduced the chances of analysts anticipating a major crisis.[43]

[43]ESRI, *Medium-Term Review*: 2003–*2010* (2003), 105.

CHAPTER 5

Academia

Reasoning will never make a man correct an ill opinion, which by reasoning he never acquired.

Attributed to Jonathan Swift[1]

1 Introduction

There is a crucial disagreement between the Honohan and Nyberg reports over the role played by academic economists in the period. The Honohan Report argued that by 2003/2004 the 'majority' view of economists outside of the official organisations was that property prices were overvalued and that a fall was inevitable. Honohan went even further, contending that 'most' studies predicted that such an event would trigger 'recessionary pressures'. His position almost directly contradicts Nyberg's contention that 'the vast majority' of academics were strongly supportive of the expansion of property-related lending by the banks, and that there was a general belief in academic circles that a soft landing was the worst-case scenario for the banking sector. The discrepancy is a pivotal one for our purposes, and establishing the reality is a crucial first step for this chapter. The two reports offer minimal help in this regard, since they do very little to justify their respective positions. Honohan does reference a warning that he himself issued in 2004 about

[1] See http://quoteinvestigator.com/2015/07/10/reason-out/. Accessed 2 February 2016.

C. M. Casey, *Policy Failures and the Irish Economic Crisis*,
https://doi.org/10.1007/978-3-319-90182-4_5

the vulnerability of the Irish economy and particularly about the rate of credit growth. However, this clearly does little to prove that such concerns were widely held.[2]

The striking picture that emerges from a systematic reading of the academic commentary on the Irish economy in the period is that the vast majority of economists never came down strongly on either side. The key journals were replete with articles about the remarkable transformation of the Irish economy from the mid-1990s, with far less attention paid to contemporary economic vulnerabilities or the future. Within the context of these publications, this is perhaps unsurprising. The Celtic Tiger was exceptional by both Irish and international standards, and analysts still struggle to fully explain it. An economist interrogating the origins of the Irish success story had the benefit of significant amounts of quantitative data and an existing literature with which to engage. In this respect the disposition towards historical analysis was probably also self-reinforcing. Furthermore, academics took a perfectly understandable personal interest in the Irish success story. Even those who held misgivings could take gratification from the dramatic reversal after entire careers spent interpreting the causes of Ireland's economic malaise. Antoin Murphy pointed to the personal pleasure he derived from seeing many of his graduate students return to Ireland after decades of watching the majority of them emigrate.[3]

We can safely assume that academics were not apathetic about the future of the Irish economy or how the property and construction booms would end. However, as Brendan Walsh put it in a 2001 interview, academic economists are not paid to forecast, and prediction in the face of economic uncertainty is inherently unscientific. A retrospective or theoretical subject matter was certainly more conducive to academic rigour. Similarly, unlike economists working in the official organisations or in the newspapers, academics were under no obligation to monitor the contemporary economy as part of their core roles. In fact the surest path

[2] Honohan Commission, *The Irish Banking Crisis: Regulatory and Financial Stability Policy 2003–2008. A Report to the Minister of Finance by the Governor of the Central Bank* (2010), 89 and Nyberg Commission, *Misjudging Risk: Causes of the Systemic Banking Crisis in Ireland. Report of the Commission of Investigation into the Banking Sector in Ireland* (March 2011), 50, 90.

[3] Antoin E. Murphy, 'The 'Celtic Tiger'—An Analysis of Ireland's Economic Growth Performance', RSC no. 2000/16, European University Institute, 2000, 23.

for career advancement, publication in high-ranking international journals, presumably discouraged a focus on the Irish economy, which in a global context could have been considered 'tiny and boring'.[4]

The relative dearth of academic articles that considered the prospects for the Irish economy thus becomes more comprehensible if we accept the premise that even those academics who had relevant expertise were not particularly incentivised to consider the subject in their formal academic writings. One can certainly argue that academics could express their opinions in other fora, and to a certain extent they did. However, a simple analysis of the references to individual academics in the economics pages of *The Irish Times* in the period is quite instructive in this regard. The quantitative data presented in Chapter 6 demonstrate that with one or two exceptions academic economists had minimal opportunity to express their views in the period, particularly in comparison with economists within the banks and stockbrokers. The marked exception is Jim O'Leary, who wrote regular opinion pieces throughout. However, if anything O'Leary serves to confirm the pattern, since he was already established as a regular contributor when he moved from Davy Stockbrokers to Maynooth.

One could give the Honohan and Nyberg reports the benefit of the doubt and argue that their contentions pertained to radio and television interviews, but without any citations to that effect it seems to be unlikely. What is much more probable is that the reports serve to illustrate how the positions taken in the period have been widely misremembered, and the importance of a thorough reading of the material produced at the time. Given the concerns expressed by the IMF, *The Economist* newspaper and some private-sector economists, it is quite likely that a number of academics held misgivings about the property market that they did not publish. In a global context, Steve Keen has contended that many Austrian and post-Keynesian economists expected an international crisis but that the vast majority did not issue public warnings. The apparent imperviousness of Irish policymakers to warnings from the formal organisations would hardly have encouraged an academic to take a public stance. We should avoid attempts at quantification with words like 'many' or 'most' in this context because in the absence of contemporary

[4]Vincent Browne, 'Facing the Future with "Qualified Optimism"', *Irish Times*, 10 November 2001, 7 and Michael Lewis, *Boomerang: The Biggest Bust* (London, 2011), 90.

survey data it is simply impossible to know the prevalence of such views among those who did not publish their opinions. For our purposes, a debate over the extent to which academics held unpublicised concerns is both somewhat fruitless and a needless distraction insofar as privately held misgivings would have had minimal effect on the wider debate.[5]

We will therefore focus on the positions that academic economists did take in their articles about the Irish economy in the period. This chapter will first provide some contextualisation before considering contemporary interpretations of the Celtic Tiger and their implications for the future. It will then turn to some of the views expressed on the core themes in the other chapters, namely competitiveness, fiscal policy, property and construction, and the financial sector. Finally, it will consider some of the predictions that were made about the future of the Irish economy. The chapter is based on a systematic reading of all of the relevant material published in the *Economic and Social Review* (ESR) and the *Journal of the Statistical and Social Inquiry Society of Ireland* (JSSISI) as the two key Irish economics journals in the period, as well as the *Irish Banking Review* up to the point that it was discontinued in mid-2004. Many additional relevant publications on the Irish economy from the period will also be included, particularly those written by influential economists. Several contributions from outside the 2000 to 2006 period will be addressed where they are deemed to have been especially significant in shaping how the economy was understood.

2 Institutional Context

Relevant contributions were published by researchers based across the Irish universities and abroad. However, a brief examination of the size and focus of the UCD (University College Dublin) and TCD (Trinity College Dublin) economics departments provides some useful insight. In the years 2004–2006, the UCD department employed approximately 26 full-time academic staff, while TCD averaged approximately 17 from the start of the decade. A relatively small proportion of these academics wrote on subjects pertinent to the exposure of the Irish economy. For example, only five of the academics listed in the Trinity department in 2005/2006 had published articles relevant for our purposes. Table 1 lists

[5]Steve Keen, *Debunking Economics: The Naked Emperor Dethroned* (London, 2011), 326.

Table 1 Academic economists

Name	*Affiliations*	*Research areas*
Frank Barry	UCD	FDI, the European Union
Morgan Kelly	UCD	Institutions, development, economic history
Cormac Ó Gráda	UCD	Famines, economic history
Kevin O'Rourke	UCD/TCD	International economic history
Brendan Walsh	UCD	Ireland, unemployment, the European Union
Anthony Murphy	UCD/Oxford	Housing
Philip Lane	TCD	EMU, globalisation, fiscal policy, finance
Patrick Honohan	World Bank	Banking and finance, EMU
Maurice Roche	NUI Maynooth	Irish housing and farming land, agriculture
Paul Krugman	Princeton	International macroeconomics

some of the key relevant academics, their then institutional affiliations, and some of their primary areas of focus in the period.[6]

A noticeable characteristic of the discourse among Irish academic economists is that analysts made decidedly little reference to whether they or their peers subscribed to theoretical schools. Debates over the nature of the Irish boom therefore did not explicitly fall along these lines. The left-wing critique of Irish economic policy in the relevant journals came primarily from sociologists. However, these articles did not significantly add to the discourse on the aspects of the Irish economy that precipitated the crash and are therefore not a core focus of our analysis. A second interesting feature is the disproportionate contribution of economic historians to the relevant debates. This was perhaps a function of both the debate over the genesis of the Irish boom and the potential relevance of international precedent in determining how it might end.

In an analysis of the journal output of Irish economists from 1970 to 2001, Alan Barret and Brian Lucey found Patrick Honohan to be the most prolific author, as well as the second most prolific adjusting for journal quality. Honohan was also conspicuous as the foremost Irish financial economist, with extensive international experience. On an annualised basis the two most prolific were Philip Lane and Kevin O'Rourke, both of whom started publishing in the 1990s. Of the economists listed in the table above, Kelly was found to have been the highest ranked in

[6]UCD Economics Department Staff Lists 2004/5 and 2006/7; TCD University Calendars 2000–2006; and https://ideas.repec.org/.

terms of publications in both the top five and the top ten international journals. At a broader level, the authors found that the journal publication record of Irish economists had become increasingly internationalised over the three decades observed, though this was not matched by a corresponding increase in publications in the top international journals. A conspicuous proportion of the economists who contributed most to the debate on the Irish economy had pursued doctoral study at highly ranked international universities, notably O'Rourke and Lane at Harvard, Kelly at Yale, Ó Gráda at Columbia, Honohan at the London School of Economics, and Murphy at Oxford. This presumably suggests that they were potentially both well-trained and cognisant of the Irish economy in its broader international context.[7]

Given that publication in high-ranking journals is a key metric for measuring the performance of both individual academics and their departments, the rankings of the Irish economics journals were clearly very significant. The *SCImago Journal Rank* (SJR) given for the ESR in the period ranged from a low of 0.123 in 2001 to a high of 0.284 in 2004, while total citations ranged from 35 to 107 per annum. A simple impact assessment based on citations over the past ten years puts the ESR at 278th place on a ranking of economics journals internationally. There was no SJR given for the JSSISI for the period, but its performance since suggests a somewhat similar picture. A comparison with the rankings and citations of large journals with an international focus is not a reflection on the performance of the Irish journals, which given their geographical focus actually do quite well. However, an ambitious academic would clearly have been encouraged to publish abroad. At the top of the table, the Harvard-based 'Quarterly Journal of Economics' received an SJR of 19.95 and 5579 citations for 2006. Seeking publication in such highly ranked journals would have significantly discouraged a focus on the Irish economy given its size. What is noticeable however, is that several of the academics who contributed most to the discourse on the Irish economy across various fora were also among

[7]Alan Barrett and Brian Lucey, 'An Analysis of the Journal-Based Output of Irish-Based Economists, 1970–2001', *Economic and Social Review*, vol. 34, no. 2 (Summer/Autumn 2003), 118, 123, 133, 137, 142 and http://www.centralbank.ie/about-us/pages/oursen-iorteam.aspx/. Accessed 11 November 2015.

the most successful at securing publication in highly ranked international journals in the period.[8]

3 Origins and Interpretations of the Celtic Tiger

Economists were as unprepared for the scale of the 1990s boom as they were for the scale of the crash in 2008. Initial cynicism that the growth figures represented nothing more than distortions induced by the transfer pricing activities of the multinationals was dispelled as employment began to grow dramatically. Once the boom was underway, a prevailing view emerged that it was a process of belated convergence with the living standards of the rest of Western Europe. While economists assumed that they had a good understanding of how and why the boom had happened, this chapter will demonstrate that there is no single conclusive explanation and that the topic was still very much up for discussion. The debate was more than academic, insofar as it had serious implications for the Irish economy's ability to sustain very high growth rates into the new millennium. We will also consider some explanations of why the Celtic Tiger happened when it did, and some of the unanswered questions about the role of the multinationals. Again, these issues had very direct implications for how the contemporary economy was understood and for the policy advice issued in the period.[9]

In explaining the origins of the Celtic Tiger economists pointed to a wide range of contributory factors, including everything from high levels of education to low levels of employment regulation. However, there are two particularly compelling accounts of why Ireland was able to achieve such extraordinary growth figures, which are worth considering briefly. The more influential interpretation was convergence theory, first advocated by Ó Gráda and O'Rourke and subsequently by Honohan and Walsh. Convergence theory argues that poor countries should grow

[8]www.scopus.com. Accessed 1 December 2014 and https://ideas.repec.org/top/top.journals.simple10.html. Accessed 1 December 2014.

[9]Brendan Walsh, 'The Transformation of the Irish Labour Market: 1980–2003', *Journal of the Statistical and Social Inquiry Society of Ireland*, vol. xxxiii (May 2004), 84; Brendan Walsh, 'The Irish Economic 'Miracle': How Do We Explain the Timing of the Boom?', *New Economy*, vol. 6, no. 4 (December 1999), 225; and Philip R. Lane, 'Profits and Wages in Ireland, 1987–1996', *Journal of the Statistical and Social Inquiry Society of Ireland*, vol. xxvii, part v (May 1998), 227.

more quickly than richer countries if they enjoy comparable levels of human capital, largely because physical capital can be used more productively in poorer countries and technologies may be imported. Honohan and Walsh argued that on this basis one could have, and some did, predict Irish convergence towards European living standards in 1973, and that the real question is why it took so long. By way of explanation, they suggest that the entire period from the early 1970s can be perceived as one long business cycle, with a prolonged recession in the early 1980s. According to this assessment, the boom was stalled through the poor policy choices made in the wake of the oil crises, and the protracted failure to address the ensuing debt crisis. The implication of convergence theory was that as Irish living standards caught up with those of richer countries growth would inevitably fall back to more normal rates.[10]

The competing fundamental explanation for the Irish performance was regional boom theory, as advocated by Paul Krugman and Frank Barry. Krugman contended that in view of its population size, its high levels of trade and the mobility of its labour force, the Irish economy could be best considered as a regional economy within Europe. Regional economies like those within the US have the potential to grow more rapidly than national ones, and the exceptional level of Irish growth could be understood on this basis. The key differential is that a regional economy can benefit from mass immigration during a boom, whereas in a more closed national economy labour shortages will inevitably dampen growth. Assuming that physical capital levels also continued to grow the Irish boom could be sustained, albeit on the basis of higher inputs rather than higher productivity. As Barry observed this was a distinctly double-edged sword, since while it meant that Irish living standards could exceed those of rich national economies, it also implied that the gains of the 1990s were readily reversible. Predicting the future

[10] Paul R. Krugman, 'Good News from Ireland: A Geographical Perspective', in Alan W. Gray (ed.), *International Perspectives on the Irish Economy* (Dublin, 1997), 43, 51, 53; Walsh, 'The Irish Economic 'Miracle': How Do We Explain the Timing of the Boom?' (1999), 226–227; Cormac Ó Gráda and Kevin H. O'Rourke, 'Living standards and Growth', in J.W. O'Hagan, *The Economy of Ireland: Policy and Performance of a European Region* (Dublin, 2000), 198–226; Patrick Honohan and Brendan Walsh, 'Catching Up with the Leaders: The Irish Hare', *Brookings Papers on Economic Activity*, 2002, no. 1, 1, 4, 5, 7; and Frank Barry, Aoife Hannan, and Eric A. Strobl, 'The Real Convergence in the Irish Economy and the Sectoral Distribution of Employment Growth', in Frank Barry (ed.), *Understanding Ireland's Economic Growth* (1999), 13.

and acting accordingly was thus heavily dependent on how analysts interpreted the past and present.[11]

If convergence theory and regional boom theory compete to explain the 'why' of the Celtic Tiger, then another key debate was why it happened when it did. There are three standout theories in this respect, which are all mutually complementary and could very plausibly have conspired to produce the Irish boom in the mid-1990s. Brendan Walsh has argued that the strong historical link between Irish and UK unemployment rates was a function of the propensity of Irish people to emigrate. For much of the 1960s and 1970s the Irish unemployment rate closely tracked that of the UK, with a differential of 3–4%. The relationship broke down in the 1980s due to a fall in demand for unskilled labour in the UK, causing Irish unemployment rates to increase markedly. This in turn dampened wage demands, reversing the trend of deteriorating Irish wage competitiveness, and was paradoxically crucial in generating the subsequent boom.[12]

The second theory, as expounded by Antoin Murphy, focuses on the coincidence of the early '90s boom in the USA with the formation of the European Single Market. This encouraged US firms to establish European subsidiaries, generating a significant increase in foreign direct investment (FDI) that Ireland was best-placed to attract, benefiting from the 'US growth that was waiting to happen somewhere in Europe', by straddling two economic 'tectonic plates'. Clearly Ireland's advantage in attracting this US FDI was influenced by its relatively low wages, and the theory is thus compatible with both convergence theory and with Walsh's contention about the effect of the UK recession on Irish wages.[13]

Paul Krugman's highly influential 1997 paper suggested a third factor that goes a long way towards explaining the timing of the Irish boom. Changes in the composition of world trade in the 1990s dramatically reduced the importance of transport costs and hence the disadvantages of a peripheral location. Ireland was thus well-placed to attract

[11]Paul R. Krugman, 'Good News from Ireland' (1997), 40–42 and Frank Barry, 'The Celtic Tiger Era: Delayed Convergence or Regional Boom?', ESRI, *Quarterly Economic Commentary, Summer 2002* (2002), 1–7.

[12]Ó Gráda and Kevin H. O'Rourke, 'Living Standards and Growth' (2000), 28 and Walsh, 'The Transformation of the Irish Labour Market' (2004), 102–110.

[13]Antoin E. Murphy, 'The 'Celtic Tiger'—An Analysis of Ireland's Economic Growth Performance' (2000), 4, 13–14.

investment from key industries. Once initial investments in these sectors were secured, it sent positive signals about Ireland as a location to similar firms, thus establishing a self-reinforcing process through information cascades. The experiences of these new firms once they arrived were therefore just as important as the initial investments.[14]

One of the striking features of the academic discourse in the period is the enormous focus on FDI, despite the fact that multinational firms accounted for a surprisingly small proportion of job creation in the period. Remarkably, the upsurge in FDI explained just 20% of the new jobs created, including spillovers. Similarly, the level of attention paid to the high-tech manufacturing sector sat slightly incongruously with the fact that most of the job creation was happening elsewhere. In the period from 1989 to 1997 employment in the market services sector contributed two-thirds of net new jobs, with just the remaining third coming from manufacturing and construction. While increased foreign investment and the manufacturing boom undoubtedly played a causal role in generating the boom in the broader economy, the relative extent of its importance was never explicitly established. A robust investigation of the role of FDI and manufacturing in precipitating the subsequent employment boom in market services, together with a comprehensive explanation of exactly how the process might have occurred, is conspicuously absent from the discourse.[15]

There was a universal recognition throughout the period that a significant proportion of the apparently enormous output of the multinationals in Ireland was attributable to distortions caused by transfer pricing manipulation. As Barry suggests, transfer prices are the prices charged for 'the transfer of goods and services between a parent company and its foreign affiliates', and are supposed to reflect market value. However, in practice this is very difficult for national authorities to enforce, and firms have an enormous incentive to allocate as much output as possible to

[14] Krugman, 'Good News from Ireland: A Geographical Perspective' (1997), 50–51.

[15] Honohan and Walsh, 'Catching Up with the Leaders' (2002), 1; Dermot McAleese, 'The Celtic Tiger: Origins and Prospects' (2000), 48; Dermot McAleese, 'The Irish Economy: Recent Growth, European Integration and Future Prospects', Address at Cantro Informação Europeia Jacques Delors, Lisbon, 12 October 2001; Krugman, 'Good News from Ireland: A Geographical Perspective' (1997), 43; and Frank Barry, Aoife Hannan, and Eric A. Strobl, 'The Real Convergence in the Irish Economy and the Sectoral Distribution of Employment Growth', in Frank Barry (ed.), *Understanding Ireland's Economic Growth* (1999), 19–20.

subsidiaries in low-tax economies. By establishing a base in Ireland firms could therefore reduce their global tax liabilities significantly. Interviews conducted with key decision-makers in US multinationals in 2001 confirmed that the favourable corporate tax rate was a critical factor in their decisions to locate in Ireland. This incentive had a profound impact on the profile of the firms that established Irish subsidiaries. Manufacturing investment was overwhelmingly concentrated in sectors with highly valuable patent rights, particularly pharmaceuticals, chemicals, computers and software, and cola concentrates, where very high outputs could be attributed to the Irish operation. In some cases this reached farcical levels, with one chemicals subsector recording a net output per worker of $2.5 million in 1998. Similarly, workers producing cola concentrates in Ireland were attributed with outputs that were a multiple of those of their European counterparts.[16]

Analysts recognised that the central role of the corporate tax rate for multinational investors represented a key vulnerability, since it was a strategy that was replicable by competitor countries, particularly new accession states in Eastern Europe after 2004. The European Parliament estimated that even increasing the corporate tax rate for exporting firms from 10 to 12.5% would reduce FDI inflows to Ireland by 7%. As Walsh observed, this would be nothing compared to the potential impact of an enforced harmonised European tax rate. For the broader purposes of this chapter there are two important insights to take from these concerns about the exposure of the economy to the multinational sector. Firstly, analysts were worried that the over-reliance on footloose multinationals represented a key vulnerability for the Irish economy. Crucially however, none proposed an alternative development strategy that put more emphasis on indigenous firms. Secondly, although excessive dependence on the construction sector was subsequently recognised as an economic

[16] Frank Barry, 'FDI, Transfer Pricing and the Measurement of R&D Intensity', *Research Policy: Policy and Management Studies of Science, Technology and Innovation*, vol. 34, 2005, 673–675; Patrick McGunnigle and David McGuire, 'Why Ireland? A Qualitative Review of the Factors Influencing the Location of US Multinationals in Ireland with Particular Reference to the Impact of Labour Issues', *Economic and Social Review*, vol. 32, no. 1 (January 2001), 43–67; Honohan and Walsh, 'Catching Up with the Leaders' (2002), 1–2; Brendan Walsh, 'Taxation and Foreign Direct Investment in Ireland', in H.G. Grubel (ed.), *Tax Reform in Canada: Our Path to Greater Prosperity* (2003), 224; and Brendan Walsh, 'The Role of Tax Policy in Ireland's Economic Renaissance', *Canadian Tax Journal*, vol. 48, no. 3, 2000, 670.

vulnerability, analysts had been concerned about over-reliance on the multinationals for years and were perhaps less alarmed by this new dependency than they might otherwise have been.[17]

Summary

The scale of the 1990s boom caught analysts by surprise. While economists subsequently believed that they had arrived at a strong and agreed understanding of the causes of the Celtic Tiger, the picture is somewhat more complicated. Rather than a single comprehensive account, there were a number of compelling explanations in the literature, which in some cases determined how analysts perceived the fundamental nature of the Irish economy. Furthermore, while the assumption that the FDI boom underpinned the subsequent employment boom was a reasonable one, the extent of its causal significance was never convincingly demonstrated. Although analysts understood that a development strategy based on foreign investment was both limited and vulnerable, nobody ever managed to devise a plausible alternative. A tendency has subsequently emerged to caricature the 1990s boom as having been more robust than it was actually considered at the time, partially because the multinational sector has continued to perform strongly but also in order to castigate the construction-led strategy that followed.[18]

4 Competitiveness and Fiscal Policy

The decision to join the European Monetary Union (EMU) was the subject of significant debate in the late 1990s. A lengthy analysis by the Economic and Social Research Institute (ESRI) concluded that on balance membership would bring modest benefits, even if the UK remained outside. Several academic commentators were decidedly more concerned, notably Frank Barry, Peter Neary and Rodney Thom. Neary and Thom concluded that the union would be most suitable for the countries at Europe's economic core, which Ireland was decidedly not given its

[17] Brendan Walsh, 'Taxation and Foreign Direct Investment in Ireland', in H.G. Grubel (ed.), *Tax Reform in Canada: Our Path to Greater Prosperity* (2003), 223; Walsh, 'The Transformation of the Irish Labour Market' (2004), 83–84; and Frank Barry, 'FDI, Transfer Pricing and the Measurement of R&D Intensity', *Research Policy: Policy and Management Studies of Science, Technology and Innovation*, vol. 34, 2005, 676–677.

[18] Jim O'Leary, 'External Surveillance of Irish Fiscal Policy During the Boom' (2011), 4. Available from www.irisheconomy.ie. Accessed 24 May 2014.

trade structure and asynchronous business cycles. Crucially, they warned that inappropriately low interest rates could drive inflation given that the economy was already booming. If the UK remained outside, the authors cautioned that this risked severe competitiveness losses against Ireland's main trading partner. What received conspicuously little attention was the enormous impact that EMU membership could have on credit flows within Europe.[19]

Like the international and domestic organisations, several other academic commentators were also highly aware of the risks to the Irish economy emanating from inflation. From the turn of the millennium, analysts warned that competitiveness was being eroded through wage and price increases, notably in housing. Commentators were also cognisant that the timing of EMU was far from ideal from an Irish perspective, since falling interest rates served to exacerbate the situation. The erosion of competitiveness was all the more worrying given the fact that wage restraint had been a fundamental driver of the employment boom in the 1990s. Prices had become increasingly expensive by European standards, an imbalance that was made particularly visible by the common currency.[20]

Like so many of the warnings issued in the period however, those published by academics lacked any sense of crisis because most analysts did not revise their core beliefs that the Irish economy was fundamentally

[19]Terry Baker, John Fitzgerald, and Patrick Honohan, 'Economic Implications for Ireland of EMU', ESRI Policy Research Series Paper no. 28 (Dublin, 1996), 346, 351–352; Frank Barry, 'Dangers for Ireland of an EMU Without the UK: Some Calibration Results', *Economic and Social Review*, vol. 28, no. 4 (October 1997), 333–349; John Fitzgerald, 'Comment on "Dangers for Ireland of an EMU Without the UK: Some Calibration Results" by Frank Barry', *Economic and Social Review*, vol. 29, no. 1 (January 1998), 99–102; and J. Peter Neary and D. Rodney Thom, 'Punts, Pounds, and Euros: in Search of an Optimal Currency Area', *Irish Business Administration Research* (November 1997), 10, 14–15. Available from http://researchrepository.ucd.ie/bitstream/handle/10197/707/ibar1997.pdf?sequence=3.

[20]Garret Fitzgerald, 'The Euro and Macro-economic Policy-Making', *Irish Banking Review* (Spring 2002), 2–4; Dermot McAleese, 'The Celtic Tiger: Origins and Prospects' (2000), 50; Philip R. Lane, 'Profits and Wages in Ireland, 1987–1996', *Journal of the Statistical and Social Inquiry Society of Ireland*, vol. xxvii, part v (May 1998), 238; Lane, 'Profits and Wages in Ireland, 1987–1996' (1998), 223–227; Philip R. Lane and Patrick Honohan, 'Divergent Inflation Rates in EMU', IIIS Discussion Paper, no. 5, 11 July 2003; and Jim Power, 'The Changing Dynamics of Irish Inflation', *Irish Banking Review* (Spring 2003), 33.

sound. Again the missing link was the extent to which the construction boom was masking structural unemployment, and how precipitously construction activity could fall. By the end of the period, Honohan and Leddin had recognised that a prolonged period of labour market weakness was a distinct possibility as the property and construction boom receded. However, there is no indication that they came close to appreciating the extent of the vulnerability.[21]

The most consistent academic critic of fiscal policy in the period was Philip Lane. Lane warned that the boom was eroding the social consensus that had hitherto been fundamental in maintaining wage moderation, and that the political system was poorly placed to meet the renewed challenge of balancing competing taxation and expenditure demands. Public expectations of continued tax reductions had become embedded, while voters had simultaneously become increasingly critical of the deficiencies of public services, particularly in health. The tension for politicians, therefore, was between securing the favour of the electorate and ensuring fiscal sustainability. Lane recognised that the tax reduction programme had likely overshot and that the tax base needed to be widened. Despite these warnings however, the fact that he did not anticipate the collapse of the construction and property sectors meant that like almost all contemporary analysts Lane decisively underappreciated the scale of the problem. The fact that a highly regarded academic who paid considerable attention to Irish fiscal policy underestimated the vulnerability of the Exchequer is highly revealing for our purposes. The failure of commentators and decision-makers in the official organisations to foresee the crisis clearly cannot be attributed to just incompetence or a lack of vigilance.[22]

Summary

Academic commentators were highly aware of the fact that competitiveness erosion posed a risk for the Irish economy. By the end of the period, Honohan and Leddin had recognised that the construction boom had temporarily offset the harmful effects of excessive inflation. There was

[21] Patrick Honohan and Anthony J. Leddin, 'Ireland in EMU: More Shocks, Less Insulation', *Economic and Social Review*, vol. 37, no. 2 (Summer/Autumn 2006), 286.

[22] Philip R. Lane, 'What Should We Do with the Surpluses' (October 1999), 3–5; Power, 'The Changing Dynamics of Irish Inflation', *Irish Banking Review* (Spring 2003), 45; Philip R. Lane, 'Assessing Ireland's Fiscal Strategy: Recent Experiments and Future Plans', in Tim Callan et al., *Budget Perspectives 2004* (ESRI, 2003), 21; and Walsh, 'Taxation and Foreign Direct Investment in Ireland' (2003), 219.

no indication, however, that any commentator apart from Morgan Kelly realised the extent of the structural weaknesses in the Irish economy, or how dramatic the reversal could be when the construction boom ended. While Honohan and Leddin recognised that construction activity was masking the effects of competitiveness losses, Philip Lane appreciated that the fiscal position had become unsustainable over the medium term. Again, an understanding of the nature of the problem did not equate to a realisation of the extent of the vulnerability. Nonetheless, these exposures went unrecognised by many other commentators, and we should allocate credit where it is due. It is crucial then, that the unforeseen key development that multiplied the scale of both the employment losses and the fall in tax revenue was the degree and speed of the collapse of the construction and property sectors.

5 Property and Construction

One noteworthy contribution from the period was from Jim Power at the very beginning of the decade. Power warned that inappropriately low interest rates had further fuelled housing demand, and that prices had become 'dangerously high'. The point of interest is not Power's disquiet, which was shared by a number of commentators at the time, so much as his subsequent about-face on the issue. In April 2007 Power debated with Morgan Kelly on RTE's (Raidió Teilifís Éireann) 'Prime Time', arguing strongly that the market was sound and that prices reflected the economic and demographic fundamentals. After the housing crash, Power described the incident as one of the biggest embarrassments of his life. The key question is why Power changed his mind about the property market between 2000 and 2007. The most obvious explanation would be that he believed prices to have been overvalued in 2000 but to have subsequently corrected. However, in the Prime Time debate he explicitly argued that prices had tracked the fundamentals over the previous ten years. Nyberg's suggestion that years of continued economic success served to silence doubters seems particularly pertinent here. Power's case was even more dramatic, in that he actively changed his mind to the extent that he was prepared to champion the prevailing view.

Paradoxically as house prices continued to grow, doubts were assuaged by the fact that the day of reckoning never came.[23]

A striking feature of the discourse was that commentators who believed that house prices were broadly appropriate often warned that a crisis would become likely if significant increases continued. Brendan Walsh, for example, argued in 1999 that current prices could be justified by economic and demographic fundamentals, but that the current rate of inflation could not continue. Seven years later, in 2006, Walsh was still of the opinion that a house price collapse was unlikely, despite the fact that prices had more than doubled in the interim. He supported the position with the contention that falls in nominal prices had been rare historically and that building land was still artificially scarce. It is difficult to imagine at what point commentators would have broadly agreed that prices were unsustainably high. Although Walsh had previously warned that the boom in construction activity must be expected to reverse over the medium term, he was decidedly sanguine at this juncture, contending that observers of the Irish economy should not be overly worried about the end of the construction boom given the high immigration rate and the prospect of economic booms in neighbouring countries.[24]

Given Walsh's status as one of the preeminent Irish economists of the day, the basis for his confidence that Irish property and construction would enjoy soft landings is particularly instructive. While we must constantly be wary of succumbing to hindsight bias, Walsh's rationale seems to have been questionable even from a pre-crisis standpoint. Most incongruous is the contention that nominal house price falls were historically rare given that a sizeable proportion of Ireland's regional neighbours had experienced them in the recent past. It seems likely that Walsh was either ignoring these episodes, or that he was basing this argument solely on Irish historical experience. Walsh's belief that prices would remain strong because of an artificial land scarcity ignored the reality that construction

[23] Jim Power, 'One Year of the Euro', *Irish Banking Review* (Spring 2000), 11; *Prime Time*, 17 April 2007 (RTE, 2007). http://www.youtube.com/watch?v=Gd6ZwqLePC0. Accessed 4 June 2014; Liam Collins, 'Just Who Is Morgan Kelly', *Irish Independent*, 30 November 2012. http://www.independent.ie/opinion/analysis/just-who-is-morgan-kelly-26699342.html. Accessed 4 June 2014; and Nyberg Commission (2011), *Misjudging Risk*, 97.

[24] Walsh, 'The Irish Economic 'Miracle': How Do We Explain the Timing of the Boom?' (1999), 226–227; Neary, 'An Interview with Brendan Walsh' (2006), 299; and www.cso.ie.

output was running at more than quadruple its historical level. Similarly, the assumption that a high immigration rate would help to encourage a soft landing in the construction sector showed scant appreciation of the reversibility of migration flows. Given that Irish migration patterns had exhibited an historic transformation just a decade earlier the perspective seems excessively conservative. Lastly, the fact that Walsh took solace in the prospect of booms in neighbouring countries indicates a limited appreciation of how fundamentally the basis of Irish growth had shifted from exports to construction. The implicit assumption that an export boom would have offset the employment effects of a potential collapse in the construction industry is highly questionable.[25]

The most strident academic publication in favour of prevailing residential property valuations was by Maurice Roche, writing for the ESRI in 2003. Roche dismissed the claims of the IMF and *The Economist* that Irish prices were overvalued, and warned that such sensationalism could be self-fulfilling. He argued that both organisations had failed to incorporate supply-side factors, and based on his own model concluded that at worst prices were overvalued by under five per cent. Though Roche believed that there might have been a bubble in the late 1990s, he contended that prices had since reverted to their fundamental values, and that much of the recent price increases could be attributed to rising land costs. Anthony Murphy subsequently challenged Roche's use of factors like land prices, average mortgage loans and user costs to explain prices. The main objections were the quality of the land price data used and Murphy's belief that these factors would logically be expected to move in tandem with rising prices as endogenous variables. He thus suggested that it was unsurprising that Roche found prices to be appropriate, since his choice of explanatory factors would invariably suggest that prices were close to fundamental values. Even more significantly, as we saw in relation to the Central Bank's model in Chapter 4, the inclusion of two of these variables just shifted the problem to a possible credit or land price bubble.[26]

[25] For nominal price falls, see Chapter 6, 220–221.

[26] Murphy, *Housing and National Competitiveness* (2004), 2–3, 12, 24, 33, 34, 36–38; Maurice J. Roche, 'Will There Be a Crash in Irish House Prices?', in ESRI, *Quarterly Economic Commentary: Winter 2003* (2003), 1–12; Maurice J. Roche, 'Irish House Prices: Will the Roof Cave In?', *Economic and Social Review*, vol. 30, no. 4 (1999), 343–362; and Maurice J. Roche, 'The Rise in House Prices in Dublin: Bubble, Fad or Just Fundamentals?', *Economic Modelling*, vol. 82, no. 2 (2001), 281–295.

Roche also pointed critics to the high nominal house price increases experienced in Ireland in the late 1970s and early 1980s, a boom that he contended had ended without a crash. The fact that Roche took comfort from the 1970s boom is very surprising, given that price increases were then in the context of very high general inflation and in real terms were dwarfed by the increases observed from the mid-1990s. Even more significant was the fact that real prices subsequently fell by an enormous 27% in real terms between 1981 and 1987. Rather than allaying concerns, the episode should have made analysts considerably more wary about the likelihood of a significant price correction, and ought to have been paid far more attention than it was.[27]

Roche's model predictably offered comfort to Irish policymakers who were banking heavily on a bright future for the Irish property market. As observed in Chapter 3, the IMF consultation from 2004 reported that the Irish authorities had rebuffed warnings on the basis that some analysts had pointed to supply-side justifications for high valuations. The fact that the inclusion of land prices as an explanatory variable was inherently problematic was evidently less important than the fact that the proponents of the model reached desirable conclusions. Murphy himself found that 2003 prices were approximately 20% above their fundamental values and suggested that they were therefore likely to fall back in the medium term. He also pointed to falling rents, in real and nominal terms, stressing that the disparity could not be expected to last.[28]

As contended in previous chapters, the domestic organisations paid far less attention than the international agencies to the potential benefits of increasing the ongoing costs of homeownership. Similarly, there was strikingly little published by academics on the issue, with Lane and Murphy as the notable exceptions. Murphy argued that the bias of fiscal policy towards property had encouraged over-investment in housing and generated large inefficiencies, suggesting that the money would be

[27] Maurice J. Roche, 'Will There Be a Crash in Irish House Prices?', in ESRI, *Quarterly Economic Commentary: Winter 2003* (2003), 1–12; David Duffy, 'A Descriptive Analysis of the Irish Housing Market', in ESRI, *Quarterly Economic Commentary: Summer 2002* (2002), 5, 8, 9; and ESRI, *Medium-Term Review*: 2005–*2012* (2005), 90.

[28] IMF, *Ireland: Staff Report for the 2004 Article IV Consultation* (*IMF Staff Country Report No 4/*348) (Washington: IMF, 2004), 18–19; Murphy, *Housing and National Competitiveness* (2004), 2–3, 12, 24, 33, 34, 36–38; and see pages 80–81.

better spent elsewhere. While he did not make the connection explicitly, the point was particularly pertinent given his contention that the user cost of housing is perhaps the most important concept in housing economics, and is directly determined by property-related taxes and charges. There was almost no call for an increase in ownership costs elsewhere in the material published by academics in the period. This is one of the key distinctions between domestic and international analysts in their analyses of the housing boom. It is particularly striking given that such measures would almost certainly have reduced demand.[29]

Both Murphy and Frank Barry also argued that landowners should be taxed on increases in land values attributable to Government decisions. The influence of land scarcity on housing costs had been substantial, with the proportion of house prices attributable to site costs rising from 15% to over 40% during the course of the boom. Murphy contended that the main causes of this scarcity were land hoarding and infrastructural deficits rather than a deficit of zoned land or planning delays. Initiatives to tax land hoarding or to ensure that taxes levied on beneficiary landowners paid for part of the costs of new infrastructure would have had a clear impact in alleviating these issues. By confronting these impediments to supply policymakers could have driven down the price of development land, with very significant benefits for housing affordability. Barry has contended that since property developers did not constitute a numerous group, the 'unhealthy relationship' that they enjoyed with politicians was attributable to financial contributions rather than votes. While other issues were also undoubtedly at play here this argument does seem rather compelling, particularly in light of Elaine Byrne's findings on the importance of developer donations for party funding in the period.[30]

There are two final points of interest on property in the contemporary academic publications. Firstly, Hogan and O'Sullivan found that

[29] Murphy, *Housing and National Competitiveness* (2004), 10, 28; Anthony Murphy, 'Modelling Irish House Prices: A Review and Some New Results' (2005). Available from http://www.nuff.ox.ac.uk/users/murphya/Centre.htm; Lane, 'What Should We Do with the Surpluses' (1999), 7; and Lane, 'Assessing Ireland's Fiscal Strategy: Recent Experiments and Future Plans' (2003), 21.

[30] Murphy, *Housing and National Competitiveness* (2004), 1–10; Frank Barry, 'Future Irish Growth: Opportunities, Catalysts, Constraints', in ESRI, *Quarterly Economic Commentary: Winter 2005* (2005), 16–18; and for Byrne's findings on party funding, see Chapter 7.

increased housing wealth had essentially no impact on the propensity of Irish households to consume. They took this to imply that households were unconvinced that house price increases constituted a permanent addition to their wealth. While this scepticism arguably played a part, the phenomenon can also be explained by Irish attitudes to housing. If a homeowner had no expectation to move house for the remainder of her lifetime, then the additional value attributed to that house was locked in and could not be spent on additional consumption. While one could borrow more using the house as collateral, this would have to be repaid with other income. If one planned to upsize, then the price gap between one's existing and future houses would most likely have increased relative to income during the boom, actually dampening other consumption. The only conceivable way that Irish consumption could have increased significantly on the back of increased property values would be if a large cohort of households downsized once their children reached adulthood and left home. Given the cultural aversion to downsizing, Hogan and O'Sullivan's finding is perhaps unsurprising, as relatively few of the net beneficiaries of the housing boom elected to sell in order to boost their general consumption.[31]

A final noteworthy issue was the flotation of the hitherto state-owned Telecom Éireann in 1999. An astonishing 500,000 Irish citizens (approximately a sixth of the adult population) bought shares in the company, after an Exchequer-funded campaign directed at new and small investors. After a short-lived success the share price collapsed, and was followed by the break-up of the company. As Moore McDowell argued, the episode served to sour the market for future flotations. Even more significantly, it almost certainly dissuaded a sizeable proportion of fledgling investors from future excursions into the stock market. The timing was critical insofar as the Telecom Éireann episode occurred just as property prices were appreciating at a record rate. Bacon's contention that many new investors saw housing as something tangible and familiar, with an easily understood return, seems pertinent here. If Telecom Éireann shares had performed strongly it might well have encouraged at least some prospective property investors to look elsewhere. In a similar vein, survey data collected by Robert Shiller in the USA demonstrated that the Enron and accounting scandals had encouraged both individual and

[31] Vincent Hogan and Patrick O'Sullivan, 'Consumption and House Prices in Ireland', ISSC Discussion Paper Series, Working Paper 2003/15, 1, 8.

institutional investors away from the stock market and into residential property.[32]

Summary

There was not discernibly more concern about the sustainability of the property boom in 2006 than there had been in the late 1990s. While prices had more than doubled in the meantime, the years of continued price growth heightened and assuaged fears concurrently. In some instances, those who argued that property prices were justified expressed concern that additional increases were not warranted, and that if the boom continued the market would become unsustainable in the future. Conversely, Roche contended that a divergence from the fundamentals had already happened, and that prices had since corrected. The house price increases of the 1970s and the subsequent declines in real terms received far less attention than they deserved, particularly since many people mistakenly believed that Irish house prices had never significantly fallen.

Strikingly little attention was paid to the potential beneficial effects of addressing the fiscal bias towards homeownership. Similarly, while the discussion that did take place about the unduly favourable treatment of landowners was astute and radical, there was far too little of it in the academic discourse overall. The fact that increases in housing value did not drive additional private consumption is interesting insofar as it implies either a scepticism about the boom or a somewhat unusual relationship with housing by international standards. Finally, the Telecom Éireann flotation should be considered as an important event insofar as it dissuaded fledgling investors from further stock purchases, and potentially further encouraged the national appetite for housing.

[32] Donal Palcic and Eoin Reeves, 'An Economic Analysis of Privatisation in Ireland, 1991–2003', *Journal of the Statistical and Social Inquiry Society of Ireland*, vol. xxxiv (October 2004), 7; Moore McDowell, 'The Rationale and Scope for Privatisation in Ireland', *Journal of the Statistical and Social Inquiry Society of Ireland*, vol. xxix (January 2000), 51; Bacon et al., *Economic Assessment of Recent House Price Developments* (1998), iv, vi, 28, 30, 85; and George A. Akerlof and Robert J. Shiller, *Animal Spirits* (Princeton, 2010), x–xi, xxv, 35.

6 Finance

There was remarkably little published on the Irish financial sector by academics in the period. This is very likely attributable to the fact that financial economics is quite a specialised field, and there were few Irish academics who felt that they had the expertise to write about it authoritatively. One notable contribution in the ESR was from Charles Goodhart from the London School of Economics. Goodhart contrasted the stability of the global financial system from 1945 to 1970 with the more turbulent period that followed. Pertinently from an Irish perspective, he suggested that the post-war period was marked by relatively little intellectual concern about bank failures because they were so rare. One can similarly assume that the remarkable stability of the Irish banking system throughout the history of the state (with the significant exception of the AIB bailout in 1984) encouraged analysts to focus their attention elsewhere.[33]

In 2003 Honohan and Lane warned that high inflation in some countries within the EMU was informing low or even negative real interest rates. They presciently suggested that this could precipitate an expenditure-led boom, exacerbating inflation and fuelling property prices, and ultimately lead to excessive private debt accumulation. Ireland had exhibited the lowest real interest rates in the union, with a remarkable average of minus one per cent. Crucially, the authors estimated that the fall in Irish interest rates could justify close to a doubling of house prices. In a subsequent paper Honohan and Leddin contended that negative interest rates had driven construction spending in particular. Without the option of a monetary policy response, a rise in inflation was considered to be procyclical and self-reinforcing insofar as it automatically generated a fall in real interest rates. Academics clearly appreciated the inflationary impact of EMU and its attendant ramifications for Irish economic stability. Honohan was also at the forefront in warning about the enormous exposure of the financial sector to wholesale funding. Nevertheless, without an appreciation of the extent of the reversibility of the construction boom or the attendant exposure and vulnerability of

[33] Charles A.E. Goodhart, 'What Can Academics Contribute to the Study of Financial Stability', *Economic and Social Review*, vol. 36, no. 3 (Winter 2005), 189–191, 199.

the Irish banks, these reservations did not constitute anything like a full recognition of the risks facing the Irish economy.[34]

7 Predictions

In a 1999 paper Philip Lane argued that economists had an obligation to be 'Cassandra-like' in highlighting risks to the economy, particularly because a widely held 'boom psychology' could discount the potential for a reversal. The comparison to Cassandra is a revealing one: firstly, since she was ignored by decision-makers, and secondly, because the economic discourse in subsequent years was far from characterised by predictions of catastrophe. It is important to stress that there were no clear mathematical solutions to many of the key questions pertaining to the Irish economy in the period. Brendan Walsh questioned whether sophisticated economic analysis had much to offer in terms of determining the likelihood of a soft landing. In particular, he pointed to the fact that there was no way of definitively determining how big the construction sector should be relative to the rest of the economy. Similarly, the Central Bank stressed that fundamental property prices were not directly observable and must be estimated. Crucially then, one could not accurately predict the future on the basis of the Irish quantitative data alone, and historical precedent was an important guide. Expert interpretations were thus inherently subjective because they were determined by which historical examples analysts considered to be relevant to the Irish boom. They were also inevitably emotionally informed. A striking difference between the pessimists (like Caroline Gavin, Morgan Kelly and the IMF mission in 2000) and more sanguine commentators was the breadth of the historical horizons that informed their analyses. The optimists either consciously or subconsciously took comfort from the perceived historical stability of Irish house prices, while the pessimistic predictions were informed by the experiences of other countries in recent history.[35]

[34] Lane and Honohan, 'Divergent Inflation Rates in EMU' (2003), 5, 7–10, 31; Honohan and Leddin, 'Ireland in EMU: More Shocks, Less Insulation' (2006), 271; and Patrick Honohan, 'To What Extent Has Finance Been a Driver of Ireland's Economic Success?', in ESRI, *Quarterly Economic Commentary: Winter 2006* (2006), 70–71.

[35] Lane, 'What Should We Do with the Surpluses' (1999), 4; Neary, 'An Interview with Brendan Walsh' (2006), 299; and CBFSAI, *Financial Stability Report* (2005), 29, 30–32.

Most academic economists did not publish predictions of how the Irish boom would end. Some of those who published on the contemporary economy certainly expressed concern about key vulnerabilities, but there was little appreciation of how sizeable the risks were. Again, the context in which one viewed the Irish economy was key. The metamorphosis from the export-led boom of the 1990s to the construction-led boom of the 2000s, while rapid, did not happen overnight. Nor was the upward trend in house prices entirely consistent: prices fell for five months after the dotcom crash in 2001, and the rate of increase never returned to the heady levels of the late 1990s. By comparison with these earlier increases, the rate of house price inflation from 2001 to 2004 seemed relatively modest. There was no single unambiguous moment at which analysts who had been studying the Irish economy for years should have fundamentally revised their opinions. To radically alter one's perspective would have required a step back in order to take stock of how fundamentally the postmillennial economy differed from the 1990s boom.

Before considering what made Morgan Kelly different from other academics analysing the Irish economy, it is worth considering his relevant predictions. Kelly's first publication on the contemporary Irish economy was an *Irish Times* comment piece in December 2006, followed by a working paper the following February. A version of the paper was subsequently published in the ESRI's 'Quarterly Economic Commentary' in July 2007. Unsurprisingly, the prediction that house prices would fall by 40–60% drew most attention at the time and is what has earned Kelly the most recognition since. Crucially however, Kelly used similar methodology to the IMF's 2000 study of international house price booms in recent decades, observing that during a bust real house prices typically fall by 70% of the price increase witnessed during the boom. He was certainly more forthright in insisting that Irish prices would follow the established pattern, but the Fund was also far from ambiguous in its language. What Kelly did recognise, unlike anybody else at the time, is that residential construction and real estate activity could fall rapidly from constituting 18% of national income to a more typical 5%, and warned that unemployment could surge to over 15%. Crucially, he also appreciated this could precipitate a 'collapse' in fiscal revenue. This required the imagination to envisage a deleterious economic reversal on a scale that was far beyond the immediate experience of Irish analysts, which is perhaps the key attribute that marked Kelly apart.[36]

Kelly therefore combined a pessimistic forecast for house prices with a unique understanding of the potential scale of the implications for construction activity and the Exchequer. While his recognition of these interlinkages was vital however, it is also important to recognise that he paid no attention to the commercial real estate sector. Even more importantly, he initially contended that the large banks were well capitalised and that interest-only and 100% mortgages were the primary concern. The extent of the exposure of the banks to large developers and commercial real estate was overlooked entirely. The point here is not to detract from what was by far the most insightful contribution in the period, and crucially Kelly was subsequently the first academic to recognise the extent of the vulnerability of the banks. However, as Pete Lunn has argued, we must not succumb to the temptation to assume that even a sceptical analyst would immediately recognise the full extent of the threat.[37]

An obvious question then, is why other academic economists who published on the contemporary Irish economy did not come to similar conclusions. Academics certainly did not suffer from an undue deference towards policymakers and were quick to criticise everything from the public-sector benchmarking process to privatisation. Nor was there a clear skills-shortage, and several Irish economists published in highly regarded international publications. A crucial distinguishing characteristic seems to be that prior to 2006 Kelly had no professional interest in the contemporary Irish economy. While other academics had gradually acclimatised to high house prices and the growth of the construction sector, Kelly came to the situation with a relatively fresh perspective. This is somewhat corroborated by the fact that the most energetic concerns about house prices raised by institutional commentators were from the

[36] Morgan Kelly, 'How the Housing Corner Stones of Our Economy Could Go into Rapid Freefall', *The Irish Times*, 28 December 2006; and Morgan Kelly, 'On the Likely Extent of Falls in Irish House Prices', UCD Centre for Economic Research, Working Paper 7/1 (2007), 1, 8–9, 14.

[37] Kelly, 'On the Likely Extent of Falls in Irish House Prices' (2007), 14; *Prime Time*, 30 September 2008 (RTE, 2008). http://www.youtube.com/watch?v=11CCxv2ueiQ. Accessed 4 June 2014; Patrick Honohan, 'Resolving Ireland's Banking Crisis', UCD Economic Workshop Conference 'Responding to the Crisis' (Dublin, 12 January 2009a), 6; and Lunn, 'The Role of Decision-Making Biases in Ireland's Banking Crisis' (2011), 9.

IMF, whose analysts were also less immersed in the Irish economy than domestic commentators.

Given that the IMF and the OECD published comparable studies examining the recent history of boom/bust cycles in house prices and construction in order to contextualise the Irish boom, it is striking that those contributions have been essentially forgotten while Kelly has become a household name. High-profile international publications like *Vanity Fair*, *The Guardian* and *The New York Times* carried features about Kelly as the economist who predicted the Irish property crash. Between 2006 and mid-2012, he was referenced in 174 articles in *The Irish Times*. By contrast, the IMF and OECD studies prompted almost no discussion in the mass media. On first sight this seems somewhat surprising, since one would assume that if anything warnings from the big international organisations would have carried more weight. Kelly did appear on television debates and made subsequent predictions, and he was much more explicit in spelling out the implications for the Irish economy. However, the discrepancy seems to be too significant to be explained by these features alone. The answer lies in the annual distribution of the references to Kelly. Figure 1 suggests that very little attention was paid to him when he published the initial research, but that he drew

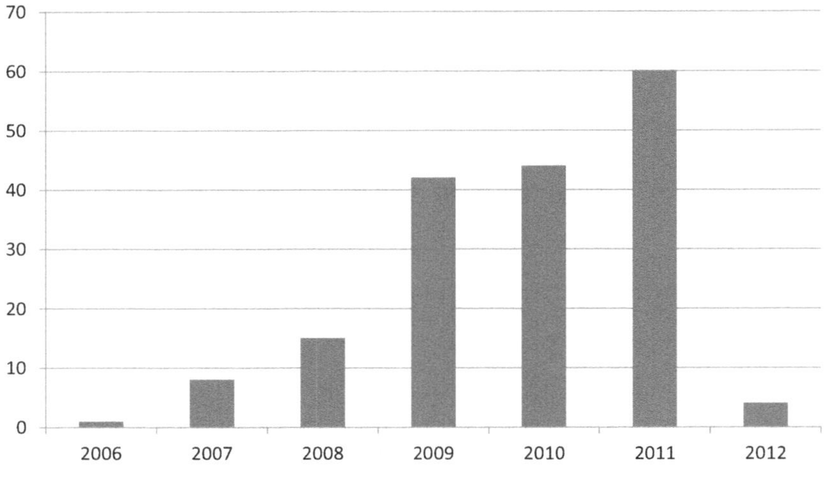

Fig. 1 Articles that referenced Morgan Kelly in *The Irish Times* (*Data Source* Factiva)

enormous focus as the crisis hit. Like the historical studies conducted by the international organisations, Kelly's analysis did not significantly change the discourse at the time, but the story of a single prescient analyst presumably offered the potential for a much more compelling narrative in retrospect.

Summary

There were few predictions in the academic literature about how the Irish boom would end, with only one observer who publicly warned of the scale of the risks. The fact that there was no definitive way to assess whether property prices or the size of the construction sector were excessive meant that analysts relied significantly on subjective opinion. A striking feature of the debate on what would happen to house prices was that the pessimists looked to the examples of boom/bust episodes in other countries. There was no single discernible moment at which the drivers of Irish growth changed, or house prices became unambiguously detached from the fundamentals.

Morgan Kelly's contribution was not a radical departure from what went before it in terms of methodology. He was, however, far more forthright than others in arguing that the Irish property market would suffer a crash similar to those experienced elsewhere. He was also unique in that he grasped the scale of the implications for employment and for the Exchequer. What he initially did not appreciate was the exposure of the banks, and he essentially ignored commercial real estate. While Kelly has been remembered as the economist who predicted the crash, he received remarkably little public attention at the time and, as he has since suggested himself, we should be careful not to overestimate his impact on the discourse at this juncture.[38]

8 Conclusion

It is important to differentiate between those academics who focused on the contemporary Irish economy and those who did not. The academics who did very likely enjoyed a greater level of autonomy than the individuals within the official institutions insofar as they were less curtailed in what they could say. While academics are notoriously reluctant to change their opinions, there is not a strong sense in the literature that this had

[38] Michael Lewis, *Boomerang: The Biggest Bust* (2012), 93.

a major impact. There were no real examples of analysts who nailed their colours to the mast early on and were forced to continue justifying themselves thereafter. Nor were academics notable for their explicit predictions that the Irish economy would enjoy a soft landing. Most of the publications on the contemporary Irish economy towards the end of the period could be accused of failing to ask the important questions more so than arriving at the wrong answers. The relative lack of discussion about the key risks certainly does suggest that many of the academics who published on the contemporary economy significantly underappreciated the likelihood and potential depth of a downturn. It is clear from the literature that Kelly was the only academic economist who publicly anticipated a serious recession in the period. Honohan and Leddin's concern that the construction boom could be followed by a lengthy period of labour market weakness, or Murphy's warning that house prices were overvalued by 20%, did not constitute a realisation of anything like the extent of the risk to the economy.

The fact that no academics came close to predicting the scale of the boom in the 1990s supports the contention made at the end of the last chapter: analysts have been consistently overly conservative in their projections about what will happen to the Irish economy over the last two decades. Given the extreme fluctuations in the growth figures this is perhaps understandable. However, as Naseem Taleb has argued, there is little point in successfully predicting the run-of-the-mill movements if one misses the rare seismic event. While we must be mindful that the crisis clearly seemed far less inevitable in advance than it does in hindsight, there are several striking shortcomings in the contemporary interpretation of the Irish economy. It is also clear from the material on the Celtic Tiger that while there was a prevailing understanding of the boom, it was by no means universally accepted. Its fundamental nature as either a belated-convergence or a regional boom was still hotly contested. Furthermore, nobody conclusively demonstrated the causal significance of the FDI boom for the subsequent employment boom in market services, yet the central importance of the relationship was widely taken as axiomatic. The fact that economists had only a partial understanding of the recent past and its profound influence on the present is perfectly normal. However, it should encourage us to revisit the assumption that they could have been expected to accurately predict the future.[39]

In addition to the difficulties they faced in understanding the fundamental nature of the Irish boom, academics struggled to conceive of an alternative development strategy. Economists could express concern about the risk of a flight of the multinationals, or appreciate the limitations of the status quo in terms of shortfalls like the scarcity of linkages with the broader economy or the lack of higher-functions performed in the Irish subsidiaries. However, nobody ever attempted to propose a comprehensive alternative approach. Interestingly, the original idea of developing Ireland into a hub for electronics, chemicals and pharmaceuticals emanated from a report by analysts from the University of East Anglia in 1968. Similar creativity and radicalism would have been very welcome from Irish academic economists in the boom period. While academics did not face the same obligations as analysts in the official organisations, they could offer an alternative perspective and valuable insight, and policymakers could have certainly made better use of their expertise.[40]

Barry's denunciation of the policy moves to address house price inflation as having been conservative in the extreme could also be extended to the discourse on the subject by academics. The near-absence of calls for a recurring property tax or charges for utilities like water or sewage is in marked contrast to the contributions from the international agencies. One could cynically suggest that domestic commentators were unlikely to recommend additional taxes that they themselves would be subject to. However, this explanation falls short in view of the fact that only Murphy and Barry called for policymakers to address the very favourable tax treatment of landowners. Both shortcomings are symptomatic of a broader dearth of imaginative suggestions to address the scale of property price growth. In this regard, academics were certainly influenced by a limited appreciation of the potential ramifications of the property boom, but were probably also more cognisant of the domestic political realities than outside commentators.[41]

[39] Nassim Nicholas Taleb, *The Black Swan* (London, 2010), xxi–xxiii.

[40] Dermot McAleese, review of *The Making of the Celtic Tiger: The Inside Story of Ireland's Boom Economy*, by Ray MacSharry and Padraic White in *Studies: An Irish Quarterly Review*, vol. 90, no. 359 (Autumn 2001), 333.

[41] Barry, 'Future Irish Growth: Opportunities, Catalysts, Constraints' (2005), 16.

In terms of considering what distinguished Morgan Kelly from other academics analysing the Irish economy there are several salient characteristics. As we have already established, he came to the situation in 2006 with a relatively fresh perspective and was perhaps less seduced than others by the remarkable longevity and apparent resilience of the boom. Furthermore, the fact that the Irish economy was not his core area of study meant that Kelly was paradoxically well-placed to challenge the prevailing consensus. A relative outsider had less at stake in making a bold prediction than would have a commentator whose core area of expertise was the Irish economy. Lastly of course, Kelly showed an ability to see past the remarkably positive headline indicators, and come to a radically fresh opinion about the future of the Irish economy. This required a recognition of the potential of both property prices and the construction sector to suffer a dramatic reversal. It was this insight and an understanding of the attendant interlinkages, supported by an appreciation of the lessons of recent international experience, which was lacking in the relevant publications elsewhere.

There is little evidence to suggest that academics were dissuaded from dissenting for fear of popular or political opprobrium. An economist who was particularly concerned about how the boom would end could have focused on vulnerabilities like eroding competitiveness or the excessive reliance on construction without attracting significant hostility. The examples of the IMF or the OECD studies on property booms, or indeed of Kelly's study, suggest that formal publications on even relatively contentious issues drew scant public attention before the crash. This in turn suggests that an individual academic could have done relatively little to influence policy. Nonetheless, examples like Jim O'Leary's criticism of the benchmarking process indicate that academics were more than happy to criticise policy decisions even when they had little chance of securing their reversal.[42]

Several of the academics who did comment on the contemporary economy were remarkably sanguine, with Brendan Walsh and Maurice Roche as the most striking examples. In this respect, they seem to have been affected by the same influences as the institutional analysts. They had access to all of the relevant data but failed to predict the crash because they had strong preconceptions about the likelihood of a deep

[42] Jim O'Leary, 'Benchmarking the Benchmarkers', in ESRI, *Quarterly Economic Commentary, Winter 2002* (2002).

recession happening to a country like Ireland. While analysts were mindful of the 1980s recession, and of the fact that it was largely attributable to policy errors, most exhibited remarkably little concern about a future crisis. Even when academics did criticise policy, there was almost no appreciation of how dramatically Irish economic fortunes could reverse. Again, analysts had a very positive perception of the Irish economy to which they tacked their misgivings, rather than fundamentally revising their opinions. The contemporary publications give a strong impression that analysts considered a deep Irish recession to be a very unlikely prospect given the prevailing conditions. When one discounts the possibility of a crash, it is possible to justify remarkable asset prices and sectoral concentrations. Roche's invocation of the Irish housing boom of the 1970s reveals a more widespread tendency to rely primarily on Irish historical experience for guidance. Given the dramatic transformation of the economy over the previous decade, the lessons from Irish history were clearly inadequate and in some cases misinterpreted, and analysts would have been well-served by taking a broader perspective.

CHAPTER 6

The Newspapers

News is what somebody does not want you to print. All the rest is advertising.
Anonymous.[1]

1 Introduction

Newspapers and speculative asset bubbles have shared a close history. In this respect, Shiller points to the importance of newspapers in disseminating ideas to a large number of people, the commercial pressures for journalists to capture the public attention and hence the liberal deployment of superlatives, and of course the overwhelming deadline pressure for journalists to produce a coherent narrative about market developments. Rather than merely reporting on proceedings, newspapers and other media outlets actively shape thought formation and the discourse that is fundamental to how market events play out. Galbraith has observed that newspapers are often pivotal in supporting those who champion deregulation, and deriding those who call for state intervention. As we shall observe, the newspapers played a somewhat more complicated role in the Irish context.[2]

[1] http://quoteinvestigator.com/2013/01/20/news-suppress/. Accessed 27 May 2015. This chapter is derived, in part, from an article published in New Political Economy, 2018 (Copyright Taylor and Francis) available online: http://www.tandfonline.com/doi/full/10.1080/13563467.2018.1426562.

[2] Robert J. Shiller, *Irrational Exuberance* (Princeton, 2000), 71–75 and John Kenneth Galbraith, *The Great Crash 1929* (London, 2009), 206–207.

C. M. Casey, *Policy Failures and the Irish Economic Crisis*,
https://doi.org/10.1007/978-3-319-90182-4_6

The performance of the Irish media during the boom has already been the subject of some scrutiny, notably by both the parliamentary Banking Inquiry and by a small group of academics from Dublin City University (DCU). One of the most prominent examinations to date comes from Julien Mercille, who applied Herman and Chomsky's 'Propaganda Model' to explain the role of the media in fuelling the property boom. In particular, he focuses on the importance of media management and advertising in influencing how the boom was reported. While many of the potential conflicts of interest he raises are certainly legitimate, this chapter will argue that they are insufficient to explain why both the property boom and Ireland's economic prospects were viewed in a more positive light than they warranted. We will then examine an alternative interpretation of why the newspapers were overly optimistic, centring on the same analytical shortfalls observed among analysts more generally, combined with the overreliance on external expertise and the functioning of the newspapers as conduits. Mercille does pay some attention to expertise, and the key issue is how much weight to attach to the different aspects of the Propaganda Model, rather than a disagreement over whether or not ownership and advertising played a role. The objective of this chapter is to refocus attention and put the importance of analytical shortcomings and expertise centre stage.[3]

In previous chapters we have examined the contributions of analysts on the basis of where they were employed rather than where they published. For example, an academic writing in an Economic and Social Research Institute (ESRI) publication was treated in the Academia Chapter, and a Central Bank analyst publishing in an academic journal was considered in the Domestic Organisations Chapter. Importantly for both the structure and the core argument of this chapter, this arrangement would be totally misleading for our treatment of the newspapers. While the ESRI might include papers from external sources as a supplement to its main publication, much of the core analysis in the newspapers came

[3] Declan Fahy, Mark O'Brien, and Verio Poti, 'From Boom to Bust: A Post-Celtic Tiger Analysis of the Norms, Values and Roles of Irish Financial Journalists', *Irish Communications Review*, vol. 12 (2010), 5–20; Declan Fahy, 'A Limited Focus? Journalism, Politics and the Celtic Tiger', in Mark O'Brien and Donnacha Ó Beacháin (eds.), *Political Communication in the Republic of Ireland* (Liverpool, 2014), 129–146; and Julien Mercille, 'The Role of the Media in Sustaining Ireland's Housing Boom', *New Political Economy*, vol. 9, no. 2 (2014), 282–301.

from external experts. We will address this issue in more detail later in the chapter, but it is necessary to stress from the outset that the analysis from outside agents was fundamental to the economic commentary in the newspapers and will be treated as such.

There was far more debate on construction and property than on the financial sector, competitiveness or fiscal policy, and it will thus take up much of the chapter. It is important to stress that the four categories clearly overlap enormously, and while delineations are necessary for the sake of structure, they are very much permeable boundaries. The key subject matter of this chapter is the newspapers as institutions, rather than the individuals who wrote in them. The challenge is to present the key themes and debates on the Irish economy in a way that accurately conveys the nature of the discourse while sparing the reader an endless rattling-off of examples. The chapter is thus not intended as a compendium of what contributors wrote or as a criticism of individuals. Articles that are important in evaluating the contributions of individuals may not be important in the context of the overall discourse in the newspaper. Furthermore, what is of interest here is what the newspapers wrote about third-party research rather than the research itself. The objective is to convey the extent to which a reader would have understood the vulnerability of the economy and the housing market, and to come to an understanding of the source of any evidential bias emanating from the necessary compromises entailed in running a newspaper, combined with the unnecessary failure to meaningfully offset their effects.

Newspaper digitisation and keyword-based searches have already been used effectively to enhance historical research elsewhere. One noteworthy example is Gentzkow and Shapiro's analysis of how frequently politically partisan words and phrases were used in particular publications. Their study found that readership and consumer preferences had a much more significant impact than ownership on the slant taken by newspapers. Digitisation was also essential in a recent study conducted by Fonseca Gavis et al., since analysing 159 newspapers over four decades would otherwise have been prohibitively time-consuming. There are clear costs associated with these keyword-based searches, however, particularly the risk that highly relevant articles will not be returned. Although the sample used here is sufficiently manageable that the search criteria could be relatively broad, it is crucial to remain vigilant for references to other articles and writers who had an impact on the discourse but were not returned in the search.[4]

In terms of methodology this chapter is based on an analysis of the articles on the Irish economy in *The Irish Times*, *The Irish Independent* and *The Economist* newspapers in the period from 2000 to 2006. For the *Times* and the *Independent*, the writer used the *Factiva* database, which returns 11,016 results for the *Times* under the broad subject category of 'Economic News'. The *Independent* is only included in the database from June 2003, and it returns 4737 articles between then and the end of the period. The enormous benefit of *Factiva* is that it displays the title and date, the author (where included) and the first two or three lines of the returned articles without requiring the reader to open each one. It is therefore often possible to pick out the relevant articles without having to enter them all individually. An additional benefit is that the articles returned under economic news are all correctly tagged, so the returns are at least about economics.

The significant downsides are also twofold. Firstly, in many cases not all of the necessary information is given. For example, the *Independent* articles in particular often omit the author and the relevant page numbers. A consultation with the newspaper's own website suggests that these omissions originate from there rather than from *Factiva*. They are therefore likely to be present in any archive of digital content (as opposed to photographic reproductions of the original pages). Secondly, there are clear examples of where important articles on the economy are not properly tagged and are therefore not returned under economic news. For example, almost none of the articles David McWilliams wrote for the *Independent* are correctly tagged or attributed. Given his importance to the discourse we will separately examine his articles on the housing market in *The Sunday Business Post*, which he contributed to throughout the period. Similarly, several articles in the *Times* refer to other relevant pieces that are not returned. These shortcomings

[4] Matthew Gentzkow and Jesse M. Shapiro, 'What Drives Media Slant? Evidence from U.S. Daily Newspapers', *Econometrica*, vol. 78, no. 1 (January 2010), 35–71; Matthew Gentzkow, Edward Glaeser, and Claudia Goldin, 'The Rise of the Fourth Estate: How Newspapers Became Informative and Why It Mattered', in Glaeser and Goldin (eds.), *Corruption and Reform: Lessons from America's Economic History* (Chicago, 2006), 187–230; and Ángela Fonseca Galvis, James M. Snyder Jr., and B.K. Song, 'Newspaper Market Structure and Behaviour: Partisan Coverage of Political Scandals in the United States from 1870 to 1910', *Journal of Politics*, vol. 78, no. 2 (2016), 368–381.

notwithstanding, the database allows for an analysis based on almost 16,000 economics articles from the two main Irish daily broadsheets. In the case of *The Economist*, it was possible to use photographic reproductions from *The Gale Group* database because there were far fewer articles pertinent to Ireland. A search of the terms 'Ireland' or 'Irish' for the period yields 1215 results. Many of these are irrelevant for our purposes, but quite a number of the articles provide a highly illuminating counterfactual to the analysis published in the Irish newspapers.

2 The Propaganda Model and the Mercille Application

Herman and Chomsky argue that the media are heavily shaped by the elite private and Government interests that control and finance them. Their 'Propaganda Model' stresses the ability of powerful groups to shape the news agenda and to marginalise dissent in order to benefit their own interests. Mercille draws parallels to Antonio Gramsci and his concept of 'Hegemony', whereby the population is induced to follow the rules of the elites on the basis that they are in the collective interest. The Propaganda Model contends that elites control what is printed through five filters:

(1) Ownership,
(2) Advertising and Income,
(3) Experts,
(4) Flak, and
(5) Anticommunism.[5]

'Flak' is described as a negative response to a media publication. It generally takes the form of hostile phone calls, letters or legal threats. There is certainly some evidence that this played a role in the Irish context. One journalist subsequently interviewed suggested that during the boom even the threat of litigation was often sufficient to get a story pulled. One particularly memorable example from the period was an apparently 'withering letter' sent by Marie Hunt from CBRE Gunne to

[5] Edward S. Herman and Noam Chomsky, *Manufacturing Consent: The Political Economy of the Mass Media* (London, 2008), xi, 1–2 and Mercille, 'The Role of the Media in Sustaining Ireland's Housing Boom' (2014), 9.

The Economist in response to its warnings about the Irish property market. The inclusion of 'anticommunism' in the model is indicative of its origins in the Cold War period and was clearly not a feature in Ireland at this juncture.[6]

Before moving on, there are a few important clarifications about the Propaganda Model. Firstly, the authors argue that the contention that powerful people are able to set the confines of the discourse is not a conspiracy theory but in fact closely resembles what they term a 'free-market' analysis. This means that one need not share their political views to acknowledge the potential applications of the model. Furthermore, they appreciate that the confines in which journalists operate are not entirely inescapable. The policies informed by the model are imperfectly enforced and permit some dissent, though Herman and Chomsky argue that this is kept at the margins. They similarly contend that while journalists do expose corporate and Government misconduct their critiques are restricted. These aspects are particularly important for our purposes because extensive evidence of core newspaper coverage that fundamentally challenged elite interests would suggest that the *intended* aspects of the Propaganda Model had limited impact in the Irish context.[7]

Mercille attributes the role of the media in sustaining the Irish property bubble to their incentives to promote elite interests. He argues that these incentives derive from four factors: the organisational links between the media and the political and corporate establishment, the neoliberal ideologies held within news organisations, advertising dependencies, and the reliance of the media organisations on experts from elite institutions. The reader will note the departures from Herman and Chomsky: flak and anticommunism are omitted, ownership is replaced with organisational linkages and ideological bias has been introduced. It is certainly apparent that the Irish media were overly sanguine about the Irish property boom in the period, and about the economy more generally.

[6] Herman and Chomsky, *Manufacturing Consent* (2008), 24; Mark O'Brien, 'The Irish Press, Politicians, and the Celtic Tiger Economy', in Shane Schifferes and Richard Roberts (eds.), *The Media and Financial Crises: Comparative and Historical Perspectives* (2014), 78; Joe Humphries, '"Economist" Accused of Scaremongering Over House Price Prediction', *The Irish Times*, 31 May 2003; Unattributed, 'Economist's Nul Points', *The Irish Times*, 5 June 2003; and Conor Cruise O'Brien, *States of Ireland* (London, 1979), 181.

[7] Herman and Chomsky, *Manufacturing Consent* (2008), xlix–l, xii, 1, 8.

It is also perfectly likely that all of the influences that Mercille proposes existed to a greater or lesser extent, and had some impact on the coverage of the property market. This does not mean, however, that each of the factors carries significant explanatory value. The key point of interest is the extent to which the failure of the newspapers to issue unambiguous warnings about the property market can be attributed to each factor.[8]

It is important to stress that this analysis is confined to the sample from the economics sections of the two Irish newspapers. Mercille's criticisms of the property section in the *Times* in particular seem irrefutable. However, to suggest that any one of these four factors had an important impact on what was published in the main body of the newspapers requires one to demonstrate that without the influence of the factor the treatment of the property market would have been significantly different. Perhaps the single most striking feature of the two Irish newspapers in the period (in marked contrast to *The Economist*) is their enormous dependence on external experts of various hues for their economic analysis. This was reflected both in the coverage accorded to these experts and in terms of the parameters of what newspaper journalists could envisage in their own analyses. One example was the treatment of the shock scenario in the ESRI's 2005 Medium-Term Review, which was termed a 'nightmare scenario' in the *Independent*. The discourse in the newspaper presented the false dichotomy of whether the ESRI shock scenario or a more benign outcome would come to pass. Significantly, a more deleterious future was never considered. It is entirely unsurprising that the many journalists who depended heavily on external experts to augment their own analyses were no more insightful than those experts themselves, whether in the private sector, academia or the domestic and international institutions.[9]

Mercille acknowledges that both David McWilliams and Morgan Kelly warned about the property boom, but argues that they were 'effectively drowned out in a sea of articles either denying there was a bubble, remaining vague about it, or simply talking about something else'. The contention that McWilliams was in any way drowned out is particularly

[8] Mercille, 'The Role of the Media in Sustaining Ireland's Housing Boom' (2014), 1–2, 6–9.

[9] Mercille, 'The Role of the Media in Sustaining Ireland's Housing Boom' (2014), 9 and 'The Threat Isn't the End of the World—But It Could Be the End of an Era', *The Irish Independent*, 19 January 2006.

difficult to justify. In the boom period he wrote regular columns in two newspapers, presented several television programmes, hosted a national radio show and wrote a best selling book. He was almost certainly the most widely recognised economist in the country. McWilliams himself has since argued that he used these platforms to warn as many people as possible about the looming property crash. To suggest that the public at large was unaware of his misgivings about the property boom is to both do him a discredit, and to unduly absolve voters and market participants. The much more challenging question is why people were so convinced of the strength of the market despite the fact that warnings were so heavily publicised. A 2005 survey revealed the extraordinary statistic that only one in five hundred people expected major house price falls in the coming year. Once we accept that McWilliams' commentary was a prominent feature of the media discourse it becomes clear that any efforts by elites to restrict dissent were rather limited in their efficacy. George Lee's position as Economics Editor of Raidió Teilifís Éireann (RTÉ) similarly undermines the contention that dissenters were successfully silenced or kept to the margins.[10]

Intentionality is a key distinguishing attribute between the four factors that Mercille proposes. In order for organisational links or advertising dependencies to encourage a decision-maker within the newspapers to accept or reject an article, she or he would have to be conscious of these influences and of a potential personal or institutional incentive for acting in accordance with them. By contrast, an editor could favour particular expert contributors or a given ideology either consciously or subconsciously, and with or without consideration of the personal or professional outcomes. The aspects of both the original Propaganda Model and Mercille's modification that assume intentionality sit rather uneasily in the Irish context. Ownership is one clear example, since *The Irish Times* was owned by a trust. This presumably informed Mercille's decision to focus instead on the personnel who held non-executive management

[10] Mercille, 'The Role of the Media in Sustaining Ireland's Housing Boom' (2014), 12; David McWilliams at the Committee of Inquiry into the Banking Crisis, 26 February 2015. https://inquiries.oireachtas.ie/banking/hearings/david-mcwilliams-early-warnings-divergent-contrarian-views/. Accessed 31 March 2015; http://www.davidmcwilliams.ie/about. Accessed 18 March 2015; Paul Melia, 'Survey Sees No End to Boom in Property', *The Irish Independent*, 21 March 2005; and Donal Donovan and Antoin E. Murphy, *The Fall of the Celtic Tiger: Ireland and the Euro Debt Crisis* (Oxford, 2013), 159–163.

roles in both the media organisations and the banks, which we will turn to presently. There are other problems with the applicability of the remaining factors however, and advertising dependencies were not uniformly significant either. Strikingly, RTÉ relied on property for between just 0.3 and 0.9% of its advertising revenue in the period.[11]

The Irish banks were certainly well represented on the boards of the Irish media organisations. While this presumably could have made the job of a journalist more uncomfortable if he or she was to repeatedly raise concerns about the future viability of the banks, there is no evidence to suggest that commentators in any sphere recognised the extent of the vulnerability prior to late 2006. In the absence of evidence that journalists were more prescient than other analysts, it is difficult to understand why pressure on behalf of elite interests would have even been required. Furthermore, such organisational linkages were by no means the preserve of corporate or Government elites. David Begg, as General Secretary of The Irish Congress of Trade Unions (ICTU), was a Governor of *The Irish Times* trust. Significantly, Begg also wrote comment pieces in the newspaper and was simultaneously on the board of the Central Bank and the chair of its audit committee. If a senior executive from one of the banks had enjoyed such authority in the media and regulatory bodies they would quite rightly have since been subjected to rigorous scrutiny. There is of course no evidence that Begg ever acted inappropriately in these roles, but clearly ICTU also wielded considerable influence and there is no suggestion that the *Times* displayed a pro-union bias. These linkages were certainly not a guarantee of favourable partiality. [12]

[11] Houses of the Oireachtas, *Joint Committee of Inquiry into the Banking Crisis*, vol. 1, no. 16, Paul Mulligan, 26 March 2015, 983.

[12] Mercille, 'The Role of the Media in Sustaining Ireland's Housing Boom' (2014), 7–8, 15. http://www.ictu.ie/about/staff.html. Accessed 18 March 2015; Central Bank of Ireland, *Annual Report 2005* (2006), 4, 5, 74, 76; David Begg (2002), 'Vote Yes for Prosperity with Freedom and Social Justice', *The Irish Times*, 4 October 2002, 14; David Begg (2002), 'Unions Maintain Social Value of Consensus Deals', *The Irish Times*, 16 December 2002, 14; David Begg, 'Employers Can Afford Generous Pay Rises', *The Irish Times*, 3 May 2006, 16; Patrick Honohan, 'Resolving Ireland's Banking Crisis', UCD Economic Workshop Conference 'Responding to the Crisis' (2009a), Dublin, 12 January 2009, 8; and O'Brien, 'The Irish Press, Politicians, and the Celtic Tiger Economy' (2014), 79.

The fact that McWilliams and Lee were able to regularly raise concerns about the property boom despite the potential conflict of interest facing non-executive directors of their respective organisations suggests that such factors were not all-pervasive and that others may well have been able to do the same. There were also several other prominent examples of where journalists published articles antithetical to the interests of the banks, notably criticism of customer overcharging in the *Independent* and extensive coverage of the banking scandals by journalists like Fintan O'Toole and Colm Keena in the *Times*. It is highly suggestive that the word 'Ansbacher' returns 748 *Times* articles in the period. If the *Times* clearly did not shirk from reporting the banking scandals then it is difficult to understand why it would intentionally downplay the vulnerability of the property market in order to benefit the banks.[13]

To attribute any apparent bias on the part of newspaper managers in favour of the property boom to the pursuit of a perceived gain (or to avoid a loss) requires some evidence that they would have acted differently without the influence of these incentives. If decision-makers already had little concern for the future of the sector because of flawed analysis, then the two conscious influences could at most have exacerbated an existing disposition. The most compelling evidence that newspaper managers were genuinely convinced by the strength of the housing boom was the acquisition in 2006 of the property websites 'MyHome.ie' by *The Irish Times* and 'PropertyNews.com' by Independent News and Media (INM), which owned the *Independent*. Contentions that such acquisitions constituted a major conflict of interest clearly have significant merit. However, the timing gives crucial insight into the causal direction. Nobody is suggesting that either paper expressed consistent concern about the housing market prior to these acquisitions and changed tack afterwards. The faith of the newspaper managers in the market informed the acquisitions rather than the other way around. Any

[13]Cyril Hardiman, 'Irish Banks "Poor Value" Against Euro Rivals', *The Irish Independent*, 14 July 2005; 'Banks Net €2.5bn a Year by "mugging" clients', *The Irish Independent*, 11 May 2006; Donal Donovan and Antoin E. Murphy, *The Fall of the Celtic Tiger: Ireland and the Euro Debt Crisis* (Oxford, 2013), 144; and All quantitative data were collected using 'Factiva'. Searches include all of the newspaper articles for the period (rather than just the economics section) unless otherwise stated. There are approximately 269,923 articles in the entire Irish Times database and 111,777 in the Irish Independent.

failure to warn about the vulnerability of the market in editorials can thus be attributed to a significant degree to misplaced conviction within the senior ranks of the newspapers.[14]

By way of empirical analysis Mercille points to the fact that the Irish newspapers used the phrases 'housing bubble' or 'property bubble' far more after the crash than they had during the boom, suggesting that this is indicative of an intended obfuscation. He contends that coverage of a 'housing boom' was not comparable because it has positive connotations. He defines a bubble as 'abnormally inflated housing prices' and suggests that the Irish case would clearly have met this definition on the basis of P/E (price/earnings) and P/I (price/incomes) ratios. In particular, he points to *The Economist's* use of these ratios to warn about property markets internationally. One major difficulty here is that there was no single agreed definition of a bubble in the newspaper publications in the period. *The Economist* actually used two conflicting definitions in one issue: firstly (like Mercille) suggesting that a bubble is evident when prices deviate from the fundamentals, but then suggesting that bubbles can never be positively identified until they burst. The *Independent* exhibited similar confusion, suggesting in 2004 that if there was a bubble it could only be identified after it burst, and then in 2006 that 'not all bubbles burst'. One does not have to accept the idea that a bubble can only be identified in retrospect, but it does explain why journalists would have used the term far more after the crash than during the boom. Insofar as the word 'bubble' carries these connotations it is actually more loaded than 'boom'. The property market was discussed obsessively in the period, with the term 'house prices' appearing in 1483 articles in the *Times*. A reading of the economics articles shows that the debate over the sustainability and future of the market was one of the key themes in the discourse.[15]

While *The Economist* did use P/E and P/I ratios to establish the existence of a price bubble in Ireland, it also included significant caveats. It accepted that lower interest rates could justify a higher P/I ratio, though

[14] Mercille, 'The Role of the Media in Sustaining Ireland's Housing Boom' (2014), 8.

[15] Mercille, 'The Role of the Media in Sustaining Ireland's Housing Boom' (2014), 1, 5, 11; 'House of Cards', *The Economist*, 31 May 2003, Issue 8326, 2–5; 'Heading for a Brick Wall', *The Economist*, 31 May 2003, Issue 8326, 15–16; 'Interest Hike Would Burst Property Bubble', *The Irish Independent*, 24 September 2004; 'Will the Property Bubble Burst at This Rate', *The Irish Independent*, 30 January 2006.

added that they did not explain the scale of the increase. Lower interest rates could also inform a higher P/E ratio because they would reduce the cost of mortgage repayments relative to rents. As we saw in Chapter 5, Lane and Honohan contended that the fall in Irish interest rates with the advent of European Monetary Union (EMU) could justify close to a doubling of prices. Other factors that could have influenced a long-term change in the P/E or P/I ratios include smaller family sizes, higher-quality houses, changes in relevant taxes and regulation, and a shortage of land in major cities. Clearly none of these factors came close to explaining all of the Irish price increases, and while interest rates were likely to have shifted to a permanently lower range with EMU, they were still liable to rise within that range. The point is to illustrate that the ratios of income and earnings to prices are not fixed and that a change is not necessarily indicative of a speculative bubble. Journalists could be overly sanguine about the property boom because of genuine conviction and questionable analysis, rather than bad faith.[16]

Mercille's contention that the boom was never seriously challenged because it was 'advantageous to key sectors of the Irish corporate and political establishment' raises more questions than it answers. As to how Teachtaí Dála (TDs) outside of the Government parties could have been induced to ignore the vulnerability is hard to imagine. The most visible political upshot of the boom was the consignment of senior Fine Gael and Labour parliamentarians to fourteen years on the Opposition benches. By 2005 Pat Rabbitte was reduced to criticising the Government for its management of 'a strengthening economy but a weakening society'. Similarly, the writer has been unable to find evidence that any of the left-leaning academic critics of economic policy in the boom period issued warnings that came close to recognising the precariousness of the property market. The possible explanations are that political and academic policy critics were silenced on the issue, that they were complicit in the obfuscation, or that they failed to recognise the exposure. If we are willing to attribute the failure of political and academic critics to appreciate the problem to genuine analytical shortcomings, then it is perfectly plausible that newspaper managers and journalists

[16]'Castles in Hot Air', *The Economist*, 31 May 2003, Issue 8326, 8–10 and Lane and Honohan, 'Divergent Inflation Rates in EMU' (2003), 10.

were subject to those same shortcomings without the need for pressure from elite interests.[17]

The contention that those within Irish newspapers exhibited a neoliberal ideology is both up for debate and insufficient to explain the failure of journalists within those newspapers to warn about the property market if they were cognisant of its vulnerability. As will be demonstrated later in the chapter, high-profile columnists within *The Irish Times* like Vincent Browne and Fintan O'Toole were at times genuinely radical. The *Times* editorials were consistently critical of fiscal decisions that favoured the well off. In the *Independent*, the reliefs that allowed the wealthy to minimise their tax liabilities were regularly condemned. While the Propaganda Model allows for some marginalised challenges to elite interests, these contributions were unequivocally in the mainstream of the publications. The relatively frequent contributions on equity issues from organisations like Think-Tank for Action on Social Change (TASC), Conference of Religious of Ireland (CORI), The Combat Poverty Agency and the trade unions could be dismissed as tokenism, or as being peripheral to the central coverage of the economy. However, if the *Times* was intended to propagate elite interests while its editorials and several of its major columnists frequently did the opposite, its performance in this respect must be called into serious question. The challenges to elite interests were too high profile and mainstream to be compatible with the thesis that such sentiments were effectively side-lined.

Summary

The Propaganda Model predicts that challenges to elite interests will be restricted and marginalised in the media. If the evidence suggests that such critiques were extensive and in the mainstream of the newspapers, then it calls into question how applicable at least some of the aspects of the model were to these publications in the period. Contrary to Mercille's assertion, McWilliams was a very prominent voice in the contemporary discourse. Similarly, the readiness of the *Times* to criticise wealthy individuals and the banks is apparent from the amount of attention it devoted to the Ansbacher scandal. To rely on the Propaganda

[17]Mercille, 'The Role of the Media in Sustaining Ireland's Housing Boom' (2014), 4 and 'Boom Times, but Not for Quality of Our Society', *The Irish Independent*, 1 April 2005.

Model to explain why journalists and newspapers failed to give sufficient warnings about the property boom, one needs evidence to suggest that they would have done so in the absence of its various explanatory factors.

Given the remarkable reliance of journalists and newspapers on external experts, it is entirely unsurprising that the media showed no more prescience than these experts themselves. Similarly, given that academics and Opposition politicians, often the most vociferous critics of economic policy, failed to anticipate the crash, it is perfectly plausible that journalists and newspaper managers also came to the wrong conclusion of their own accord. The purchases of property websites by the newspapers certainly seem to offer corroborating evidence in this regard. If this faith in the market was genuine and widespread, then it can go a long way towards explaining the failure to issue sufficient warning. In such an event, pressure from elite interests would clearly have been unnecessary. The disparity between the use of the word 'bubble' before and after the crash is at least partially explained by how the term was understood by journalists themselves. Furthermore, while P/E and P/I ratios could certainly be important tools in evaluating property prices, they are liable to fluctuate even in the absence of speculation. They are therefore not entirely objective indicators of a bubble, and it is quite apparent that many analysts reached overly benign conclusions through genuine, if clearly flawed, analysis.

3 Experts

The reliance on external expertise certainly did engender a pro-property market bias into much of the commentary in the newspapers. While several of the prominent economics journalists had relevant degrees, O'Brien's point that McWilliams and Lee stood out because they had worked as economists before becoming journalists seems key. It is thus helpful to distinguish between those journalists who self-identified as economists and those who did not. The non-economists often cited multiple external economists in their news reports and relied heavily on them for their own analysis. It is rare to find an example of where a non-economist seriously qualified or critiqued an economist opinion that they cited, even in the cases where two opinions used were incompatible. Many of the articles in the *Times* give the distinct impression that journalists considered the expertise of external economists to far outweigh their own and believed that it was not their job to challenge them. It is therefore often impossible to even identify the opinions of journalists themselves. For a typical reader, a very large proportion of the facts, analysis and opinions that they would have encountered thus originated from agencies external to the newspapers. As will be demonstrated below, very many of the key contributors were from private organisations with a significant stake in the property market.[18]

A reading of the economics articles from both Irish newspapers reveals the striking extent to which each relied on the same small group of commentators for citations and analysis. Table 1 illustrates the number of opinion pieces written by thirty-two prominent economists in the period that were published in *The Irish Times*, as well as the number of articles in which each contributor was cited. A citation is counted as an article in which an opinion or a fact is attributed to an analyst other than the writer. If the person is referred to in the context of something they did (like attending a conference, changing job or publishing a report), it is not counted as a citation unless it meets this criterion. Citations are highly important insofar as the people who supplied journalists with the facts and opinions that dominated the economic discourse played a key part in informing the decisions of market participants. Commentators are ranked in order of citations.

The private-sector economists are included on the basis that they were heavily cited in the *Times* in the period. Where academics were cited with any frequency they are also included, as are others who had a particular research interest in Ireland. What is immediately striking is the prominence of economists from the banks and stockbrokers. The bank economists had an obvious conflict of interest insofar as their employers were exposed to the property market. The economists from two of the major brokers, Davy and Goodbody, also faced a conflict of interest since their organisations were owned by Bank of Ireland and Allied Irish Bank (AIB) for much of the period. The potential conflict of interest for all of the brokers and Friends First (a life assurance company) was that their own managed funds could very possibly have been exposed to the Irish property market or broader economy, which the *Times* made no effort to clarify.

It is important not to caricature the contributions from the bank economists, and they often predicted a fall in the rate of house price

[18]www.linkedin.com. Accessed 19 March 2015 and O'Brien, 'The Irish Press, Politicians, and the Celtic Tiger Economy' (2014), 82.

Table 1 Citations and articles authored in *The Irish Times*, 2000–2006

	Analyst	*Organisation*	*Cited*	*Authored*	*Institution type*
1	Austin Hughes	Irish Intercontinental Bank (IIB)	295	19	Private
2	Jim Power	Bank of Ireland/Friends First	255	11	Private
3	Dan McLaughlin	ABN Amro/Bank of Ireland	246	55	Private
4	Alan McQuaid	Bloxham Stockbrokers	146	2	Private
5	Dermot O'Brien	NCB Stockbrokers	133	3	Private
6	John Fitzgerald	ESRI	93	5	Research institute
7	Danny McCoy	ESRI/IBEC	86	21	Combination
8	Colin Hunt	Goodbody Stockbrokers	86	12	Private
9	Robbie Kelleher	Davy Stockbrokers	82	11	Private
10	Pat McArdle	Ulster Bank	81	5	Private
11	Eunan King	NCB Stockbrokers	78	3	Private
12	Jim O'Leary	Davy/NUI Maynooth	73	90	Combination
13	John Beggs	Allied Irish Bank (AIB)	57	13	Private
14	Oliver Mangan	Allied Irish Bank (AIB)	56	12	Private
15	Colm McCarthy	DKM Economic Consultants	42	10	Private
16	Marian Finnegan	Sherry Fitzgerald	27	7	Private
17	Brendan Walsh	University College Dublin (UCD)	18	4	University
18	Moore McDowell	University College Dublin (UCD)	12	0	University
19	Sean Barrett	Trinity College Dublin (TCD)	12	3	University
20	Patrick Honohan	ESRI/World Bank	10	5	Combination
21	Frank Barry	University College Dublin (UCD)	10	0	University
22	Joe Durkan	University College Dublin (UCD)	9	0	University
23	Dan O'Brien	Economist Intelligence Unit	8	25	Research institute
24	Philip Lane	Trinity College Dublin (TCD)	7	9	University
25	Frances Ruane	TCD/ESRI	7	6	Combination
26	Dermot McAleese	Trinity College Dublin (TCD)	3	0	University
27	Kevin O'Rourke	UCD/TCD	3	1	University
28	Anthony Leddin	University of Limerick (UL)	1	5	University
29	Antoin Murphy	Trinity College Dublin (TCD)	1	1	University

(continued)

Table 1 (continued)

	Analyst	*Organisation*	*Cited*	*Authored*	*Institution type*
30	Rodney Thom	University College Dublin (UCD)	1	2	University
31	Cormac Ó Gráda	University College Dublin (UCD)	0	5	University
32	Morgan Kelly	University College Dublin (UCD)	0	1	University
	Total		1938	346	

growth. Pat McArdle from Ulster Bank even warned that the longer the price boom continued the greater the likelihood of an eventual bust, and argued in favour of measures to cool the market if it continued to boom. Nonetheless, the economists from the banks and estate agencies had a direct professional interest in the market to an extent that would not have been shared by analysts employed by the newspapers or by economists from organisations with no direct stake. It therefore seems likely that in a counterfactual scenario without the bank and estate agent contributions there would have been less unreservedly positive analysis. Similarly, it would have been almost unthinkable for these commentators to issue unambiguous warnings of significant price falls, let alone a market crash. However, given that so few analysts from any sphere realised the extent of the vulnerability, it is by no means certain that in the counterfactual scenario there would have been much more in the way of unequivocal concern.[19]

It is thus important to recognise that while more internal expertise would have improved the situation it was by no means a panacea. This was evident from 2005 when the *Times* appointed Marc Coleman as Economics Editor. Coleman had significant experience in both the Irish Department of Finance and the European Central Bank (ECB). He thus rightly self-identified as an economist and was notably more forthright in giving his own opinion and analysis than his predecessors. Nonetheless, the *Times* continued to rely heavily on external experts, and the appointment of a more assertive editor did not radically alter the tone of the

[19] Dominic Coyle, 'Housing Market Collapse "Unlikely"', *The Irish Times*, 9 June 2004 and Brendan Keenan, 'Cowen Urged to Act as Rising House Prices Baffle Experts', *The Irish Independent*, 22 October 2004.

commentary. Even when journalists employed by the newspapers were prepared to argue a point they were markedly more equivocal than the experts from the private organisations. This is not a negative reflection on the journalists concerned: economic forecasting and analysis is inherently difficult, and conveying uncertainty was only responsible. By contrast, however, an economist from an estate agency could be totally unequivocal about the prospects for the property market and still be doing their job, insofar as that job was to promote the interests of their employer.[20]

The main fault of the two Irish newspapers vis-à-vis the property market then, was not ignoring the possibility of overpricing or an eventual correction. The problem emanated from their reliance on external expertise to augment their analyses, and the extent to which their coverage was shaped by representatives from the industries that had most to gain from talking up the market and downplaying the risks. There is no suggestion of a conspiracy theory or bad faith on the part of the newspapers here. The relevant journalists were required to submit multiple articles daily. If a journalist had reservations about his or her economic qualifications, then it made perfect sense to go to outside experts for opinion and analysis. Given the time pressure involved it is quite understandable that an individual journalist would tend to rely heavily on the people they knew would be prepared to respond and to do so quickly. It was in the aggregate that these dependencies became problematic. Similarly, budget constraints within the newspapers probably go a long way towards explaining their internal expertise shortfalls. It is not reasonable to expect that the Irish newspapers would have enjoyed resources comparable to *The Economist*. However, it was the role of the newspaper editors and managers to ensure that the overall tone and coverage of their publications were not heavily skewed by external interests by working to offset any resultant bias. Their performances to that end are difficult to defend.

As Herman and Chomsky contend, the provision of information and analysis by companies should be considered as an effective subsidy to news agencies. They also point to the fact that elites go to significant pains to make things as easy as possible for journalists so as to secure their positions as dominant sources. There are plenty of benign motives that would encourage a private-sector economist to allocate some of his

[20] www.linkedin.com. Accessed 19 March 2015.

or her day to talking with journalists, including the promotion of one's organisation and the personal satisfaction of contributing to a debate. But these incentives also would have applied to an academic, and there is clearly a pronounced discrepancy in favour of the private-sector organisations. Part of this could conceivably have emanated from a preference on the part of journalists for private-sector economists. However, a word search of the phrases 'top economist' or 'leading economist' in the *Times* does not immediately suggest a marked bias in this respect. The high number of citations from the ESRI similarly suggests that such a bias was not a decisive factor. What is more likely is that private-sector economists considered giving an opinion to journalists to be part of their core roles in a way that academics did not, and made themselves more available to journalists on a daily basis. This is supported by Pat McArdle's subsequent contention that he was expected to secure a high media profile. Regardless of the reasons for the bias, one indisputable upshot of the relationship was the ability of private-sector economists to shape perceptions of the markets in which their employers operated through the newspapers.[21]

One could of course counter that the newspapers assiduously identified the organisations that external experts worked for. However, we have to consider the impact of this from the perspective of a typical reader. While many readers would presumably have treated the ebullience of the estate agents with at least some degree of scepticism, their spokespeople were generally portrayed as market experts and there was little explicit recognition of the fact that they faced a conflict of interest. In the case of the bank economists, it is by no means clear that many readers would have given any thought to their dual interests. In the case of the Davy and Goodbody stockbrokers, it is highly unlikely that a significant proportion of readers were even aware of the fact that they were owned by the banks. Identifying the contributor's employer and title could have served to establish their expert credentials as much as to qualify what they said. There was certainly plenty of information and analysis in the *Times* in particular that would have helped an economically minded and dispassionate reader to come to their own conclusions. But a very large proportion of readers would certainly have depended heavily

[21] Herman and Chomsky, *Manufacturing Consent* (2008), 20–21 and Houses of the Oireachtas, *Joint Committee of Inquiry into the Banking Crisis*, vol. 2, no. 12, Pat McArdle, 7 May 2015, 84.

on the newspapers themselves to help them mediate between competing arguments. The newspapers instead published analyses with wildly differing predictions for the future and made no real attempt to equip their readers with the tools to critique them. Given that many people were essentially looking for reasons to justify their desires to buy, all that was required of the industry experts was to create a degree of ambiguity and present concerns about the market as being a matter of opinion.

Summary

The newspapers were enormously dependent on external expertise for their economic analysis. They accorded particular prominence to private-sector analysts, especially those from the banks, stockbrokers and estate agents. There is no reason to assume that this emanated from any intentional bias on the part of the newspapers, and it is probably explained by busy journalists relying on those who made themselves most available. However, the upshot of this was that the newspapers accorded enormous coverage to the views of organisational representatives with major conflicts of interest. This allowed these experts to actively shape the markets in which their employers operated using the newspapers as conduits. It was the responsibility of newspaper editors and managers to ensure that the coverage and analysis of their publications were not skewed by external agencies, and there is significant evidence that they failed in this respect. It is important to stress that even if more alternative expertise had been available to the newspapers we cannot assume that they would have been more prescient in their warnings. However, they almost certainly would have published less material that barefacedly talked up the market, with the estate agents particularly culpable in this regard.

4 Property and Construction

4.1 *The Irish Times*

It is important to distinguish between the various types of warnings about property that analysts could issue in the period. An article could recognise that prices were rising too quickly without worrying that actual price levels were excessive. In turn, an analyst could appreciate that prices themselves were too high but not necessarily anticipate a fall. Finally, even those analysts who anticipated some sort of fall did not necessarily grasp the attendant implications for the broader economy. It was therefore perfectly possible for journalists and external experts to warn that price increases were excessive without recognising the vulnerability of the market, the Exchequer or the banks.

There were fairly clear warnings about the property sector published in the *Times* throughout the period. For example, Garret Fitzgerald expressed concern about the exposure of the housing market and construction sector to a US recession in early 2001. Jim O'Leary raised the prospect of possible price falls in 2003 and then warned about the reliance on the construction sector in 2005. He questioned the sustainability of building double the number of residential units required to meet underlying demand and labelled the industry a pyramid scheme 'on a truly enormous scale'. The editorials in the *Times* became warier from 2004 onwards, warning about the threats posed by continued price increases, the possibility of price falls, the reliance of the economy on construction for growth and employment, and unsustainable mortgage growth. One feature the editorials shared with commentary from many other quarters was the contrast between the willingness to identify that continued price increases would make price levels unsustainable and a marked reluctance to ever assert that such a juncture had been reached. Prior to Morgan Kelly's article in late 2006 (which is addressed in Chapter 5), the most prescient quantitative warning came from Constantin Gurdgiev, who argued in 2005 that the ESRI's worst case scenario of 30% price falls was too moderate and that anyone who bought after 2001 would be left in negative equity.[22]

Given his significant professional experience, it is interesting to note the warnings that Marc Coleman issued in the *Times* from his appointment as Economics Editor to the end of 2006. Again, any publications elsewhere or beyond that date are outside the remit of this analysis. In 2005 Coleman warned of a slight overvaluation in the housing market, the reliance of the Exchequer on housing and the unsustainable reliance

[22]Garret Fitzgerald, 'Right State Action Can Stave Off Recession', *The Irish Times*, 24 March 2001, 18; Jim O'Leary, 'Bricks and Mortar Hold Value but Can It Last?', *The Irish Times*, 10 January 2003, 55; Editorials, *The Irish Times*: 22/4/2004, 1/4/2004, 12/8/2005, 19/08/2005, 5/9/2006 (Note, not all editorials are correctly tagged but it is reasonably easy to identify them because of their page numbers, style, headlines and length); and 'What's Next? Experts Give Their Views', *The Irish Times*, 31 December 2005.

on construction for generating employment and growth. He suggested that a smooth landing was still likely but not a guarantee. In March 2006 he pointed to the exposure of the economy to a housing crash. In June he warned that the imbalances in the economy were worsening, and that if the numbers employed in the construction sector reverted to the EU average it would entail 100,000 job losses, a warning he reiterated in September. He also pointed to the OECD and IMF concerns about price overvaluation and called for remedial action. On the basis of Coleman's articles a reader would clearly have been well aware of the nature of many of the growing risks to the economy, if perhaps unprepared for the potential scale of the crash.[23]

The treatment of the official domestic and international institutions in the *Times* is quite pertinent. The most significant analyses of the Irish economy, like the ESRI's Medium-Term Reviews or the Central Bank's Financial Stability Reports (FSRs), were annual publications. The newspapers shared the predilection of many daily publications for the immediate over the important. A key publication might be the focus of several articles for a day or two, and if there was a particularly significant insight it might change the discourse thereafter. However, the coverage in the newspapers is suggestive of journalists under time pressure to find the most newsworthy points. Unsurprisingly, the realities of journalism in the period therefore served to discourage a proper consideration of the full significance of these reports. For example, in August 2000 there were four articles published in the *Times* on the IMF's Article IV Consultation the day after its publication. Strikingly however, there was no coverage of its study on the recent history of asset booms, which had fundamental ramifications for how the Irish property boom should have been understood.

Again, the prominence given to the concerns voiced by these organisations suggests that any attempt to marginalise opinion that challenged the property market had limited success. There were repeated references to the IMF's warnings that Irish housing risked overvaluation from 2003. Nor did such coverage require any particular assiduousness on the part of the reader: in April 2004 the front page of the *Times* carried the headline 'Central Bank and IMF Warn on Property Prices'. A front-page headline the following year read 'OECD Believes

[23] Marc Coleman, *The Irish Times*: 5/8/2005, 1/10/2005, 3/3/2006, 4/3/2006, 2/6/2006, 6/7/2006, 13/9/2006, 16/7/2006, 29/12/2006.

Irish Property Market over-valued by 15%'. In 2006 Coleman reported that the Central Bank's warnings were supported by 'a chorus coming from the OECD, the European Central Bank, the International Monetary Fund and the Economist Magazine'. Nevertheless, the papers also allowed the warnings issued by these organisations to be undermined by interested organisations, in a misguided effort to achieve balance. This balancing of competing opinions sometimes teetered on the absurd. In 2005 the *Times* reported Marian Finnegan of Sherry Fitzgerald's opinion that the OECD's finding on house price overvaluation was 'academic', since it would take a shock bigger than the terrorist attacks of 9/11 to cause a market crash in a strong economy. Finnegan's position flew entirely in the face of the international history of asset booms. But the net effect on the typical reader would presumably have been to muddy the waters and significantly undermine the impact of the OECD finding. The implicit position of the *Times* was that equal consideration should be accorded to formal international organisations on the one hand, and to representatives of the banks and estate agents on the other, with little effort made to adjudicate or to establish the glaring conflicts of interest on one side.[24]

Again, we must be careful not to present the role of the private-sector economists as having been monolithic. Davy and Goodbody issued repeated warnings about property despite their ties to the banks. In 2003 the *Times* reported Goodbody's concern about a housing bubble risk and a potential disorderly correction. In 2004 the stockbroker warned that a housing market collapse had become a significant risk. It is important to stress that such warnings did not equate to an appreciation of the depth of a potential crash. The broker was relatively sanguine about residential construction by 2006, with the worst case scenario envisaged as a fall to 60,000 units by 2008 and economic growth of 2.5%. Similarly, Davy warned of a significant fall in housing output 'and probably price' in 2004, while Merrion Stockbrokers predicted zero nominal house price growth and small falls in real terms over the coming two years. Despite warnings about the remarkably low yields in the

[24] *The Irish Times*: 10/4/2003, 7/8/2003, 23/9/2004; Una McCaffrey, 'Central Bank and IMF Warn on Property Prices', *The Irish Times*, 22 April 2004, 1; Emmet Oliver, 'OECD Believes Irish Property Market Over-Valued by 15%', *The Irish Times*, 7 November 2005, 1; Marc Coleman, 'Economy Vulnerable to Housing Crash', *The Irish Times*, 4 March 2006, 13; and 'Predicting Prices Is Academic', *The Irish Times*, 10 November 2005, 8.

housing sector, Davy was decidedly bullish about construction by 2006, anticipating output of 75,000 residential units as far ahead as 2010.[25]

A critic of the *Times* would not have to look hard for evidence that it extensively published articles from private-sector interests that talked up the market. Attributing this to intentional bias in the absence of compelling evidence is to unfairly assume bad faith on the part of the people who worked at the newspaper, while perhaps overestimating the attention to detail paid to the overall message of the economics section. A more plausible explanation is that the dependence on private-sector economists for analysis and information allowed special interests to transmit an unduly favourable view of the property market using the *Times* as a conduit. We should be wary of unduly criticising newspaper managers for failing to recognise the extent of the vulnerability of the market, given that so many professional economists also fell short in this respect. The fact that management at the newspaper did not identify or meaningfully offset the extent to which its coverage was shaped by vested interests should therefore be considered its major shortcoming. One not atypical piece was piece written by Ronan O'Driscoll from CB Hamilton Osborne King in January 2003, arguing that sales would remain buoyant and that interest rates and long-term mortgages had made new houses 'highly affordable'. The article was essentially indistinguishable from a sales piece, pointing to 'superb new projects coming up for first time buyers early in the new year'. As the boom started to falter in late 2006, the *Times* published an opinion piece by the Managing Director of Sherry Fitzgerald, Michael Grehan. Grehan assured readers that 'what's actually happening is that, while the market is levelling out, prices are still increasing but at a more sustainable pace. Instead of creating anxiety in the market, this should, in fact, be instilling confidence'.[26]

The fact that there were well-organised interests who had a stake in property prices increasing but no countervailing organised interests with sufficient incentive to challenge such articles was crucial. The *Times* itself should have filled such a space, but mistakenly considered 'balance' to be the accordance of comparable weight and credibility to vested and

[25] *The Irish Times*: 26/3/2003, 14/11/2003, 6/3/2004, 10/3/2004, 18/8/2004, 30/3/2006, 20/7/ 2006, 5/10/2006.

[26] Ronan O'Driscoll, 'New Home Sales Will Stay Buoyant', *The Irish Times*, 2 January 2003, 23 and Michael Grehan, 'No Reason to Brace Yourself for a Crash', *The Irish Times*, 26 October 2006, 6.

relatively objective groups. Property interests were dutifully on hand to offset the impact of unwelcome analysis on the public discourse, with one article in June 2003 criticising RTÉ for its allocation of significant coverage to 'scaremongering' on the part of *The Economist*, on the basis that the newspaper's analysts knew 'little or nothing about house values here'.[27]

There are far too many examples of articles informed by industry experts who championed the boom to reference them all, and we will briefly confine ourselves to those that illustrate a broader point. As Table 1 demonstrates, Dan McLaughlin of Bank of Ireland was one of three economists cited in over two hundred *Times* articles in the period. His analysis of the property market was therefore crucial. In 2003 he argued that housing markets were more resilient than others and less susceptible to bubbles and other factors contributing to volatility. He also contended that nominal falls were rare (a point to which we will return shortly) because prices were sticky downwards, adding that while real falls were more common they were not much cause for concern. In 2005 McLaughlin spoke to a meeting of chartered surveyors about 'a golden age of construction' in Ireland, commenting that it was 'amazing that nobody wants to take credit for this'. He contended that such growth in construction activity challenged those who pointed to a failure in the housing market, and that 'the golden age is not yet over'. Similarly, at the top of the table, Austin Hughes was of the opinion that housing demand and prices would continue strongly, and urged the Government not to intervene in the market. Jim Power, as the third most frequently cited economist ranked, maintained that there was no prospect of a crash and that prices were 'close to fair value'. While these three contributors were regularly cited in the same articles, between them they account for a remarkable 796 citations in the *Times* (41% of the citations counted across the 32 economists) and thus the fact that they were collectively so confident had a fundamental impact on the discourse in the newspaper.[28]

[27]'Economist's Nul Points', *The Irish Times*, 5 June 2003.

[28]Dan McLaughlin, 'Housing Market More Resilient than Others', *The Irish Times*, 17 October 2003, 54; 'Tiger Economy Returns with a Celtic Panther', *The Irish Times*, 11 February 2004, 4; Marc Coleman, 'Housing Demand Set to Stay Strong', *The Irish Times*, 28 September 2005, 18; Laura Slattery, 'IIB Warns Against Plan to Cool House Prices', *The Irish Times*, 5 September 2006, 19; and Marc Coleman, 'Consumer Caution to Hit Growth—Friends First', *The Irish Times*, 7 July 2005, 16.

The reliance on external agencies for information clearly ensured regular coverage for those organisations able to provide it. It seems to have been an accepted norm that if a journalist cited a private organisation's research findings that they would include a brief comment from a representative. This was generally quite understandable and is clearly not suggestive of any ill-intent. However, without remedial action by newspaper managers such relationships could have a distorting influence on how market developments were reported. This was very much the case with the ESRI/PTSB (Permanent TSB) House Price Index. On a monthly basis and year after year, the newspapers would include a one-line analysis on house price developments from a Permanent TSB spokesman. While other organisations tended to use an economist for such occasions, PTSB displayed remarkable candour by deploying its head of marketing, Niall O'Grady. The problem was not that PTSB relentlessly talked up the market, and such efforts would have lost all credibility. All that was necessary was to cushion the impact of any slowdown in price growth and to suggest that such 'moderation' was a welcome sign of stability. O'Grady was cited in the *Times* in 82 articles, and was thus well positioned in 2006 to assure 'young people' that fears of a crash were misplaced and that they should not be dissuaded from buying.[29]

4.2 *The Irish Independent*

The *Independent* similarly accorded significant attention to warnings issued on the property market. When the IMF expressed concern in September 2003, the paper deferentially referred to it as a 'prestigious agency'. A fortnight later two articles were written about a warning of a possible bubble issued by the European Commission. The same week the *Independent* reported Davy's concerns about possible 'price and volume' adjustments in the market. In a rare acknowledgement of the role of vested interests in the discourse, one columnist even cautioned first-time buyers that there were far more parties invested in prices rising than falling. The same article warned that in a low-inflation environment nominal price falls were much more likely to occur than they had in the past. Subsequent articles characterised residential property as a house of cards and warned that the longer high price growth continued the higher

[29] *The Irish Times*: 28/10/2003, 1/5/2004, 2/6/2004, 17/8/2004, 21/6/2006.

the chance of a subsequent fall. One particularly interesting piece by P.J. Drudy from Trinity College contended that a three-bed semi-detached house still only cost in the region of €100,000 to build, and pointed to huge profits accruing to banks, estate agents, solicitors, developers, landowners and the state. The *Independent* also published articles warning about the economic dependency on construction and about the potential macroeconomic implications of a sharp drop in prices.[30]

On given days, particularly in the wake of key reports, fears over house price falls dominated the economics section. When the ESRI raised the prospect of 30% price falls as the shock scenario in its 2005 Medium-Term Review it prompted four articles in the *Independent* on the same day. The inevitable industry response that followed pointed to very strong demand and the 'extremely favourable' prospects for the market 'to the end of the decade and beyond'. On 28 January 2006 three articles collectively warned that 40% of houses were being sold to investors, of the gulf between build costs and prices, of the unsustainability of mortgage growth, and of the possibility of a potential price crash. An article by McWilliams argued that the state did so little to address price increases because credit allowed it to reconcile the competing political objectives of placating the powerful and keeping the electorate docile. The paper continued to publish regular warnings on the market throughout the rest of the year.[31]

Like the *Times*, however, the *Independent* was also replete with articles from external experts talking up the market, very often the same people. One questionable argument from Jim Power was that because a price fall would damage the wider economy gradual rises were in the interests of everyone. A subsequent article that is unattributed in the database gratefully observed that the housing boom had created so many winners and so few losers, noting that there was very little risk of Irish buyers falling into negative equity. Such sentiments were of course highly dubious even at the time. Several industry experts doggedly considered demand in terms of the fundamentals throughout. When construction

[30] *The Irish Independent*: 19/9/2003, 1/10/2003, 7/10/2003, 16/10/2003, 4/12/2003, 18/3/2004, 31/3/2004, 9/4/2004, 7/10/2004, 16/10/2004, 6/01/2005, 18/08/2005, 18/10/2005, 1/12/2005.

[31] *The Irish Independent*: 16/12/2005, 17/12/2005, 28/1/2006, 8/2/2006, 23/3/2006, 12/4/2006, 15/5/2006, 1/8/2006, 22/8/2006, 14/9/2006, 15/9/2006.

output outpaced Dan McLaughlin's demand estimates, his response was to conclude that the immigration and population data must be wrong. The *Independent* also published pieces from industry representatives that could have just as easily been advertisements. In December 2004 Dara Deering as head of EBS Mortgages wrote that 'even though rental incomes have fallen off in recent months, property investors will tend to take the longer-term view. Property provides a tangible asset with high rates of return over the long term, and more importantly high levels of security and stability'.[32]

While there were certainly economists in the banks and particularly the stockbrokers who expressed some unease, several of the estate agents were unrelenting. Marian Finnegan from Sherry Fitzgerald was entirely unperturbed by the fact that first-time buyers had largely abandoned Dublin in favour of the commuter counties, maintaining that the property market 'will continue to provide us with a stable and resilient vehicle in which to invest without the angst which spiralling prices may have created'. She derived enormous comfort from the relatively low number of houses relative to the population, suggesting that 'until this gap is breached there is no possibility of a significant slowdown in the property market'. It is worth emphasising the importance of this: the *Independent* published an article written by an industry expert advising its readers that a market crash was impossible. One incident that encapsulates both the dependence of the newspaper on industry experts and their varying degrees of confidence was the simultaneous publication of short articles by Marie Hunt from CBRE Gunne, Marian Finnegan, Austin Hughes and Dan McLaughlin in which they were asked to rate the performance of the market out of ten. The bank economists, McLaughlin and Hughes, gave it seven and eight respectively. Hunt awarded the market nine points while Finnegan gave it full marks, pointing to its 'phenomenal performance' and contending that 'property still looks like providing fantastic opportunities in the years ahead'.[33]

[32] Jim Power, 'Don't Bank on Any House Price Collapse', *The Irish Independent*, 3 October 2003; *The Irish Independent*: 4/8/2005, 22/10/2004; and Dara Deering, 'Housing Market Buoyant on Strong Foundations', *The Irish Independent*, 30 December 2004.

[33] Marian Finnegan, 'Ten Years on, How Affordable Now Is the Irish Housing Market', *The Irish Independent*, 20 May 2005; Marian Finnegan, 'How Much Longer Can It Last?', *The Irish Independent*, 17 June 2005; and *The Irish Independent*: 13/1/2006.

The professional incentive to talk up the property market clearly encouraged some of the private-sector economists to do so. However, we should not assume that all of the experts who contributed to the newspaper discourse acted in bad faith. There is one piece of evidence in particular that strongly suggests that some analysts could have been driven by misplaced conviction. In June 2006 the bookmaker 'Paddy Power' offered bets on residential property price increases. It seems safe to assume that there was virtually no chance that a bookmaker would offer odds that ran counter to its own analysis. It is therefore highly suggestive that the shortest odds were for a remarkably bullish 12–13%. By November the bookmaker had revised its forecast sharply downwards, estimating price growth of approximately 6%. Notably however, it still offered 6/1 odds on an increase of less than 3% or a fall. According to the *Independent*, a rush of betting from 'pessimists' encouraged the bookmaker to halve these odds the following month. However, on the basis of its own analysis Paddy Power still predicted the most likely outcome to be a rise of between 4.25 and 5%. This was remarkably close to the predictions made by four bank and real estate economists interviewed by the *Independent* three weeks later. If an organisation that was clearly incentivised to make accurate forecasts was excessively optimistic, then it is fair to assume that in at least some cases industry experts were similarly informed by genuine but misplaced conviction.[34]

4.3 David McWilliams

McWilliams was the most consistent critic of the Irish residential property market as a speculative bubble in the period. He first warned of an imminent price crash in the late 1990s, though predicted that such an event would occur within two years. He explicitly pointed to credit as the key driver of the boom from very early on and warned of mutually reinforcing lending growth and house price increases driven by irrational expectations. McWilliams regularly drew comparisons to recent international housing bubbles, such as those in Japan, California and Massachusetts in the late 1980s and early 1990s, observing that significant negative equity had been experienced in many countries and that there was no reason to expect Ireland to be exempt. One element that is

[34] *The Irish Independent*: 23/6/2006, 17/11/2006, 8/12/2006, 30/12/2006.

conspicuously missing in the articles examined is an attempt to use historical precedent to gauge the extent that prices were liable to fall. Even in the absence of such explicit analysis however, it is highly apparent that McWilliams expected such falls to be substantial. A marked difference between McWilliams and many other commentators is that he clearly perceived the Irish property boom in the context of the history of international asset booms, recognising that such manias were a regular occurrence. While he did not predict bank collapses, he did recognise that the Irish banks were overexposed to land and were liable to experience share price collapses and possible takeovers. He was also one of the few commentators to appreciate that Irish house prices had fallen in real terms through much of the 1980s.[35]

4.4 *'The Ireland That We Dreamed of'*

Before finally leaving the coverage of the property market in the Irish newspapers it is worth dispelling the misconception that by the end of the boom opinion was divided between those who predicted a hard or a soft landing. Some of the more ebullient long-term forecasts anticipated no landing at all. In November 2005 Eunan King from NCB Stockbrokers argued that falling household size and inward migration

[35] *The Late Late Show*, Exact Date Unknown (RTE). https://www.youtube.com/watch?v=vzNO4u8AU3Y. Accessed 5 January 2016; Stephen O'Brien, '"Boom and Bust" Cycle Predicted for Celtic Tiger', *Irish Independent*, 23 March 1999; David McWilliams, 'Irish Economy Mirrors Asia's Before the Bust', *The Irish Times*, 16 January 1998; David McWilliams, 'Housing Proposals Should Focus on Credit Availability', *The Sunday Business Post*, 1 July 2000; David McWilliams, 'Ireland Looks Like Japan Before the Bubble Burst', *The Sunday Business Post*, 28 October 2000; David McWilliams, 'It Happened in California, and It Could Happen Here', *The Sunday Business Post*, 4 February 2001; David McWilliams, 'Borrowing Bubble About to Burst', *The Sunday Business Post*, 10 November 2001; David McWilliams, 'Life After the Bubble Bursts', *The Sunday Business Post*, 15 December 2001; David McWilliams, 'Let's Borrow Some Money', *The Sunday Business Post*, 27 July 2002; David McWilliams, 'You Can Bet Your Bottom Dollar', *The Sunday Business Post*, 16 March 2003; David McWilliams, 'Paying a Mortgage, Not Rent, Is Dead Money in Today's World', *The Sunday Business Post*, 5 October 2003; David McWilliams, 'Gold in Them There Streets', *The Sunday Business Post*, 7 November 2004; David McWilliams, 'Property Buzz May Yet Have Nasty Sting in Tail', *The Sunday Business Post*, 22 February 2006; and *Prime Time*, 16 October 2003 (RTE, 2003). https://www.youtube.com/watch?v=cxtkjZFfuZI. Accessed 26 March 2015.

would underpin demand for between 50,000 and 70,000 houses for the next fifteen years. The reader will note that such estimates implied in the region of a million additional homes. NCB also forecast that a 90% mortgage drawn down in 2005 would represent just 69% of the value of the house by 2009. The following March the broker anticipated that the economy would continue to grow at an average of 5% per annum until 2020. On New Year's Eve 2005, Ken MacDonald as Managing Director of Hooke and MacDonald asserted that property prices would double over the coming ten years, particularly in Dublin. Such confidence was by no means unique in such circles. At an industry conference in June, 70% of attendees had reportedly forecast that the average Dublin house price would reach €750,000 by 2015.[36]

4.5 *The Economist*

The Economist contrasted strongly with the *Times* and *Independent* in its coverage of the Irish property market. Expertise was a key differential. The staff list on *The Economist's* website does not suggest an enormous discrepancy in the number of economics journalists employed. However, the self-assuredness exhibited by staff at *The Economist* was far removed from the diffidence to external experts that characterised many of their Irish counterparts. This was highlighted in November 2005 when Pam Woodall, as a key contributor behind *The Economist's* analysis of housing markets, presented at a conference in Dublin. Woodall pointed to housing booms in countries like the USA, the UK, Ireland, Australia and New Zealand as 'the biggest financial bubble in history' and predicted 20% falls over the next five years. Few Irish journalists would have had the confidence to independently make such an assertion. The lack of comparable expertise and self-certainty explains in large part why Irish journalists were so reliant on industry economists for analysis.[37]

[36] 'Borrowed Time and Money', *The Irish Independent*, 1 August 2006; Colm Keena, 'Immigration to Sustain Housing Demand', *The Irish Times*, 29 November 2005, 18; 'Migrants Will Boost Record Demand for Houses', *The Irish Independent*, 29 November 2005; Marc Coleman, 'One Heroic Assumption Too Many', *The Irish Times*, 23 March 2006, 3; 'What's Next? Experts Give Their Views', *The Irish Times*, 31 December 2005, 3; and Ailish O'Hora, 'Average Dublin House in 2015 to Hit €750,000', *The Irish Independent*, 2 June 2005.

[37] www.economist.com. Accessed 25 March 2015 and Marc Coleman, "House Prices 'Set for Soft Landing'", *The Irish Times*, 22 November 2005, 18.

A second key difference was that because *The Economist* was published weekly, and because Ireland was fairly far down its list of priorities, it only addressed the Irish housing market intermittently. This cancelled out a lot of the 'noise' that characterised the coverage of the subject elsewhere and allowed the publication to deliver a unified message, with no opportunity for vested interests to create confusion. The newspaper evidently had significant faith in its readership, and published the arguments supporting its position in considerable detail. The upshot is that while a diligent reader of the Irish newspapers would have been aware of the divergence of expert opinion about the likelihood of a property crash, a subscriber to *The Economist* would have been better equipped with the tools to consider the problem themselves, and would have been much more cognisant of the Irish boom in a broader international and historical context. *The Economist* would thus have helped to immunise its readers against some of the more transparent arguments made by industry experts who talked up the boom. For example, the newspaper rightly argued in 2004 that any arguments supporting rising prices that relied on demographic changes should be treated with scepticism in a market where rents were not rising at a similar pace. The reader will remember that in Ireland rents at this juncture were actually falling. Similarly, as discussed in Chapter 3, the growing number of vacant units should have quickly dismissed explanations of this nature.[38]

The Economist first warned of 'bubble-like' symptoms in Ireland in 2002, pointing to record P/I ratios and the fact that it lay at the extreme end of house price inflation, with average annual increases of 20% from 1996 to 2000. The newspaper also cautioned that house price bubbles are more dangerous than equity bubbles insofar as they are driven by debt, and that the worst case scenario was price falls across many countries. Furthermore, the Japanese and German experiences demonstrated that real house price declines were unlikely to be masked in a low-inflation environment, since it would take sellers too long to wait out nominal falls. In 2003 the newspaper warned that the Irish P/I ratio was 40–50% above its long-term average, and estimated an overvaluation of 42%. It predicted a fall of 20% over the next four years, allowing for the effects of permanently lower interest rates and income increases in the interim. In stark contrast to Marian Finnegan's composure as first-time

[38]'Castles in Hot Air', *The Economist*, 31 May 2003, Issue 8326, 8–10.

buyers were pushed out of Dublin, and her belief that prices would remain stable in the absence of a fundamental shift in economic performance, *The Economist* warned that the market would invariably start to wobble once this group was priced out, and that a change in sentiment was all that was required to burst the bubble.[39]

The newspaper observed that low interest rates had driven an Irish 'property frenzy', particularly in Dublin, where prices had quadrupled in a decade. Ireland was deemed to be 'peculiarly vulnerable' because policymakers were unable to prick the bubble by raising interest rates. In 2005 *The Economist* labelled the international property boom 'the biggest bubble in history', unprecedented in its duration, geographical spread and scale (surpassing even the US stock bubble of the 1920s), and it warned readers to 'prepare for the economic pain when it pops'. The newspaper commended the OECD's methodology for establishing Irish house price overvaluation, but observed the sensitivity of such analysis to an interest rate fluctuation. Crucially, *The Economist* estimated that a rate increase of just one per cent would be sufficient to push Irish overvaluation from 20% to as much as 50% given the low base level and the high number of variable mortgages. This is clearly a crucial qualification and should have garnered much more attention from the OECD and other commentators. Again, the fact that journalists in *The Economist* actually had the time and skill set to critique OECD methodology does not cast the Irish newspapers in a particularly flattering light.[40]

4.6 Nominal Price Falls, Advice to Individuals, and Internal Expertise

One widespread belief that repeatedly surfaced in the newspapers and elsewhere was that nominal house price falls had been historically rare. There is surprisingly little collated evidence in this regard, and most

[39] 'Going Through the Roof', *The Economist*, 30 March 2002, Issue 8266, 77–79; 'As Safe as What?', *The Economist*, 31 August 2002, Issue 8288, 63; 'Betting the House', *The Economist*, 8 March 2003, Issue 8314, 82; 'Castles in Hot Air', *The Economist*, 31 May 2003, Issue 8326, 8–10; 'Have the Property Gurus Really Got It Right?', *The Irish Independent*, 7 October 2006; 'House of Cards', *The Economist*, 31 May 2003, Issue 8326, 2–5; and 'Hot Property', *The Economist*, 13 September 2003, Issue 8341, 86.

[40] 'Why Worry?', *The Economist*, 11 December 2004, Issue 8405, 77–78; 'In Come the Waves', *The Economist*, 18 June 2005, Issue 8431, 73–75; and 'Hear That Hissing Sound?', *The Economist*, 10 December 2005, Issue 8456, 88.

studies tend to focus on real falls. Real falls are of course important insofar as they reduce the value of the house relative to wages and affect the profitability of development, but so too are nominal changes given that the size of the homeowner's mortgage remains constant and its relationship to the nominal house price therefore determines net equity. Efforts to dismiss the relevance of either real or nominal changes were clearly misguided. Articles in the *Independent* and *The Economist* at least recognised that the incidence of nominal price falls in the past was unlikely to offer much guidance for the future, given that in many countries inflation rates were at their lowest point in half a century. However, even the premise that nominal falls had been rare was a dubious one. Within the EU15 (the fifteen European Union members prior to 2004), Britain, Sweden, Finland and the Netherlands had all experienced very significant nominal falls since 1978. Furthermore, German prices were actually falling in the period. Thus, a third of Ireland's regional neighbours had recent experience of such falls. Switzerland, Japan and Norway had also suffered very large falls from the late 1980s. Similarly, insofar as Ireland's economy could be likened to that of a US region given its high migration flows, nominal declines in Boston, New York and San Francisco in the early 1990s should have given cause for concern. In view of the almost unparalleled scale of Irish price increases and the well-established relationship between the size of a boom and the subsequent bust, nominal falls had certainly not been so rare elsewhere to justify any complacency.[41]

While the newspapers had a significant impact on the public discourse, and thus on politics, they also directly informed the choices made by market participants. The disparate advice given to prospective buyers in the period is therefore significant. In August 2005 a reader from Dublin wrote to *The Irish Times* explaining that he had held off buying from the late 1990s because of his 'paranoia about a housing crash'. The columnist admonished his timidity and urged him to buy, describing it as 'bewildering' that the reader 'could have determined

[41] Brian Lowe, 'Is a Soft Landing the Silver Lining in Property Bubble Deflation?', *The Irish Independent*, 2 November 2006; 'A Boom Out of Step', *The Economist*, 31 May 2003, Issue 8326, 5–7; 'Heading for a Brick Wall', *The Economist*, 31 May 2003, Issue 8326, 15–16; 'Cracks in the Brickwork', *The Economist*, 3 January 2004, Issue 8356, 51–52; and Gerard Kennedy and Kieran McQuinn, 'Why Are Irish House Prices Still Falling?', *Central Bank of Ireland Economic Letter Series*, vol. 2012, no. 5, 8.

back in the late 1990s or at almost any point since that the residential property market was liable to crash to the extent that you would be faced with a position where you had negative equity on your home'. In the same year the *Independent* advised that anyone who postponed buying would face prices that would 'inevitably be higher' when they eventually did. In 2006, Niall O'Grady pointed to people who had been 'sitting on their hands waiting for negative equity to happen' and now struggled to get on the ladder. Seemingly without irony, he added that 'we wouldn't be advising FTBs [first-time buyers] to ever hold off buying'.[42]

By contrast, in 2003 McWilliams encouraged prospective buyers to avail of falling rents and avoid the risk of being consigned to years of bad debt through a price shock. In the same year, *The Economist* similarly advised readers in the countries where it identified a bubble to hold off buying until prices had fallen. In 2005 the newspaper repeated the advice and urged people to rent and to invest the money they saved in shares. Interestingly, it also argued that the myth that it was always better to buy was a remnant from the 1970s and 1980s, when very high inflation had simultaneously eroded mortgage values and pushed up rents. The intergenerational aspects of this seem particularly pertinent, and it presumably played a part in informing the paradigm of parents encouraging their adult children to make the responsible choice and buy during the boom. The estate agents were of course prepared to capitalise on such familial approval, and in 2004 Eunan O'Carroll as Managing Director of Gunne Residential justified continued price increases by reference to the 'significant parental equity' available to first-time buyers.[43]

The pivotal importance of internal expertise was particularly apparent at various points in the discourse. In 2004 Cliff Taylor as the Economics Editor of the *Times* contrasted warnings from the IMF with Maurice Roche's use of supply-side factors to argue that prices were in line with the fundamentals. Taylor clearly considered himself unqualified to

[42] Dominic Coyle, 'Q&A', *The Irish Times*, 5 August 2005, 7; 'There's a First Time for Everything', *The Irish Independent*, 8 March 2005; and Edel Kennedy, 'House Prices to Keep Rising but at a Slower Rate', *The Irish Independent*, 21 June 2006.

[43] *Prime Time*, 16 October 2003 (RTE, 2003). https://www.youtube.com/watch?v=cxtkjZFfuZI. Accessed 26 March 2015; 'Heading for a Brick Wall', *The Economist*, 31 May 2003, Issue 8326, 15–16; 'To Buy or Not to Buy? That Is the Question', *The Economist*, 5 March 2005, Issue 8416, 11; and Eunan O'Carroll, 'Price to Rise as Equilibrium Is Miles Away', *The Irish Times*, 18 March 2004, 6.

critique Roche's position, contending that 'you would need an advanced knowledge of mathematical equations- and an understanding of the assumptions underlying them- to judge between the mathematical models established to assess the state of the market'. If senior economics staff in the Irish newspapers were quite candid about their inability to adjudicate on the merits of such arguments, it is quite unsurprising that they were so ready to depend on outside experts. Spotting the flaw in Roche's argument clearly did not require the qualities that Taylor suggested, and three days later in the same newspaper Jim O'Leary pointed out that using the price of building land to explain rising house prices simply shifted the problem to a potential bubble in land prices. One occasion in particular stands out in highlighting the extent to which some journalists and subeditors were unfamiliar with their subject matter. In September 2005 an article written by the Industrial Correspondent of the *Independent* warned that just twelve foreign companies accounted for some 90% of Irish exports, including Coca-Cola, Viagra and Intel. If such a figure strikes the reader as incongruous, it should. Three days later the newspaper published a retraction clarifying that the actual figure was twelve thousand.[44]

Summary

It is clear that both the Irish newspapers published significant warnings about the property sector, including the possibility of price falls and the reliance of the macroeconomy on construction activity. However, almost all of these warnings totally missed the scale of a potential crash, with Kelly and Gurdgiev as two notable exceptions. The newspapers faithfully transmitted warnings from third-party organisations like the OECD, IMF and the Central Bank. However, they also allowed these warnings to be undermined by industry representatives in the name of balance, with almost no effort to adjudicate between the two sides. There were many articles in both the *Times* and the *Independent* that enabled industry experts to talk up the market and downplay the risks. The example of Marian Finnegan dismissing the possibility of a crash in the *Independent*

[44] Cliff Taylor, 'Room with a View to a Killing', *The Irish Times*, 6 January 2004, 11; Jim O'Leary, 'Single-Digit House Price Inflation May Be at Hand', *The Irish Times*, 9 January 2004, 5; Gerald Flynn, 'Just 12 Firms Account for 90pc of Irish Exports', 2 September 2005; and 'Foreign Firms Account for 90pc of Exports', *The Irish Independent*, 5 September 2005.

is particularly arresting. It is also highly significant that the three most prominent external economists identified were all sanguine about the market.

Contemporary and subsequent portrayals of the debate as having been between those who predicted a hard or soft landing are misleading. Several industry commentators clearly envisaged that the boom would go on unabated for many years to come. *The Economist* performed far more successfully than the Irish newspapers in terms of warning about a property crash, which can be attributed to its superior internal expertise and attendant self-confidence. Its resultant independence from external experts ensured that the newspaper's message was unified and clear. The fact that *Economist* analysts were sufficiently skilled and resourced to critique the OECD's econometric models highlights the gulf between it and the Irish newspapers. Crucially, nominal house price falls had not been rare in Western Europe in recent decades. The remarkable scale of the Irish boom should have encouraged analysts and policymakers to treat the historical lessons much more carefully.

5 The Financial Sector

Like many organisations in the period, the newspapers published regular warnings about the rate of credit expansion. At the start of the decade, for example, the *Times* reported John Fitzgerald's concern the banks were liable for a nasty shock if the economy slowed given their exposure to residential mortgages. The *Times* also transmitted regular warnings from the Central Bank, including a front-page article on the risk of a fall in property prices posed by the rapid growth of personal debt. By 2006 such warnings were a common feature of its editorials and commentary. On three occasions the newspaper likened the Central Bank's routine warnings of a property bubble and debt crisis to those of the boy who cried wolf. As one editorial observed, such regularity had served to dull the edge of its message. To Marc Coleman's credit, he did stress that the lesson of the fable was that the wolf eventually arrived.[45]

Such warnings generally pertained to increases in personal debt however, with remarkably little written about how the banks were funded or lending to property developers. This is highly conspicuous given

[45] *The Irish Times*: 25/2/2000, 2/6/2000, 20/12/2000, 13/6/2004, 30/1/2006, 1/3/2006, 4/3/2006, 2/5/2006, 1/7/2006, 5/8/2006, 9/11/2006.

that mortgage lending growth represented just 35% of the increase in private-sector credit from January 2000 to December 2006. It is not credible to attribute the discrepancy to a lack of publicly available information, since the key aggregate data on total mortgage debt and total private-sector debt were frequently published by the newspapers themselves, and should have prompted more investigation. On the funding side, as one journalist subsequently noted, the banks' own annual reports published the key data on their heavy reliance on foreign borrowing and high loan-to-deposit ratios. One key factor in informing complacency on the part of the newspapers was their propensity to accept the position of the Central Bank that the system was fundamentally sound. The fact that journalists did not further interrogate the data themselves is difficult to explain given their concerns about personal credit growth. Nor is there compelling evidence to suggest that journalists understood the problem but intentionally avoided it. In February 2005 an article in the *Times* advised readers that AIB shares offered 'exceptional medium-term value'. A subsequent article in September further advised that the Irish banks were good value and that the medium-term prospects for the sector were favourable.[46]

Even senior journalists clearly had no idea of the powers available to the Central Bank to restrict credit growth. Editorials in the *Times* urged the Bank to remind borrowers of the risk of an interest rate increase and to ensure no further slip in lending standards, but observed that the Bank was unable to do much else to curtail growing indebtedness. One could make allowances for this misunderstanding on the basis that the newspapers faced resource issues, but it would certainly have been possible to ask the Bank itself to outline its available powers. An article written by a former Assistant Director General of the Bank in the *Times* listed some of the available intrusive measures, including raising capital adequacy ratios, raising risk weightings, and banning 100% loan-to-value mortgages. The reader will remember that if such measures failed the Central Bank had the authority to put a ceiling on the rate of credit growth across the institutions, which clearly would have had a dramatic

[46]O'Brien, 'The Irish Press, Politicians, and the Celtic Tiger Economy' (2014), 80–81; Figures on Credit Obtained from the Central Bank; 'The Squeeze Tightens', *The Irish Times*, 5 August 2006, 13; Marc Coleman, 'Banking Too Heavily on Property Market', *The Irish Times*, 9 November 2006; and *The Irish Times*: 25/2/2005, 23/9/2005, 18/11/2006.

effect. While we cannot know what would have happened exactly, it is worth reflecting on the political pressure that the newspapers could have exerted had they been aware of the ability of the Bank to stop the debt spiral in its tracks.[47]

The *Independent* also regularly repeated debt warnings from organisations like the OECD and the Central Bank. However, it too perpetuated the misconception that there was not much that the Bank could do beyond issuing warnings. The newspaper was particularly assiduous about warning readers of the dangers of growing personal debt, and did so persistently. One of the more outspoken articles on the subject dubbed personal indebtedness 'the new national disease', commenting that 'many of us appear to be living as if it was a permanent summer' and 'believe the bubble will never burst'. The newspaper's coverage of the macroeconomic implications of this, however, was generally confined to repeating the warnings issued by the Central Bank. Again, the occasional simple error suggests that this could have been attributable to expertise. One short article in January 2006 warned that outstanding home loans had reached €252 billion. This figure actually pertained to total private-sector debt, and the level of mortgage debt at that point actually stood at €90 billion. The mistake was not just a typo and was repeated in the article. One could certainly excuse an inexperienced journalist for the confusion, but the fact that the mistake got past a subeditor indicates that the newspaper was potentially not well placed to challenge the position of the Central Bank.[48]

The coverage of the banking sector in the *Independent* from mid-2006 was particularly interesting. In June the ECB warned about credit growth of 11% across the Eurozone, prompting Davy to question what it made of the Irish growth level of 30%. The Central Bank warned that at current rates residential mortgage debts would more than double in

[47] Editorials, *The Irish Times*: 5/4/2005, 12/5/2005; Michael Casey, 'Watchdog Sanguine on Property Boom', *The Irish Times*, 14 October 2005, 5; and Honohan Commission, *The Irish Banking Crisis: Regulatory and Financial Stability Policy 2003–2008. A Report to the Minister of Finance by the Governor of the Central Bank* (2010), 105.

[48] *The Irish Independent*: 27/11/2003, 21/4/2004, 13/7/2004, 22/9/2004, 27/4/2005, 16/7/2005, 1/9/2005, 2/11/2005, 31/12/2005, 7/1/2006, 28/1/2006, 18/4/2006, 29/4/2006; Kevin Murphy, 'The New National Disease', *The Irish Independent*, 7 January 2006; 'Drowning in it…', *The Irish Independent*, 7 January 2006; and www.centralbank.ie. Accessed 27 March 2015.

three years. In October, Brendan Keenan reported on Patrick Honohan's warning about the reliance on overseas funding at the Dublin Economics Workshop. In late December the newspaper expressed concern about the dependence of the big banks on property and construction, with 78% of the profits of AIB, Bank of Ireland and Anglo Irish Bank coming from the sector. In an early recognition of at least part of the systemic exposure to developers, the same article warned that just over half of this was attributable to construction and property speculation alone. However, the *Independent* continued to carry stories in which third parties talked up the banks, with no attempt to qualify their optimism. In November, it reported Davy's view that there was no deterioration in credit quality and that Irish bank shares were not overpriced in a European context. The following month it reported that Goldman Sachs had upgraded Anglo Irish Bank shares to 'best buy', and had raised its earnings and price targets for both Bank of Ireland and AIB.[49]

6 Competitiveness and Inflation

There is a tendency to contrast the despondency of the recession with the giddy optimism of the boom years that preceded it. However, the discourse for much of the boom was actually far less positive than one would expect. From the turn of the millennium until mid-2001 inflation concerns were a dominant theme in the newspapers. As the global economy slowed, fears quickly grew about the threat of an economic crisis. From then throughout 2002 the mood was markedly downbeat, with quite a number of contemporaries referring to the period as a 'downturn'. Commentators were still talking about the economy in terms of 'recovery' until early 2004. Nor was any kind of boom anticipated, and remarkably more than half of Irish adults surveyed in November 2003 expected the economy to deteriorate over the following twelve months, while only a fifth anticipated an improvement. The real exuberance emerged from 2005, encouraging one *Independent* headline to observe that the 'Economic Outlook gets Better and Better'. The importance of inflation was a constant theme that received very significant attention

[49] *The Irish Independent*: 1/6/2006, 16/11/2006, 6/12/2006, 21/12/2006, 29/12/2006.

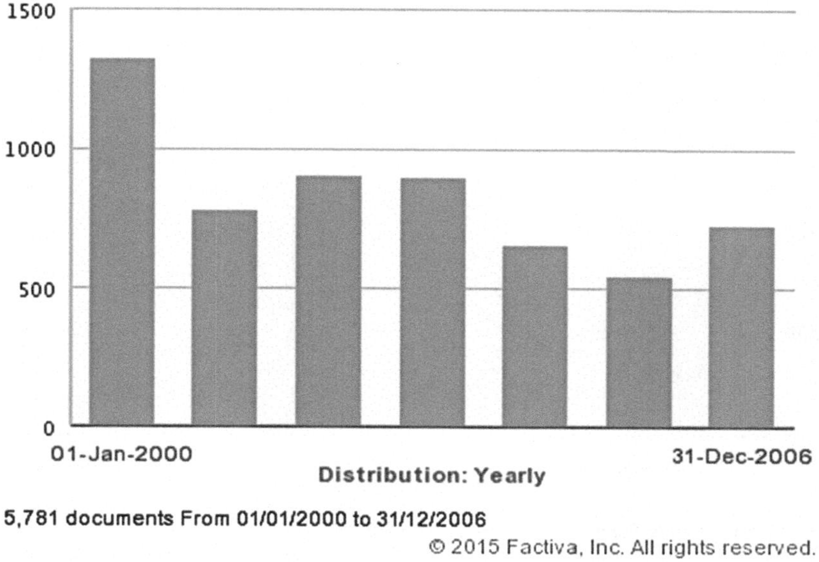

Fig. 1 *Irish Times* articles that mention 'inflation'

from both newspapers throughout the period, as demonstrated in Figs. 1 and 2.[50]

Competitiveness and inflation was one area where the reliance on third-party commentary had significant benefits. Organisations like the Small Firms Association (SFA), its umbrella group The Irish Business and Employers Confederation (IBEC), and the Irish Exporters Association (IEA) routinely warned of the associated dangers. Both Irish newspapers also transmitted numerous warnings from the Governor of the Central Bank about the need to remain competitive. In 2004 the *Independent* reported the Bank's concern that inflation posed the single biggest threat to the economy. However, the proposed policy solutions were almost universally fiscal. The role of credit in fuelling inflation was subjected to far less scrutiny. This was despite the fact that one *Times* editorial in 2006 observed that over the following twelve months

[50] *The Irish Independent*: 25/11/2003, 5/2/2004, 6/1/2005 and Graphs from Factiva.

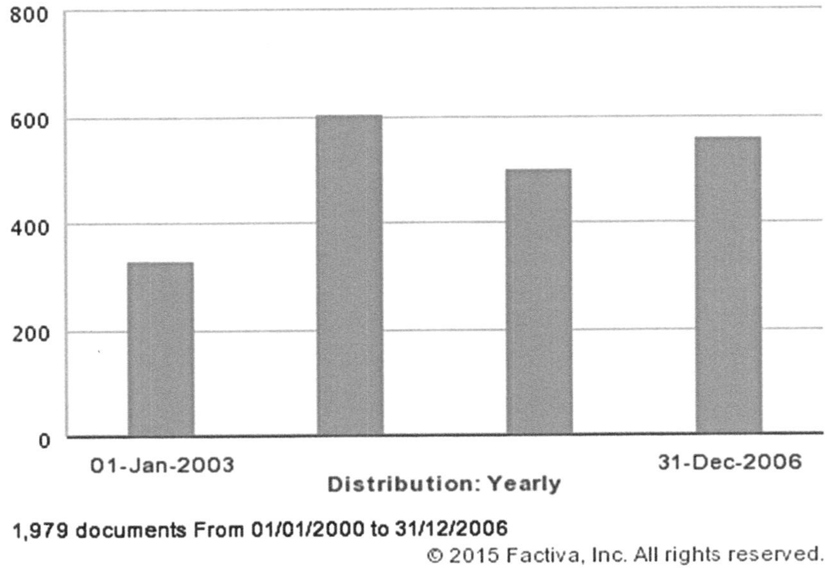

Fig. 2 *Irish Independent* articles that mention 'inflation'

additional Government spending (excluding maturing Special Savings Incentive Accounts [SSIAs]) would account for €5 billion while additional borrowing would approach €60 billion. The Bank's responsibility for addressing the inflationary aspects of credit expansion went largely unaddressed, presumably again because the newspapers were unaware of the policy measures available to it.[51]

Garret Fitzgerald was perhaps the most consistent critic of the inflationary impact of fiscal policy, and McCreevy was clearly his bête noire. The 2000 and 2001 Budgets drew remarkable ire, both at the time and for years afterwards. Fitzgerald argued that McCreevy was ideologically a Progressive Democrat (PD) rather than a Fianna Fáil pragmatist. While he readily recognised that the Minister was gifted, he argued that

[51]'Tiger Strides on, but Industry Is No Longer at Your Service', *The Irish Independent*, 17 November 2005; *The Irish Times*: 20/12/2000, 19/1/2001, 29/6/2002, 13/8/2002, 24/3/2004, 28/10/2004, 29/1/2005, 10/6/2006; and *The Irish Independent*: 28/10/2004, 30/10/2004.

his self-certainty and strong ideology made him dangerous, memorably dubbing him a 'strong-minded accountant with a gambling streak'. He witheringly observed that the Minister seemed 'unable to accept such obvious economic concepts as the need to pursue counter-cyclical rather than pro-cyclical policies'. Fitzgerald condemned as indefensible the degree of budgetary politicisation and criticised trebling the growth rate of public spending as an act of 'sheer lunacy'. He contended that either the Government forgot that it had joined the EMU, 'or else it has completely failed to understand the significance of that decision', particularly the risks posed by inflation with no devaluation option.[52]

Fitzgerald subsequently identified the key economic objective for the Government elected in 1997 as having been to dampen demand and safeguard competitiveness as Ireland entered the monetary union. He juxtaposed this with McCreevy's 'grossly irresponsible' decision to boost spending by a quarter, and argued that the 15% rise in the Consumer Price Index (CPI) over three years was the foreseeable outcome 'of these disastrous Budgets'. He explicitly attributed the policies to the Minister's inexpertise and intransigence, arguing that 'the level of economic incompetence in this whole process is deeply disturbing. It does not appear that McCreevy ever understood the inevitable consequences of his actions and he clearly refused to listen to the advice of his own officials'. Unlike many newspaper commentators in the period, Fitzgerald recognised that the damage done in the period was lasting, with Ireland suffering a 20% competitiveness loss against its main trading partners. Significantly, he did not propose a means to address the problem, believing there to be no solution in the absence of universal wage cuts. The fact that he did not call for contractionary Budgets probably emanated from either a complacency about the extent of a potential construction collapse, or from his implicit recognition of what was politically conceivable. To his credit however, Fitzgerald had clearly warned of the dangers of such rampant fiscal expansion at the time.[53]

The editorials in the *Times* were also routinely critical of the failure of policymakers to tackle inflation and pointed to the need to encourage

[52] Garret Fitzgerald, *The Irish Times*: 8/1/2000, 29/1/2000, 1/4/2000, 17/6/2000, 4/11/2000, 25/11/2000, 9/12/2000, 30/12/2000, 17/2/2001, 30/11/2002, 19/7/2003, 17/1/2004.

[53] Garret Fitzgerald, *The Irish Times*: 3/7/2004, 17/9/2005, 10/12/2005, 28/10/2006, 9/12/2006.

competition 'no matter what vested interests are at stake'. The editorials criticised the Government response of commissioning reports on the issue, arguing that 'it all smacks of a "look busy" approach while ducking hard, short-term decisions'. The newspaper was similarly critical of the decision of the benchmarking body to make recommendations that would stoke inflation without explaining its rationale. It astutely identified the similarities between the problems emanating from both the public and private sectors, pointing to the need for significant improvements in public service delivery and in competition policy, arguing that consumers were taking second place to vested interests. The effects of inflation were highly apparent by 2006, with an editorial in April pointing to the inability of Irish exporters to benefit from the pickup in the global economy. A subsequent piece in June pointed to 1000 manufacturing job losses a month, warning that construction could not be taken for granted forever.[54]

7 Fiscal Policy

Both Irish newspapers were quite energetic in critiquing fiscal policy. The *Times* was primarily concerned about economic management and equity issues, while the *Independent* paid very significant attention to how the system allowed very high earners to dramatically reduce their tax liabilities. An editorial in the *Times* in November 2002 accused the coalition of 'gross mismanagement' of spending control, and of pursuing a strategy that was 'breathtakingly cynical' politically and 'ham fisted' economically. Subsequent editorials focused on the need to ensure value for money and to control spending, and urged the achievement of crucial public-sector reforms in return for benchmarking. The newspaper called for multi-annual budgetary planning and an informed debate on spending priorities and how to pay for them. In mid-2005 it encouraged the Department of Finance to analyse the impact of construction and related lending on the broader economy and subsequently warned of the vulnerability in this respect. However, the exposure did not inform the newspaper's fundamental view of fiscal policy or the stability of the Exchequer, and the editorials were decidedly supportive of Brian Cowen's stance from his

[54]Editorials, *The Irish Times*: 14/6/2000, 29/6/2000, 16/12/2000, 25/4/2001, 13/5/2001, 14/5/2002, 10/1/2003, 1/2/2003, 28/3/2003, 11/4/2003, 23/5/2003, 13/6/2003, 12/11/2004, 8/4/2006, 10/6/2006.

appointment in September 2004. One notable editorial in January 2006 was entitled 'Rude Health of Good Economy', and observed that Cowen was presiding over an economy that was 'the envy of Europe'. The newspaper's attitude towards the Minister soured palpably towards the end of the year, observing that his claims that his job was 'not to interfere' in the property market rang hollow in view of the Government's intervention on behalf of property speculators. By contrast to the relatively warm greeting for Cowen's first Budget, the 2007 Budget was derided for its lack of prudence or vision.[55]

In terms of promoting equity issues several senior columnists in the *Times* were notably strong. For example, Fintan O'Toole argued that all non-graduates should be entitled to substantial payments to help them pursue additional education. He also criticised Government policy for having left many behind, particularly the McCreevy Budgets, observing that 'public resources became prey to the greed of a rich elite'. Garret Fitzgerald similarly argued that 'right-wing policies have left profound inequalities'. He contended that such failures were no accident, pointing to the policy decisions to grant large tax cuts, and censured the state as the most right-wing in Europe in terms of its resource allocation to public services and poverty reduction. Fitzgerald subsequently criticised the Special Savings Incentive Account (SSIA) scheme as a 'disastrous anti-social transfer of €500 million from taxpayers to the better-off section of our community'.[56]

Vincent Browne wrote critically of how the ideology of the PDs had become widely imbedded, condemning the party's low-spend and low-tax policies as socially uncaring. Browne also invoked Gramsci, complaining that basic questions of fairness and equality were almost never raised in Budget debates, or else were dismissed by 'common sense' as being eccentric or beside the point. He argued that the major issues in Irish society and politics were the disparity in terms of incomes, opportunities,

[55] Editorials, *The Irish Times*: 15/11/2002, 4/1/2003, 1/2/2003, 5/3/2003, 5/6/2003, 5/12/2003, 2/12/2004/, 12/8/2005, 5/10/2005, 5/1/2006, 1/7/2006, 5/9/2006, 21/10/2006, 18/11/2006, 7/12/2006.

[56] *The Irish Times*: 17/10/2000, 24/7/2001, 4/8/2001, 2/11/2002; David Madden, 'Winners and Losers on the Roller-Coaster: Ireland, 2003–2011', *Economic and Social Review*, vol. 45, no. 3 (Autumn 2014), 405–421; and Michael Savage, Tim Callan, Brian Nolan, and Brian Colgan, 'The Great Recession, Austerity and Inequality: Evidence from Ireland', ESRI Working Paper no. 499 (2015), 7–8.

health and educational services, and power. Echoing the Propaganda Model, Browne challenged the influence wielded by a small minority through control over parliament and the media. There were of course plenty of examples of commentators in the *Times* arguing for policies that would further imbed and deepen inequality. However, it is difficult to maintain that more egalitarian voices were marginalised or subdued in view of the remarkably robust views held by three senior columnists.[57]

The editorials in the *Times* also paid very significant attention to equity issues. In May 2000 the newspaper criticised the tax cuts that had favoured the better off in the 2000 Budget. Throughout the year it repeatedly urged the Government to ensure that in the next Budget the bulk of the benefits accrued to the less well off. It renewed the call the following year, pointing to the need to focus on social welfare recipients and the lower paid. The newspaper criticised the 2003 Budget for allocating €1.2 billion more to public-sector pay but just €500 million more to social welfare and pensions, arguing that 'there is something badly wrong with the allocation of spending resources when one relatively well-off group gets significant increases, while the poorest barely keep pace with inflation'. In 2003 the editorials became discernibly more strident, with one arguing that 'the coalition Government is presiding over an outrageous assault on the living standards of the most vulnerable and impoverished sections of our society as an alternative to higher income tax or more extensive borrowing'. A subsequent editorial argued that the 2004 Budget estimates made 'grim reading for anyone with a social conscience', and contended that the socially regressive measures were 'a shame on the Government in harder times'. In response to the Budget the *Times* berated McCreevy for having 'sucked up' to the business community, sardonically lamenting that if only 'the disadvantaged could lobby as effectively'. The newspaper welcomed Brian Cowen's efforts to address the ability of high earners to dramatically reduce their tax liabilities through reliefs. However, it noted that the closure of the schemes smacked of the Government gently closing the stable door after some of the state's wealthiest individuals had bolted.[58]

[57]Vincent Browne, *The Irish Times*: 4/12/2002, 22/10/2003.

[58]Editorials, *The Irish Times*: 17/5/2000, 19/7/2000, 18/10/2000, 24/10/2000, 2/12/2000, 28/4/2001, 22/8/2001, 1/12/2001, 2/12/2002, 5/12/2002, 16/12/2002, 15/11/2003, 4/12/2003, 17/8/2004, 27/11/2004, 3/2/2006, 7/2/2006, 28/6/2006.

For its part the *Independent* routinely railed against the reliefs open to the super-rich from 2005. In March, Brendan Keenan observed that 29 people earning over €500,000 had managed to avoid paying any income tax in 2001, and that Ministers appeared to be deeply wedded to the reliefs. Of the returns under the economics category in *Factiva* there were four similar articles in October. In November one headline read 'How to Pull Off the Trick of Paying no Tax: Simply Make Sure You're Already Loaded'. An article in February 2006 observed that Joan Burton's claim that it was a different law for the super-rich was vindicated as an uncomfortable truth by three separate reports. On the same day a piece by Senan Molony referred to the situation as 'a scandal'. An article in July was entitled 'Too Much is Never Enough for Ireland's Super-Rich', and acerbically observed that for the very wealthy the two certainties in life were death and tax avoidance. Two weeks later the newspaper noted that the top 400 earners were paying just 24.5% tax on average earnings of €1.8 million per annum, contrasting it to the 42% upper rate for normal workers. The point here is clearly not to suggest that the newspapers were overwhelmingly concerned with equity issues. However, any argument that the *Times* was characterised by a neoliberal ideology or that either publication displayed an overriding reluctance to challenge the interests of societal elites is evidently very difficult to sustain.[59]

8 Conclusion

The Propaganda Model was developed by American academics to explain the inherent biases of the mass media. In particular, Herman and Chomsky focused on foreign policy and how conflicts were treated in the American press. There is no reason to assume that all of the aspects of the model would be equally applicable in other contexts, and some of its key factors clearly had only limited relevance for Ireland in the period. The model in its original form predicts that challenges to elite interests will be restricted and marginalised in the media. The fact that mainstream columnists and the editorials in the *Times* regularly argued for fairer Budgets, criticised policy, and exhaustively covered the

[59] *The Irish Independent*: 19/3/2005, 1/10/2005, 13/10/2005, 27/10/2005, 31/10/2005, 4/11/2005, 8/12/2005, 7/2/2006, 1/7/2006, 15/7/2006, 30/9/2006.

Ansbacher scandal therefore challenges its relevance to this context. Garret Fitzgerald's excoriation of McCreevy was particularly unrestricted in its undermining of a societal elite. The high profile of McWilliams across multiple fora, including those owned by corporate interests, is also deeply problematic for any attempt to uniformly apply the model to this context.

We must be careful to clarify the nature of the bias within the newspapers, which often exhibited foresight comparable to that of analysts in many other quarters. The Irish newspapers collectively warned that property prices, the construction sector, the Exchequer and the banks were all exposed. However, for the most part they shared the inability of many other commentators to envisage the potential scale of a reversal. This is perfectly explicable: one would logically expect that most journalists would have exhibited no more prescience than the external commentators who informed their analyses. The warnings from people like Kelly, McWilliams and Gurdgiev were among the strongest issued anywhere, and cannot be dismissed as total aberrations. The newspapers were also notably diligent in reporting the unease of the IMF, the OECD and the Central Bank. Where the publications did exhibit a bias was in the number of articles that unabashedly talked up the market, often with only the flimsiest of evidence. As we have observed, this emanated from the fact that newspaper managers did not meaningfully curtail or offset the distorting influence of the industry representatives who they relied on for information and analysis. That this continued as editorials and other articles in the newspapers became increasingly concerned is particularly difficult to justify.

While there were evidentially expertise shortfalls within the newspapers, it is clear that they did go to some efforts to address the problem. The recruitment of Jim O'Leary and Marc Coleman as columnists in the *Times*, and of course of McWilliams in the *Independent*, enhanced their coverage considerably. However, it is also clear that expertise did not ensure that one would anticipate the crash. Time pressure seems to have had a remarkably damaging impact on the performance of the Irish newspapers, encouraging the reliance on external experts and seemingly inhibiting the deeper investigations that should have been the natural response to some of the headline figures. The failure of both the *Times* and the *Independent* to establish the powers available to the Central Bank is highly important and cannot be attributed to just an expertise shortfall. The almost exclusive focus on fiscal policy as a macroeconomic instrument was a direct function of this misunderstanding of the options that were actually available to key decision-makers, exacerbating the more widespread failure of economists to pay sufficient attention to the macroeconomic impacts of credit growth.

One can certainly argue that newspaper managers were restricted by the resources available to them. However, much of what was published in the broad economics sections of the newspapers was presumably of limited use to almost anyone. Monthly fluctuations in export, credit, price and inflation data are largely meaningless to many readers without an explanation of the medium-term trends and their implications. For those who require it, such data were much more readily available outside of the newspapers than they had been in the past. The continued devotion of resources to reporting such fluctuations almost certainly stems from an unquestioned belief that this is what the economics section should contain, combined with the fact that such data lend themselves to regular publication without requiring too much time on the part of the journalist. The newspapers would almost certainly have better served their readers by publishing fewer articles and devoting more time to rigorous analysis and investigation. One could argue that in-depth analysis might command a limited audience, but it is hard to imagine that articles on the monthly fluctuations of construction input prices generated widespread enthusiasm. Readers would unquestionably have derived more benefit from rigorous but accessible arguments, as both the record and popularity of *The Economist* seem to corroborate.[60]

The interviews that have been collected from journalists after the crash and the hearings at the parliamentary Bank Enquiry are certainly informative. However, it bears repeating that we should be very careful to interrogate any testimonies made after the crash against the articles that were published during the boom. The events of 2007/2008 colour the post-millennial period irrevocably, and subsequent recollections and interpretations will inevitably be informed by what followed.

Efforts to attribute blame to journalists in the period need to be kept in perspective. Many journalists evidently did not believe that they had the expertise to critique external economists, or that to do so was even their job. This obviously served to devalue the contribution of the newspapers significantly, but the institutional requirements and time

[60]O'Brien, 'The Irish Press, Politicians, and the Celtic Tiger Economy' (2014), 76.

restrictions that journalists operated within were controlled by management. Several aspects of the boom should have generated significant unease even in the absence of specific expertise or knowledge, particularly house price rises and the construction sector. However, given that the record of expert economists in this regard was so mixed we should make some allowance for the relative disadvantages faced by journalists, with many presumably concluding that if the regulators and experts were generally sanguine there was no major cause for alarm. Nonetheless, journalists clearly cannot have it both ways, and they should at least have been prepared to give due consideration to the dissenters. Brendan Keenan's self-assured dismissal of Morgan Kelly's warnings about the solvency of the banks in the wake of the state guarantee sits uneasily with his evident belief that journalists should be held to a lower standard.[61]

[61] *Prime Time*, 30 September 2008 (RTE, 2008). Available from https://www.youtube.com/watch?v=11CCxv2ueiQ. Accessed 1 April 2015 and Donovan and Murphy, *The Fall of the Celtic Tiger* (2013), 164.

CHAPTER 7

Politics

Asking the Taoiseach a question is like trying to play handball against a haystack. You hear a dull thud and the ball does not come back to you.
Joe Higgins, *Dáil Éireann*, 2003[1]

1 Introduction

The interplay between discourse and policy is particularly evident in the parliamentary debates. Here the key decision-makers were, at least notionally, required to justify their positions and explain their worldviews in detail. This attribute gives the political debates an additional dimension in our study of the discourse on Irish economic policy. As we shall see however, Ministers could maintain remarkably unsubstantiated or illogical positions without ever being held to account by parliament in a meaningful way. This emanated from both the weaknesses of democratic institutions that prevail to a greater or lesser extent in many countries, and from the failure of Opposition TDs (Teachtaí Dála) to interrogate Ministers on key points with sufficient determination. Three pertinent examples we will address later in the chapter were Charlie McCreevy's conviction that an expansionary fiscal policy had no real bearing on inflation, the widespread belief in Government that lower tax rates could

[1] Dáil Éireann debate excerpt is the copyright of Houses of the Oireachtas. Re-use permitted in line with the Oireachtas (Open Data) PSI licence. https://beta.oireachtas.ie/en/copyright-and-reuse/.

C. M. Casey, *Policy Failures and the Irish Economic Crisis*,
https://doi.org/10.1007/978-3-319-90182-4_7

inform higher spending levels, and the assertion that increased housing supply was the fundamental solution to price increases.

This chapter is based on a reading of all of the relevant parliamentary debates in the Dáil from 2000 to 2006. Such a study is greatly facilitated by the excellent transcriptions of the Dáil debates. The online database also allows for some quantitative analysis but unfortunately it is somewhat limited. Responses to written questions are not included in the study because they were generally stock answers that do little to illuminate the thinking behind policy stances. Parliamentary committee proceedings would certainly be a useful area for future research and would make an interesting study in their own right. The chapter also draws heavily on newspaper articles, particularly where key politicians are quoted at events outside the Dáil Chamber.

Charlie McCreevy's role as Minister for Finance is crucial both in terms of fiscal policy and given that he was the Minister responsible for establishing the new Financial Regulator. As in the previous chapters, housing policy and its attendant debates are of particular interest. In setting the bar by which we evaluate contributions from TDs, it is important to remember that merely recognising that house prices or general price inflation were excessive did not equate to appreciating the precariousness of the situation. Deputies often expressed concern about house prices insofar as they affected their constituents, without necessarily questioning the stability of the market and its implications for the macroeconomy. Furthermore, such problems were routinely raised by the Opposition as one of many perceived failures on the part of the Government. Referring to a key risk as one item on a long list of grievances did not suggest that a Deputy had any appreciation of the potential scale of the problem.

2 Irish Politics in the Twenty-First Century

Several commentators have pointed to a pronounced parochialism that characterised Irish politics in the twentieth century, with a strong determination on the part of TDs to maximise the share of the national pie for their own constituents. A related characteristic was the significant influence exercised by special interest groups. While these attributes had evolved somewhat, a reading of the parliamentary debates suggests that the primacy given to serving geographical and sectoral constituencies was still a dominant feature of Irish politics in the millennial period.

Before turning to how specific aspects of the economy were treated in the debates, it is important to first consider how well-positioned the Dáil was to interrogate policy.[2]

During the 2002 Budget debates Labour's Michael D. Higgins argued that the discussion presented 'a "depeopled" economy, an economy described in terms of its indicators but not broken across categories of the population'. In actuality the Budget debates, in common with debates on virtually every other topic, were dominated by concern for how policy decisions would directly affect people, with Deputies energetically advocating the interests of specific groups. In the Budget speech the previous week the Minister for Finance and Opposition spokespeople had referred to 'people' 81 times compared to the 'economy' just 21 times. The Budget speech the following year presented a similar picture, with 70 references to people and 18 to the economy. By contrast, a defining feature of the economic debates was that discussions about longer-term or systemic concerns with no natural constituency, such as macroeconomic stability or development strategy, attracted little interest from the majority of the House and were almost invariably interrupted. This pattern was repeated across the debates on key issues, with debates on financial regulation, inflation and the housing market all dominated by the needs of consumers.[3]

The preoccupations of the House will be familiar to anybody who lived in Ireland in the period. Favourite topics included road safety, nursing homes, child care, the waste of taxpayers' money, and above all the shortcomings of the health service. The common theme was the

[2] J. J. Lee, *Ireland: 1912–1985, Politics and Society* (1989), 82–85, 470, 472, 519, 546; Elaine A. Byrne, *Political Corruption in Ireland, 1922–2010: A Crooked Harp* (Manchester, 2012), 90, 217, 221, 238; Tom Garvin (2004), *Preventing the Future* (2012), 45–48, 74, 82; Mary Daly, *Industrial Development and Irish National Identity* (1992), 178; Lee Komito, 'Irish Clientelism: A Reappraisal', *Economic and Social Review*, vol. 15, no. 3 (April 1984), 173–194; and Richard Manton, 'Spokes or Strokes? Clientelism and Cycling Funding in Ireland', *Irish Political Studies* (2016). Published online, available from http://dx.doi.org/10.1080/07907184.2016.1141766.

[3] *Dáil Eireann Debate 2002*, vol. 559, no. 3: Financial Resolutions, 2002—Financial Resolution No. 11: General (Resumed), Michael D. Higgins, 12 December 2002; *Dáil Eireann Debate 2002*, vol. 558, no. 5: Financial Resolutions. 2002—Budget Statement 2002, 4 December 2002; *Dáil Eireann Debate 2003*, vol. 576, no. 2: Financial Resolutions, 2003—Budget Statement 2003, 3 December 2003; and *Dáil Eireann Debate 2003*, vol. 561, no. 6: Finance Bill 2003: Second Stage (Resumed), Seán Power, 20 February 2003.

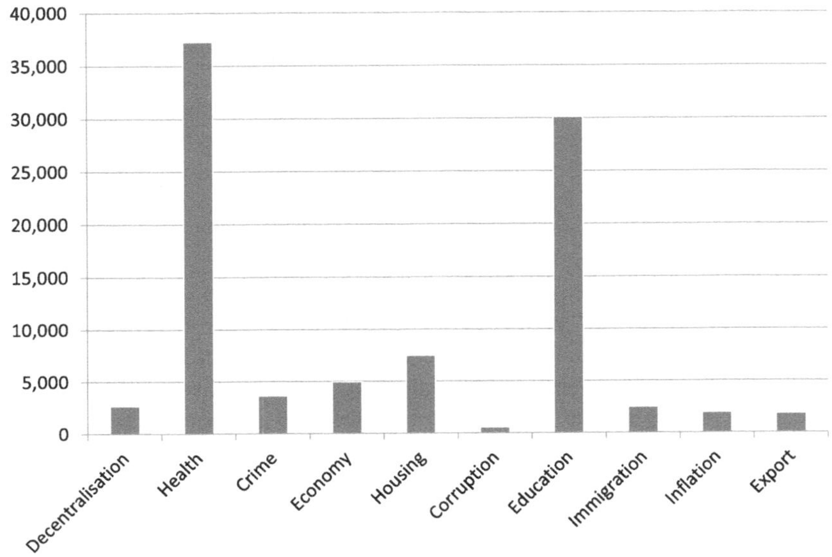

Fig. 1 Number of Dáil debates in which keywords were used, 2000–2006

propensity of politicians to raise issues with which voters could readily identify. Deputies did not feel compelled to explain in detail why the groups they promoted deserved particular attention over any other and would often raise as many issues as possible within the time allotted. As an extreme example, in one debate Fianna Fáil's Tony Killeen turned to ten separate issues in just 885 words, including the record of the Government, transport infrastructure, the National Pension Reserve Fund, the treatment of Aer Lingus employees, child benefit payments, income tax reform, decentralisation, regional airports, health strategy, and two different bypasses in his own constituency. Such contributions were clearly not conducive to any analytical rigour. Figure 1 depicts the number of debates or written answers in which keywords were used over the seven years. What is clear is that social issues, particularly health and education, received vastly more attention than more narrowly economic concerns.[4]

[4] *Dáil Eireann Debate 2002*, vol. 553, no. 3: Private Members' Business: Programme for Government: Motion (Resumed), Tony Killeen, 19 June 2002.

The level of attention that TDs paid to their own constituencies is evident from the debates, as is the extent of the associated workloads. Charlie O'Connor observed that in the first seven months after his election in 2002 he had met with 1500 constituents in his four separate clinics. Of the various criticisms levelled at Irish TDs, the contention that they were removed from the concerns of the electorate is the hardest to substantiate. Perhaps the most compelling evidence of the close relationship between Deputies and their constituencies is that prior to the abolition of the dual mandate in 2003, 101 of the 166 members of the 29th Dáil also held seats on local authorities.[5]

Deputies were remarkably unabashed about the primacy of their concern for their own constituents. One standout example was Seamus Healy demanding that his constituency received its 'fair share, which amounts to 750 decentralised jobs for County Tipperary'. However, the most explicit exposition of the symbiosis between a TD and his constituents came from Michael Ring. In a High Court challenge to the abolition of the dual mandate, Ring contended that without his seat on Mayo County Council he would lose a large component of his political base. He argued that his Dáil seat was not secured through legislative work, but by dealing with local issues like medical cards, roads and social welfare. Ring was similarly aggrieved by the fact that the 29th Dáil was the first in the history of the state in which Mayo was not represented at Cabinet. At its most acute this localism was intra-county, with Ulick Burke complaining that 1000 new jobs secured for Galway by the IDA (Industrial Development Agency) were likely to be located in the city rather than 45 minutes away in Loughrea or Ballinasloe where he felt they were needed.[6]

The priority that Deputies gave to their constituents is one possible explanation for the conspicuously generalist language used in Dáil debates. One gets the distinct impression that for many TDs the other

[5] *Dáil Eireann Debate 2002*, vol. 559, no. 4: Planning and Development (Amendment) Bill, 2002 [Seanad]: Second Stage (Resumed), Charlie O'Connor, 13 December 2002 and 'Big Increase in Dual Mandate TDs', *The Irish Times*, 22 May 2002.

[6] *Dáil Eireann Debate 2002*, vol. 533, no. 1, Nomination of Taoiseach, Seamus Healy, 6 June 2002; 'Laws on Dual Mandate are Undemocratic, TD Claims, *The Irish Times*, 29 January 2004; *Dáil Eireann Debate 2002*, vol. 553, no. 2: Private Members' Business: Programme for Government: Motion, Michael Ring, 18 June 2002; and *Dáil Eireann Debate 2002*, vol. 548, no. 4: Finance Bill, 2002: Second Stage, Ulick Burke, 14 February 2002.

Deputies in the Chamber were not the principal audience for their contributions. While non-technical language was perfectly appropriate for many topics, it inevitably limited debates on subjects like the economy or financial regulation. One cannot just attribute this to a universal lack of relevant expertise, given that both McCreevy and Joan Burton as Labour's finance spokesperson were chartered accountants, and Richard Bruton as Fine Gael's spokesperson was an economist. However, these high-profile TDs made decidedly little explicit use of these qualifications in their Dáil speeches.

Deputies also drew heavily on constituency anecdotes and reports in the popular media to substantiate their arguments. Programmes such as *Prime Time* and *Morning Ireland* played a significant role in setting the political agenda, with the former referenced in 285 debates and written answers. Although Deputies did use findings from organisations like the Central Bank and the IMF (International Monetary Fund) to bolster their positions, there was strikingly little engagement with the actual analysis. If one accepts McCreevy or Bertie Ahern's claims that they spent much of their time reading third-party reports on the Irish economy it is notable how little of the detail permeated through to their Dáil contributions.[7]

A striking feature of the debates is the marginalised role of the Dáil in drafting legislation. As if to underscore the point, McCreevy adopted the habit of leaving the Chamber during the Opposition speeches on Budget day. This reached its nadir in 2002, with the Minister for Finance, the Taoiseach and the Tánaiste all absent by the third contribution from the Opposition. Richard Bruton subsequently pointed to the inability of the Dáil to hold the Government to account, bluntly acknowledging that 'we are a joke as a house'. He observed that while the 2005 Finance Bill would be accompanied by 24 hours of solid debating it would be confined to tinkering at the edges of the tax structure. Shortly after his appointment as Minister for Finance Brian Cowen did acknowledge the need for more meaningful participation by the Oireachtas, 'rather than Members feeling that the process is done and dusted before they get to speak about it'. The highly restricted power of the Dáil to shape

[7] Houses of the Oireachtas, *Joint Committee of Inquiry into the Banking Crisis*, vol. 2, no. 38, Charlie McCreevy, 1 July 2015, 94 and Houses of the Oireachtas, *Joint Committee of Inquiry into the Banking Crisis*, vol. 2, no. 48, Bertie Ahern, 16 July 2015, 110.

legislation or to hold Government to account should thus be considered a severe limitation of the debates in the period.[8]

Summary

Several of the defining characteristics of Irish political life in the twentieth century were still very much apparent after the turn of the millennium. The first concern for many TDs was the welfare of their own constituency. Similarly, many Deputies saw economic debates as an opportunity to promote the interests of various social groups rather than to debate the macroeconomic implications of Government policy. The language used in the debates was far more generalist than that used in any of the official reports on the Irish economy or even in the newspapers. Deputies also exhibited a reluctance to engage with the analysis underpinning expert assessments, preferring constituency anecdotes or references to the popular media. Finally, neither the Government nor the Opposition leaders were under any illusion that the Dáil enjoyed a major role in economic policy formation.

3 Fianna Fáil and the PDs

An analysis of the political relationship between Fianna Fáil and the Progressive Democrats (PDs) is crucial for understanding how policy was formed in the period. The debates are particularly interesting in this regard insofar as they allow us to gain an understanding of the mentalities of the key protagonists in the two parties. Fiscal policy vacillated significantly, as demonstrated by Fig. 2. McCreevy was accused both inside and outside the house of increasing spending at an irresponsible rate in the run-up to the 2002 General Election. This was followed by a pronounced reduction in spending growth as the global economy slowed, with capital expenditure actually cut by €380 million over two years. Fianna Fáil's relatively poor performance in the 2004 Local and European Elections was widely attributed as the trigger for McCreevy's replacement with Brian Cowen, who raised the rate of expenditure

[8] *Dáil Eireann Debate 2002*, vol. 558, no. 5: Financial Resolutions, 2002: Budget Statement 2002, Dan Boyle, 4 December 2002; *Dáil Eireann Debate 2004*, vol. 585, no. 2: Management of Public Funds: Motion, Richard Bruton, 11 May 2002; *Dáil Eireann Debate 2005*, vol. 597, no. 2: Finance Bill 2005: Second Stage, Richard Bruton, 8 February 2005; and *Dáil Eireann Debate 2005*, vol. 601, no. 3: Parliamentary Questions—Budgetary Procedures, Brian Cowen, 27 April 2005.

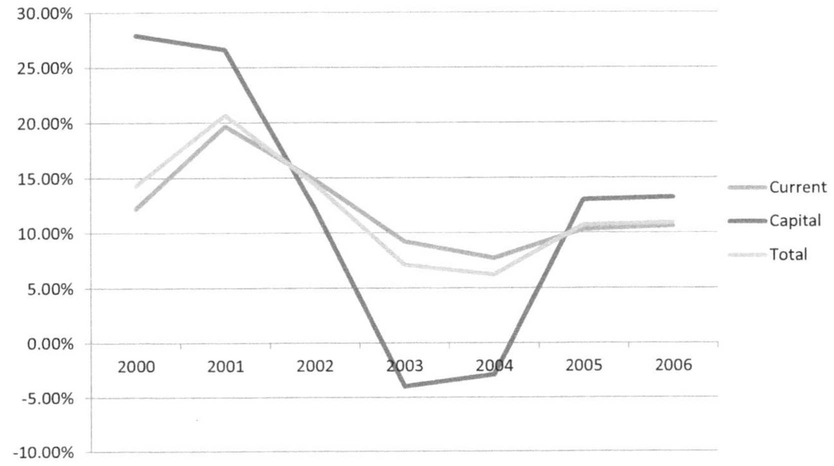

Fig. 2 Expenditure increases/decreases (Department of Public Expenditure and Reform)

increase, while the rhetoric from Bertie Ahern and Fianna Fáil acquired a distinctly leftist hue.[9]

A recurring accusation from the Opposition was that Government policy was heavily influenced by the PDs, despite their small numbers. This was an interpretation that Michael McDowell actively promoted, arguing that 'the larger party may lead. The junior party defines the direction'. The implication was particularly problematic for Fianna Fáil given that the PDs were generally perceived to be the most right-wing party in the state. A key political tension for Fianna Fáil was therefore to ensure that the ideological and rhetorical distinction between itself and the PDs did not become so blurred that it jeopardised the senior partner's traditionally strong appeal to working-class voters.[10]

[9] *Dáil Eireann Debate 2004*, vol. 594, no. 2: Financial Resolution No. 2—General (Resumed), Eamon Ryan, 2 December 2004; Notably Garret Fitzgerald, *The Irish Times*, see Chapter 6; and Data from 'Expenditure Trends', Department of Public Expenditure and Reform, http://www.per.gov.ie/en/expenditure-trends/. Accessed 25 September 2015.

[10] *Dáil Eireann Debate 2002*, vol. 553, no. 1: Nomination of Taoiseach, Seamus Healy, 6 June 2002; *Dáil Eireann Debate 2006*, vol. 627, no. 6: Housing Policy: Motion, Willie Penrose, 21 November 2006; *Dáil Eireann Debate 2004*, vol. 585, no. 2: Management of

A key figure in the implementation of fiscal policy in the period was Fianna Fáil's Charlie McCreevy. McCreevy's active role in the establishment of the PDs has been well-documented. Similarly, his affinity with the party's ethos was regularly observed, with opponents dubbing him the PDs' soulmate, Mary Harney's 'political Siamese twin' and Michael McDowell's 'ideological buddy'. McCreevy had spent much of his career chiding his party's spending excesses from the backbenches, and had been explicitly critical of the 'populist, all things to all people approach of Fianna Fáil and Fine Gael'. Upon his appointment as Minister for Finance in 1997 he committed to restrict current expenditure growth to 4%. Senior civil servants who worked closely with him have suggested that Ahern allowed him full jurisdiction over tax policy. The incongruity between McCreevy's long-held concern for fiscal stability and the fact that he presided over a doubling of current expenditure therefore stands out as one of the key paradoxes of the period. Figure 3 compares the trajectory of current spending from when McCreevy took office to what it would have been if the 4% target had been adhered to. Remarkably, in the counterfactual scenario current expenditure would have been €13.4bn lower at the point of his departure in 2004, and some €19.4bn lower by 2006.[11]

Despite his clear incapacity to curtail spending growth, McCreevy was resolute in his support for a low-tax regime. He took personal pride in having 'transformed the tax system', contending that lower taxes had helped to create jobs and to generate unprecedented growth. McCreevy

Public Funds: Motion, Richard Bruton, 11 May 2004; and 'McDowell Says PDs Are Key to any Coalition', *The Irish Times*, 25 February 2006, 1.

[11] Stephen Collins, *Breaking the Mould: How the PDs Changed Ireland* (Dublin, 2006), 25–29, 42–45; *Dáil Eireann Debate 2000*, vol. 527, no. 5: Financial Resolution No. 4: General (Resumed), Pat Rabbitte, 7 December 2000; *Dáil Eireann Debate 2002*, vol. 548, no. 4: Finance Bill 2002: Second Stage (Resumed), Caoimhghín Ó Caoláin, 14 February 2002; *Dáil Eireann Debate 2002*, vol. 548, no. 3 Finance Bill 2002: Second Stage (Resumed), Derek McDowell, 13 February 2002; *Dáil Eireann Debate 2002*, vol. 558, no. 5: Financial Resolutions 2002—Budget Statement 2002 Richard Bruton, 4 December 2002; Sean MacCarthaigh, 'McCreevy Promises to Stick to 4% Spending Limit', *The Irish Times*, 8 November 1997; Collins, *Breaking the Mould: How the PDs Changed Ireland* (Dublin, 2006), 27; Johan Christensen, *The Power of Economists Within the State* (Stanford: Stanford University Press) (2017), 92–93; and Data from 'Expenditure Trends', Department of Public Expenditure and Reform, http://www.per.gov.ie/en/expenditure-trends/. Accessed 25 September 2015.

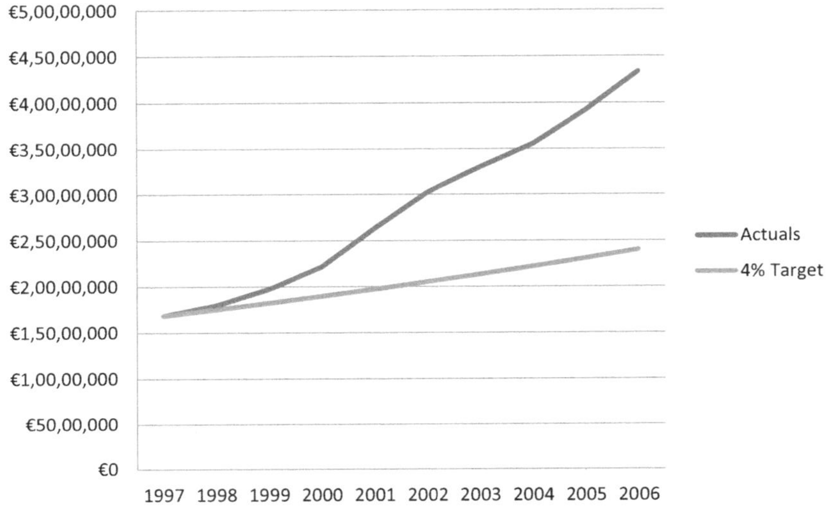

Fig. 3 Current expenditure (€000s) (Department of Public Expenditure and Reform)

was fundamentally averse to high income tax both on moral grounds and because he advocated 'a taxation system which encourages individuals and thereby creates greater wealth'. His arguments supporting the causal relationship between low taxes and growth hinged almost exclusively on his belief that lower taxes had worked for Ireland in the recent past. He made essentially no use of international examples or reference to the economic theorists whose work underpinned his worldview. Nor did he ever counter Ó Gráda's pertinent observation that the timing suggested that Ireland's low-tax regime was in fact a product of the Irish boom rather than its cause.[12]

[12] Mary Minihan, 'Papers Reveal Political Wrangling Behind State's Boom-Time Giveaway Budget', *The Irish Times*, 18 February 2013; *Dáil Eireann Debate 2004*, vol. 585, no. 3: Management of Public Funds: Motion, Charlie McCreevy, 12 May 2004; *Dáil Eireann Debate 2003*, vol. 576, no. 2: Financial Resolutions 2003—Budget Statement 2003, Charlie McCreevy, 3 December 2003; Cormac Ó Gráda, 'Is the Celtic Tiger a Paper Tiger?', in ESRI, *Quarterly Economic Commentary*, Spring 2002, 7; *Dáil Eireann Debate 2002*, vol. 550, no. 2: Finance Bill 2002: Report Stage, Charlie McCreevy, 7 March 2002; and *Dáil Eireann Debate 2003*, vol. 562, no. 4: Finance Bill 2003: Report Stage, Charlie McCreevy, 4 March 2003.

Mary Harney, as Tánaiste and leader of the PDs, was also deeply committed to low-tax policies. She advocated low personal taxation on the basis that it would attract and retain workers, describing Ireland as a 'meritocracy, where people are rewarded on the basis of merit'. Like McCreevy, she identified low capital, corporate and personal tax rates as having been fundamental causes of the boom. Harney was also a keen advocate of market liberalisation, observing that its benefits were already apparent in Ireland in terms of flight, telephone and taxi prices, and argued that 'the process of liberalisation still has a long way to go in this country'. She styled Ireland as believing in 'essential regulation but not over-regulation'. It is salient that in terms of both low-taxation and market liberalisation Harney also supported her views with perceived evidence from recent Irish experience.[13]

The most pugnacious Member on the Government benches was Michael McDowell, who memorably dismissed the Opposition as an 'array of losers' during his first Budget debate as Minister for Justice in 2002. Again, McDowell identified tax policy as having been key to Ireland's economic success, and contrasted it with what he termed the 'high tax, high spend, high unemployment strategy' which had damaged the economy in the late 1970s and 1980s. His economic philosophy was remarkably unembellished, as he explained during the Budget debates in 2005:

> I wish to look at the economics behind the Budget, but my contribution will not be technical or complicated. The key points of my contribution are capable of being delivered in six words- lower rates, higher yields, more resources. My essential point is that the lower tax rates provide higher revenue yields for the State which, in turn, lead to more generous levels of State resources. That has been my political philosophy and that of my party from its inception.[14]

[13] *Dáil Eireann Debate 2000*, vol. 527, no. 5: Financial Resolution No. 4: General (Resumed), Mary Harney, 7 December 2000; Mark Brennock, Harney Opposes Closer Integration of Europe', *The Irish Times*, 22 July 2000; and *Dáil Eireann Debate 2002*, vol. 558, no. 6: Financial Resolutions, 2002—Financial Resolution No. 11: General (Resumed), Mary Harney, 5 December 2002; and Mark Brennock, 'Harney Opposes More Tax on Wealthy', *The Irish Times*, 2 August 2004.

[14] *Dáil Eireann Debate 2002*, vol. 558, no. 5: Financial Resolutions 2002—Financial Resolution No. 4: Stamp Duties, Michael McDowell, 4 December 2002; *Dáil Eireann Debate 2003*, vol. 576, no. 4: Financial Resolutions 2003—Financial Resolution No. 5: General (Resumed), Michael McDowell, 5 December 2003; and *Dáil Eireann*

McDowell thus reconciled the tension between cutting taxes and providing social services on the basis that lower tax rates stimulated faster economic growth and ultimately generated more money for the Exchequer. He pointed to the recent performance of the Irish economy as an endorsement of this view, and argued that the Labour Party would risk Ireland's economic prosperity by ignoring the 'lower rates, higher yields and more spending formula of the past decade'. By way of evidence, McDowell argued that when McCreevy halved capital gains tax it generated so much additional activity that the yield quintupled. McDowell used similar language to Harney in advocating Ireland's transition to low rates of direct taxation on ethical grounds, contending the 'dominant political outlook in Ireland has changed to one liberating the talents and innate capacity of the people to deliver'.[15]

It is worth briefly mentioning that the idea of a trade-off between tax rates and revenues had gained significant traction in the USA after a meeting between the academic Arthur Laffer and two senior members of the Ford administration, Dick Cheney and Donald Rumsfeld in 1974. 'The Laffer Curve' is intended to demonstrate that 'under some circumstances' tax cuts can generate more rather than less revenue because they stimulate growth by increasing the incentives on work, output and employment. Laffer has since argued that the incentive affects are far larger when rates are high, and the Laffer Curve certainly does not suggest that cutting tax rates will generate higher yields under all conditions. Paradoxically, the fact that Ireland had cut rates substantially in the recent past meant that future cuts were actually less likely to generate additional yields.[16]

McCreevy's close affinity with the economic worldviews of Harney and McDowell notwithstanding, the key question is why the rest of Fianna Fáil so readily accepted economic policies that were far more in

Debate 2005, vol. 612, no. 15: Financial Resolution No. 6: General (Resumed), Michael McDowell, 8 December 2005.

[15] *Dáil Eireann Debate 2005*, vol. 612, no. 15: Financial Resolution No. 5: General (Resumed), Michael McDowell, 8 December 2005; *Dáil Eireann Debate 2006*, vol. 629, no. 2: Financial Resolution No. 5: General (Resumed), Michael McDowell, 7 December 2006.

[16] Arthur B. Laffer, 'The Laffer Curve: Past, Present and Future' (2004). Available from www.heritage.org.

keeping with the philosophy of the PDs than with the party's own traditions. While Brian Cowen rejected Harney's now storied identification with the American over the European socio-economic model, he did subscribe to another core tenet of the PDs. In March 2005, shortly after his appointment to Finance, Cowen argued 'I am in favour of low tax for the simple reason that it brings in more money for the State. I am a pragmatist. The more people at work, the higher the contribution to the State'. Like McDowell, Cowen pointed to the surge in capital gains tax receipts after the rate was reduced. Bertie Ahern was similarly convinced, arguing that 'by having lower taxes, we were able to spend more'. The Taoiseach lauded the enormous spending increases on social services that the boom enabled, observing that 'that is what our brand of socialism allows us to do', and that 'the real workers' party in this country is Fianna Fáil'.[17]

The appeal of the 'lower rates, higher yields and more spending formula' for the senior Government partner was thus quite apparent. In 2002 Labour's Derek McDowell observed that for many years Fianna Fáil had aspired to being all things to all men, and that the boom had enabled it to achieve just that. The mantra that tax cuts and spending increases could be mutually compatible provided intellectual validation, making the Government's position even more attractive. The fundamental political dilemma underpinning fiscal policy decisions had been solved: since tax cuts would ultimately generate additional funding for social services, the Government was no longer required to adjudicate in the trade-off between erstwhile competing demands. For a party leader with Ahern's political nous and drive for electoral success the formula must have been irresistible. He gave a rare direct insight into his mentality in 2003 when he suggested that 'Deputy Kenny and I have been Members of the House for long enough to know that there is a code of ethics whereby those who have been elected to the House try to remain elected. That is the code of ethics in this House'. The economic philosophy of the PDs afforded him political cover for presiding over rapid spending increases in tandem with tax cuts. Ahern's record as

[17] Derek Scally, 'Cowen Reaffirms EU Commitment', *The Irish Times*, 8 March 2001, 8; *Dáil Eireann Debate 2005*, vol. 599, no. 3: Finance Bill 2005: Report Stage (Resumed), Brian Cowen, 9 March 2005; *Dáil Eireann Debate 2004*, vol. 592, no. 4: Leaders' Questions, Bertie Ahern, 17 November 2004; and *Dáil Eireann Debate 2004*, vol. 592, no. 3: Leaders' Questions, Bertie Ahern, 16 November 2004.

the longest-serving Taoiseach since DeValera is testament to the electoral success of this strategy.[18]

For Ahern, Ireland's economic success also served as a fulfilment of the national project. He derived 'great pleasure in confounding the pundits in the City of London, Brussels and Frankfurt, who, blinkered by orthodoxy, still cannot quite understand how the Irish of all people have managed to get it right, and who are so certain that it cannot continue'. Perhaps most gratifyingly of all, the Taoiseach suggested that the potential lessons from Ireland's success were recognised 'even among Unionists in Northern Ireland'. On the same basis Noel Treacy spoke of how the nation and its people enjoyed the benefits of progress that those who won independence would have hoped for but scarcely thought possible, and how Ireland served as 'the perfect role model' for the EU accession states. Mary Coughlan invoked both earlier generations and 'our children who anticipate working in a nation striving towards its destiny, its head held high, its eye fixed firmly on the horizon and with hope in its heart'.[19]

Summary

The two Governments elected in 1997 and 2002 thus represented a confluence of PD ideology and Fianna Fáil populism at a unique historical juncture that allowed them to fulfil the primary objectives of both parties simultaneously. Regardless of whether one interprets the Celtic Tiger as a regional boom or a period of accelerated convergence it was clearly a temporary phenomenon. However, the key figures in both parties evidently believed that they had developed a strategy for permanently higher growth. McCreevy went so far as to suggest that 'we can feel confident we will never return to mass unemployment and emigration'. The party leaders were convinced that tax cuts had been fundamental in triggering the boom, and extrapolated that additional tax cuts would drive further growth. They gave no indication of where they considered the

[18] *Dáil Eireann Debate 2002*, vol. 550, no. 4: Private Members' Business—Economic Policies Motion, Derek McDowell, 20 March 2002 and *Dáil Eireann Debate 2003*, vol. 576, no. 5: Leaders' Questions, Bertie Ahern, 9 December 2003.

[19] Arthur Beesley, 'Taoiseach Attacks Economy's Doubters', *The Irish Times*, 8 April 2000; *Dáil Eireann Debate 2005*, vol. 612, no. 15: Financial Resolution No. 5: General (Resumed), Noel Treacy, 8 December 2005; and *Dáil Eireann Debate 2002*, vol. 555, no. 1: Private Members' Business—Public Finances: Motion, Mary Coughlan, 10 December 2002.

endpoint of this strategy, and nor did they imply that they considered any of the abundant new tax revenue to be in any way transient.[20]

While presiding over an unprecedented boom was clearly a political boon for Fianna Fáil, tax cuts did leave it open to accusations of being 'in thrall to right-wing economic theories'. The enormous spending growth of these years can be explained in large part by efforts to placate those constituencies that demanded public services and pay improvements. By committing itself to far higher levels of current spending, the Government further affirmed its confidence in the irreversibility of recent revenue growth. The belief that lower taxes would continue to produce higher yields was based on remarkably scant evidence drawn from recent Irish experience, rather than any international, long-term historical or theoretical perspectives. Attributing a five or tenfold increase in the capital gains tax yield over seven years exclusively to the decision to halve the rate blatantly ignored the fact that the reduction coincided with a period of economic growth and a property boom that were both remarkable by international standards. Those who used the apparent effects of the rate cut to bolster their arguments for generalised tax cuts never attempted to disaggregate the causes of the surge in revenue. One would naturally assume that the readiness of Government Ministers to treat the causality of the relationship as axiomatic was in large part down to political rhetoric. However, beyond Irish experience from the late 1980s onwards they gave no real indication of what else might have underpinned their generalised collective faith in the formula of 'lower rates, higher yields, more resources'. The apocryphal lesson of the 1997 capital gains rate reduction dramatically multiplying the yield has even survived the crash: McCreevy and others were still convinced of its veracity and applicability in 2015, with the factor seemingly having risen to twelve in the intervening years.[21]

[20] Charlie McCreevy, 'Strong Irish Economy Is Getting Stronger', *The Irish Times*, 13 September 2000.

[21] *Dáil Eireann Debate 2004*, vol. 585, no. 3: Management of Public Funds: Motion (Resumed), Martin Ferris, 12 May 2004; *Dáil Eireann Debate 2005*, vol. 599, no. 3: Finance Bill 2005: Report Stage (Resumed), Brian Cowen, 9 March 2005; Houses of the Oireachtas, *Joint Committee of Inquiry into the Banking Crisis*, vol. 2, no. 38, Charlie McCreevy, 1 July 2015, 116; and Harry McGee and Fiach Kelly, 'Renua Ireland Wants New Flat Tax on all Income', *The Irish Times*, 3 September 2015.

4 Inflation and Fiscal Policy

The various objections to the fiscal policies pursued in the period are often conflated, and it is worth quickly setting out the basis on which an interested and proactive Deputy should have raised concerns. Firstly, as many commentators observed, successive Budgets stimulated an already-booming economy. Secondly, a significant proportion of the tax derived from property and construction was transitory, and it was therefore imprudent to increase current spending commitments to a level that would be difficult to sustain into the future. Lastly, in an ideal scenario the Government would have saved significant reserves beyond those invested in the National Pensions Reserve Fund (NPRF). As we shall see, McCreevy cannot be unduly criticised in this respect, since he rightly maintained his commitment to fund the NPRF despite widespread political opposition. By running structurally neutral Budgets and increasing spending at a more sustainable level he would have naturally accumulated greater reserves, though it is clear that the political pressure to spend these or to reduce taxes would have been enormous.

The inflationary impact of McCreevy's Budgets was identified as a concern by Opposition Deputies from the start of the decade, in particular by Michael Noonan. McCreevy's stock defence was that international factors like oil prices and currency fluctuations were the primary drivers of inflation, and that fiscal policy had minimal impact in this regard. He contended that he would have to take billions out of the economy to produce any meaningful effect and rightly observed a marked reluctance on the part of the Opposition to identify where the cuts might be made. Frustratingly however, he never justified his position that fiscal policy was a minor determinant of inflation. The best he offered by way of evidence was his suggestion that 'someone recently did the sum' and found that removing £3–4 billion from the economy would only reduce the inflation rate by 0.5%, without clarifying who the person was. The belief that fiscal policy had a negligible impact on inflation was clearly not shared by the Opposition or by essentially any commentator on fiscal policy outside the house. At the start of the decade Philip Lane had explicitly advocated tighter fiscal policy as a means to combat inflation. The reader will also remember the IMF's advice that fiscal policy would have more of an inflationary impact within the common currency zone. The key failing on the part of Opposition TDs was that they never really pushed McCreevy to produce the evidence to support his position. Given that the close relationship between budgetary policy and inflation is commonly taken as a core principle of economic management this is difficult to explain.[22]

Remarkably, Bertie Ahern subsequently implied that he disagreed with McCreevy, criticising Opposition Deputies who chose 'to ignore altogether the economic effects of fiscal policy on inflation and competitiveness as if the only issue that mattered was balancing the books by spending up to the limit'. Such accusations were clearly hard to reconcile with the record of his successive Governments. Brian Cowen was of a similar mind to the Taoiseach, expressing his concern not to add to inflationary pressures through increased spending. Most remarkably of all, McCreevy himself had criticised the Rainbow Government's 1997 Budget on the basis that 'the Budget is pro-cyclical. The last thing the economy needs at this time is the stimulus which this Budget will give it'. It is very difficult to ascertain why pro-cyclicality had ceased to be a problem, and one would have expected such an intellectual reversal to warrant significant proof and debate. Even if one did accept McCreevy's position it raised profound problems in itself. In particular, it would have made the decision to proceed with European Monetary Union (EMU) difficult to defend, since this entailed relinquishing the Government's control over interest and exchange rates, two other key tools for managing domestic demand.[23]

McCreevy's failure to provide a satisfactory explanation for his disavowal of the inflationary impact of stimulatory Budgets provoked a mixed reaction from the Opposition. Joan Burton and Richard Bruton

[22] *Dáil Eireann Debate 2000*, vol. 514, no. 6: Finance Bill 200: Second Stage, Michael Noonan, 22 February 2000; *Dáil Eireann Debate 2000*, vol. 522, no. 2: Private Members' Business—Government Policies: Motion, Michael Noonan, 22 June 2000; *Dáil Eireann Debate 2001*, vol. 530, no. 3: Private Notice Questions—Budgetary Policies, Charlie McCreevy, 13 June 2001; *Dáil Eireann Debate 2001*, vol. 539, no. 2: Priority Questions—Inflation Rate, Charlie McCreevy, 27 June 2001; Dan O'Brien, 'McCreevy's Fiscal Policy Was Lacking in Sophistication', *The Irish Times*, 29 September 2004; Philip Lane, 'Tighter Fiscal Policy Needed to Fight Inflation', *The Irish Times*, 8 May 2000, 14; and For the IMF, see Chapter 3.

[23] *Dáil Eireann Debate 2006*, vol. 629, no. 2: Financial Resolution No. 6: General (Resumed), Bertie Ahern, 7 December 2006; *Dáil Eireann Debate 2006*, vol. 628, no. 1: Priority Questions—Fiscal Policy, Brian Cowen, 22 November 2006; and *Dáil Eireann Debate 1997*, vol. 473, no. 4: Financial Resolutions 1997—Financial Statement, Budget 1997, Charlie McCreevy, 22 January 1997.

paid decidedly little attention to the issue, focusing instead on the inflationary impact of increased charges administered by the state and by state-owned companies. Calling for reduced charges was undeniably more politically popular than advocating tax increases or spending cuts. By concentrating on a secondary issue however, the Opposition was surrendering the pass on a key point of economic management. This was a critical tactical mistake, since on various criteria other than pro-cyclicality McCreevy could rightly argue that his management of the economy was unassailable, as evidenced by low public debt and a series of surplus Budgets. Furthermore, the Opposition parties routinely demanded measures that would further stimulate demand, such as investing money from the NPRF into Irish infrastructure or reducing the number of people paying income tax at the upper rate.[24]

There was an enormous amount of discussion about the injustice of a system that allowed high earners to dramatically reduce their tax liabilities. By contrast, the extent of the revenue lost through other income tax breaks garnered remarkably little attention. Donovan and Murphy have suggested that reliefs and exemptions totalled €11.5 billion in 2005, by which point they actually exceeded receipts. While the exemptions principally accessible to high earners were clearly difficult to justify, at €2 billion cumulatively they constituted only one component of the broader risk posed by the erosion of the tax base. By focusing on the injustice of reliefs that benefited a small and particularly unneedy group, politicians studiously avoided the wider but more politically sensitive issue. In a similar vein, the attention accorded to issues like tax benefits for stallion owners, the tax treatment of GAA players vis-à-vis professional sportspeople, or the reimbursement of Eircom shareholders was out of all proportion to the money involved. Politicians of all hues thus demonstrated a propensity to tackle the issues that would win them broad support at the cost of addressing more fundamental risks. They correspondingly

[24] *Dáil Eireann Debate 2003*, vol. 567, no. 6: Priority Questions—Price Inflation, Richard Bruton, 28 May 2003; *Dáil Eireann Debate 2006*, vol. 617, no. 85: Priority Questions—Fiscal Policy, Joan Burton, 30 March 2006; *Dáil Eireann Debate 2002*, vol. 554, no. 5: Private Members' Business—Public Finances: Motion, Charlie McCreevy, 9 October 2002; *Dáil Eireann Debate 2003*, vol. 561, no. 5: Finance Bill 2003: Second Stage (Resumed), Joan Burton, 19 February 2003; and *Dáil Eireann Debate 2004*, vol. 593, no. 1: Leaders' Questions, Enda Kenny, 23 February 2004.

displayed a marked aversion to calling for spending cuts or tax increases that would affect a broad constituency.[25]

Like many of the other observers of the Irish economy in the period, Deputies did raise concerns about its trajectory without necessarily appreciating the scale of the risk. The general consensus into 2006 was that the economy was fundamentally strong, even among those who held misgivings. Eamon Ryan from the Green Party, for example, acknowledged Ireland's economic success while cautioning about its reliance on property development and foreign investment, especially given declining exports from indigenous companies. Some of the most astute warnings came from Enda Kenny and Richard Bruton from Fine Gael. Kenny warned of the large dependency on personal debt, consumer spending and the construction sector. He also pointed to Ireland's falling trade share and declining manufacturing employment, arguing that the effects of international competitiveness pressures were temporarily masked by a 'debt-driven property boom'. Bruton went further, arguing that the economy was at its most fragile for many years, and that construction employment was perhaps unsustainably high. He also pointed to the dependence of the Exchequer on construction activity, concluding that 'we are not in a strong position; we are, in fact, in a vulnerable position'.[26]

Such concerns notwithstanding, a central feature of the Dáil debates was the relentless political pressure from the Opposition to increase current spending and cut taxes. Kenny's take on Cowen's first Budget in 2004 was that it was at best a catch-up, and that more could have been done on pensions, child benefit, Garda numbers, health and education. Pat Rabbitte as Labour leader similarly complained that the Budget represented 'the bare minimum that could have been done'. In

[25] 'Rich Man, Poor Man', editorial, *The Irish Independent*, 7 February 2006; Donovan and Murphy, *The Fall of the Celtic Tiger* (2013), 122; *Dáil Eireann Debate 2004*, vol. 582, no. 1: Finance Bill 2004: Report Stage, 10 March 2004. http://taxpolicy.gov.ie/wp-content/uploads/2011/03/Taxrev2006vol2.pdf. Accessed 7 October 2015.

[26] *Dáil Eireann Debate 2006*; vol. 627, no. 5: Industrial Development Bill 2006: Second Stage, Eamon Ryan, 16 November 2006. *Dáil Eireann Debate 2006*, vol. 623, no. 86: Leaders' Questions, Enda Kenny, 5 July 2006; *Dáil Eireann Debate 2006*, vol. 629, no. 2: Financial Resolution No. 6: General (Resumed), Enda Kenny, 7 December 2006; *Dáil Eireann Debate 2006*, vol. 614, no. 16: Finance Bill 2006: Second Stage, Richard Bruton, 7 December 2006; *Dáil Eireann Debate 2006*, vol. 629, no. 2: Budget Statement 2006, Richard Bruton, 6 December 2006.

response to a €14 increase in social welfare payments Fine Gael's Paul McGrath questioned why this was not applied to pensions. His reaction to Cowen's commitment not to raise VAT was to ask why the Minister had chosen not to cut it. The following year Richard Bruton complained that tax cuts amounted to just €20 per person per week, or put another way, a thousand euro a year. Kenny suggested that his biggest regret about the 2005 Budget was that it did not give people enough, and that they should get more. Sinn Féin's Arthur Morgan captured the same sentiment, observing that 'the Budget was not an especially bad one as Budgets go and I welcomed it to the extent that it went'.[27]

In 2006 Cowen outlined the increases to social welfare over his first three Budgets, totalling €55 a week or 38%. Finian McGrath's immediate response was that the lowest rate was just above the poverty line. Both Labour and Fine Gael chastised the Government for its failure to remove enough earners from the upper income tax rate. Pat Rabbitte pledged that Labour would not increase taxes, while Richard Bruton rebuked what he branded 'a high tax Government'. The response to the 2006 Budget echoed those of previous years, with Labour's Roisín Shortall arguing that 'what we were presented with yesterday was the very least that people could have expected from the Government'.[28]

The political environment thus clearly incentivised the Ahern Governments to cut taxes and to increase spending as quickly as possible. There was plenty of concern in the house about the need to reduce waste and to cut inequitable benefits to the wealthy, but this was accompanied by markedly little concrete discussion or analysis of how such problems could be tackled on a scale that would offset the increasing

[27] *Dáil Eireann Debate 2004*, vol. 594, no. 2: Financial Resolution No. 2—General (Resumed), 2 December 2004; *Dáil Eireann Debate 2005*, vol. 611, no. 17: Budget Statement 2005, 7 December 2005; and *Dáil Eireann Debate 2005*, vol. 612, no. 15: Financial Resolution No. 5: General (Resumed), Enda Kenny and Arthur Morgan, 8 December 2005.

[28] *Dáil Eireann Debate 2006*, vol. 629, no. 2: Budget Statement 2006, Brian Cowen and Finian McGrath, 6 December 2006; *Dáil Eireann Debate 2006*, vol. 623, no. 86: Government Record: Motion (Resumed), Richard Bruton and Joan Burton, 5 July 2006; *Dáil Eireann Debate 2006*, vol. 623, no. 124: Government Record: Motion (Resumed), Pat Rabbitte, 4 July 2006; *Dáil Eireann Debate 2006*, vol. 628, no. 1: Priority Questions—Fiscal Policy, Richard Bruton, 22 November 2006; and *Dáil Eireann Debate 2006*, vol. 629, no. 2: Financial Resolution No. 6: General (Resumed), Roisín Shortall, 7 December 2006.

reliance on revenue from construction and property. Government Deputies were predictably enthusiastic about the continued pursuit of tax cuts and spending increases. In 2005 Sean Fleming observed that two-thirds of the workforce paid either no income tax or paid at the standard minimum rate, adding that this represented a 'tremendous achievement. I am confident we can do better'. After six years in Government the Taoiseach could point on consecutive days to having achieved both the lowest level of personal tax in Europe for someone on the average wage and having increased health spending from €4bn to almost €11bn between 1997 and 2004. There was in essence no political pressure to reverse or even to reduce the pace of either of these trends.[29]

Summary

Charlie McCreevy's conviction that fiscal policy had a negligible effect on inflation in Ireland was fundamental to the choices he made as Minister. This position had very few adherents inside or outside of the House, yet it was the subject of remarkably little debate and he was never obliged to justify it in any detail. Even if Opposition Deputies had no power to stop his Budgets being passed, one would expect them to have pursued this issue persistently throughout his tenure. Instead they moved on to the inflationary impact of state and semi-state charges, which presumably had the benefit of being more politically advantageous. This reflected a widespread predilection on the part of TDs to raise issues that would curry public favour and were politically uncontentious over those that were integral to economic stability. The Fine Gael leadership did express concern about many of the key risks facing the economy towards the end of the period. However, this did not discourage Opposition Deputies from almost unanimously calling for more tax cuts and spending increases. Fiscal policy for much of the period is best understood as a response to this political pressure, coupled with McCreevy's dismissal of its inflationary impact.

[29] *Dáil Eireann Debate 2005*, vol. 597, no. 3: Finance Bill 2005: Second Stage (Resumed), Sean Fleming, 9 February 2005; *Dáil Eireann Debate 2004*, vol. 592, no. 3: Leaders' Questions, Bertie Ahern, 16 November 2004; and *Dáil Eireann Debate 2004*, vol. 592, no. 4: Leaders' Questions, Bertie Ahern, 17 November 2004.

5 Property and Construction

The Bacon Reports were a major influence on Government housing policy insofar as they identified insufficient supply as a primary cause of price inflation. While inadequate supply was a reasonable explanation when the first report was published in 1998, it became increasingly problematic as the years went on and output levels soared. With 93,000 units built in 2006, Irish housing construction had reached a scale that was over four times the average output from 1970 to 1994. Output was two and a half times that of Germany and France and four times that of the UK on a per capita basis. Nonetheless, the Government tenaciously backed increased supply as the key solution. Bertie Ahern still contended that 'we must build more houses to stop the rate of increase in prices and ensure we keep a satisfactory level of affordability for everyone'. His brother Noel, as the Minister of State responsible for housing, similarly stressed that the Government was 'trying to encourage supply because with the current situation that is the only real solution'. There was strikingly little discussion about the need to ensure that supply was concentrated in the areas where it was most needed. When confronted with the argument that prices continued to rise rapidly despite high levels of supply, the Minister pointed to factors like immigration, strong employment and overly generous lending as drivers of additional demand. While an intuitive response would have been to curtail credit growth as one of the identified ultimate causes of the problem, Ahern instead returned to the proximate cause of unmet demand, and thus to supply as the only solution.[30]

Senior Ministers were very circumspect about making radical interventions in the housing market. This stemmed in part from the widespread perception that implementing Bacon's recommendations to dissuade investors had backfired and pushed up rents. This perceived failure seemed to cement the anti-interventionist instincts of some of

[30] Bacon et al., *Economic Assessment of Recent House Price Developments* (1998), iii, v, vii; *Dáil Eireann Debate 2006*, vol. 622, no. 79: Leaders' Questions, Bertie Ahern, 21 June 2006; *Dáil Eireann Debate 2006*, vol. 618, no. 5: Priority Questions—House Prices, Noel Ahern, 4 May 2006; *Dáil Eireann Debate 2006*, vol. 614, no. 18: Priority Questions—House Prices, Noel Ahern, 14 February 2006; and for house building comparisons, see *Housing Statistics in the European Union 2010*, 74. Available from http://www.bmwfw.gv.at/Wirtschaftspolitik/Wohnungspolitik/Documents/housing_statistics_in_the_european_union_2010.pdf. Accessed 23 March 2016.

the key decision-makers, since it appeared to corroborate McCreevy's belief that one could never be sure of the consequences of interfering with a market as fluid as housing. However, other decisions made are difficult to explain regardless of how one viewed the market. The first Bacon Report proposed a temporary reduction in capital gains tax on residentially zoned land brought into development, from 40 to 20%. The second half of the proposal was that the rate would be increased to 60% after four years, using a carrot-and-stick approach to encourage landholders to make sites available for development. McCreevy was criticised by the Labour Party in particular for the decision to maintain the 20% rate on a permanent basis, which Deputies viewed as the effective removal of the stick. More problematically, as Derek McDowell observed, the announcement was made some fifteen months before the four-year period ended, thus reducing the amount of land brought into use. Labour attributed the decision both to McCreevy's ideological aversion to capital taxes and to Fianna Fáil's fund-raising interests in the construction sector. The Minister's defence was that imposing the 60% rate would have encouraged the diversion of land from residential to commercial development. The obvious solution would presumably have been to introduce accompanying legislation to prevent such a diversion, but this was never satisfactorily addressed by either side.[31]

The logic underpinning the treatment of tax reliefs for property investors was equally hard to justify. Some key incentives for property investors were removed on Bacon's recommendation in 1998, on the basis of his concerns about speculative demand and the fact that many investors seemed to consider housing a one-way bet. These incentives were reintroduced on Budget day in December 2001 (with the expressed approval of Fine Gael), with the explanation that the economy and property market were experiencing a significant downturn and the Government was concerned about construction activity and employment. This responsiveness to market events was perfectly reasonable; the problem was that it was sorely lacking when the market bounced back. From 2004 onwards Opposition spokespeople became increasingly critical about the repeated

[31] *Dáil Eireann Debate 2006*, vol. 522, no. 2: Finance (No. 2) Bill, 2000: Second Stage (Resumed), Charlie McCreevy, 27 June 2000 and *Dáil Eireann Debate 2001*, vol. 531, no. 4: Finance Bill, 2001: Second Stage (Resumed), Derek McDowell, Pat Rabbitte, and Charlie McCreevy, 28 February 2001.

extension of a broad range of property investment reliefs without any evidence that the building industry needed the fillip.[32]

One of the most striking features of the political debate on house prices was the resolve of Noel Ahern as the relevant Minister of State to downplay the scale of the problem. In 2002 Ahern argued that 'people on good incomes will have no difficulty buying houses for themselves'. The Minister was similarly sanguine as late as 2005, suggesting that 'people have the money and, by and large, are managing'. Again, he pointed to the positive impact of high incomes, law taxes and historically low interest rates on affordability. Some of the objections to this stance were recognised by the Opposition, particularly the fact that not everyone was fortunate enough to be on a 'good income'. Deputies also objected to the unfairness of homebuyers paying high prices that were driven by supernormal profits. A key risk that garnered far less attention before its effects were felt, however, was that unprecedentedly low interest rates allowed for a significant upswing in the future. Similarly, there was almost no appreciation of the fact that if the economy faltered it would damage the ability of recent homeowners to repay their mortgages because of reduced incomes or job loses, while outstanding mortgage debt would remain unchanged. It was therefore potentially prices rather than affordability that would ultimately matter more from a financial stability perspective in the event of a shock.[33]

Deputies did intermittently raise concerns about the stability of the housing market and its significance for the broader economy. In February 2000 Labour's Sean Ryan warned that price increases were unsustainable and that the bubble would burst if they continued, reminding the house of the British experience in the 1980s. In 2004 Pat Rabbitte warned of the potential macroeconomic ramifications of such an event, arguing that the market could precipitate a serious

[32] Bacon et al., *Economic Assessment of Recent House Price Developments* (1998), iv, vi, 28, 30, 85; *Dáil Eireann Debate 2002*, vol. 548, no. 3: Finance Bill, 2002: Second Stage (Resumed), Martin Cullen, 13 February 2001; and *Dáil Eireann Debate 2004*, vol. 579, no. 5: Finance Bill 2004: Second Stage, Richard Bruton, Dan Boyle and Caoimhghín Ó Caoláin, 11 February 2004.

[33] *Dáil Eireann Debate 2002*, vol. 558, no. 3: Other Questions—Local Authority Housing, Noel Ahern, 28 November 2002; *Dáil Eireann Debate 2003*, vol. 570, no. 2: Private Members' Business—Housing Crisis: Motion, Noel Ahern, 1 July 2003; and *Dáil Eireann Debate 2005*, vol. 597, no. 3: Other Questions—House Prices, Noel Ahern, 9 February 2005.

economic collapse and that 'one must accept that there is no example in the world where such constant house price rises have not caused grief'. However, to a large extent such interspersed warnings do little to vindicate the performance of the Dáil. The potential instability of the housing market was treated by the Opposition as one of many evident social and economic problems with which to reproach the Government. There is no immediately logical way to reconcile Rabbitte's warning of a serious economic collapse with his continued demands for higher spending and support for low taxes. To the extent that he was genuinely concerned about housing, it did not inspire him to advocate policies that were in any way politically unpalatable. No Deputy in the house exhibited an appreciation of the degree of the risk posed by the market, or called for precautionary measures to ameliorate against a potential crash on anything like the scale that was needed.[34]

There was remarkably little focus on the scale of the construction sector and the attendant threat to the broader economy during the political debates. A notable exception was Richard Bruton's warning in late 2005 that the sector was responsible for 40% of employment growth, a particular cause for concern given the large number of vacant houses. He pointed to the waning export sector, asking Cowen whether construction represented a more fragile driver of economic growth. Rabbitte issued a similar warning, stressing that the over-bloated construction sector accounted for an eighth of all jobs, and that the inevitable correction would have a significant impact on the economy. The degree of the risk was again clearly unappreciated, however, and it continued to be treated as a secondary issue. Senior Ministers were highly complacent, with Cowen arguing that the level of housing output was justified by demographic and employment factors, and fatefully predicting a 'soft landing'. Government Deputies were most inclined to talk about the sector when they were lauding the extent to which policies to increase supply had worked. In defence of the Government's actions on housing, Dick Roche, as Minister for the Environment, pointed to the fact that output had reached almost four times the Western European average relative to population. Roche was similarly impressed with the increase in

[34] *Dáil Eireann Debate 2000*, vol. 514, no. 4: Planning and Development Bill, 1999 [Seanad]: Second Stage (Resumed), Sean Ryan, 16 February 2000 and *Dáil Eireann Debate 2004*, vol. 586, no. 3: Private Members' Business—Housing Provisions: Motion (Resumed), Pat Rabbitte, 26 May 2004.

construction employment from 92,000 to 233,000 since 1994, as well as the doubling of house construction as a proportion of GNP to 14%. Far from being concerned about a possible reversal from these highs, he considered the scale of the sector to be a major achievement and argued that demand would remain robust on the back of population growth.[35]

On a final point in relation to the construction industry, Fianna Fáil was routinely criticised by the Opposition for its close links to developers. One highlight was Eamon Gilmore's description of the house building industry as the party's 'commercial wing'. As Elaine Byrne has argued, both parties in Government were indeed dependent on the broad property sector for over a third of their funding. In 2002 Brendan Daly made a forthright contribution about the close long-term relationship between the party and construction interests. What made Daly's elucidation stand out from the routine criticisms by the Opposition was that he was a long-standing Fianna Fáil Deputy and former Minister, and was making an argument in explicit support of the link:

> Fianna Fáil policy since its foundation has been geared towards advancing the construction industry- the party has been synonymous with the building industry. It gave the industry life and vibrancy. Every time Fianna Fáil went out of office the building industry went into decline because people involved in the industry did not have the confidence to invest and develop it.[36]

Summary

Ministers continued to advocate increased supply as the core solution to the housing market, even as output reached unprecedented levels and prices continued to rise. Far from being concerned about the unsustainable scale of construction output, Government Deputies extolled the size

[35] *Dáil Eireann Debate 2005*, vol. 606, no. 80: Other Questions—Economic Growth, Richard Bruton, 5 October 2005; *Dáil Eireann Debate 2005*, vol. 612, no. 15: Financial Resolution No. 5: General (Resumed), Pat Rabbitte, 8 December 2005; *Dáil Eireann Debate 2005*, vol. 612, no. 15: Priority Questions—Fiscal Policy, Brian Cowen, 13 December 2005; and *Dáil Eireann Debate 2005*, vol. 610, no. 70: Housing Policy: Statements, Dick Roche, 16 November 2005.

[36] *Dáil Eireann Debate 2000*, vol. 521, no. 1: Private Members' Business—Housing Policy: Motion, Eamon Gilmore, 13 June 2000; Elaine Byrne, *A Crooked Harp* (2012), 4, 192, 193, 197, 199–204; and *Dáil Eireann Debate 2002*, vol. 548, no. 3: Finance Bill, 2002: Second Stage, Brendan Daly, 13 February 2002.

of the sector as evidence of the success of their approach. Several of the policy decisions and reversals of the period were never properly explained in the Dáil, notably the approach taken regarding capital gains tax on residential development land and the extension of incentives for property investors during a boom. McCreevy's perception that reducing capital gains rates in the past had produced favourable outcomes was probably a factor in the former decision. It is difficult to propose a convincing explanation for the latter other than its political expediency.

Noel Ahern's repeated efforts to minimise the problems posed by high house prices put him at odds with essentially every other commentator on the issue. A likely explanation is that in the absence of a definitive solution to a problem an attractive alternative is often to downplay its effects. Senior Opposition Deputies did express clear concerns about the potential vulnerability of the construction sector and the property market, and the consequent risks to the macroeconomy. However, such warnings were interspersed through the general debate, and none conveyed the impression that Deputies appreciated the scale of the threat. Nor did these misgivings temper demands for additional spending or tax cuts, and crucially the option to reduce credit growth was never meaningfully broached.

6 Intergenerational Aspects and the Kenny Report

In 2005 P. J. Drudy identified the winners and losers of the prevailing Irish housing system. The winners predictably included many of the business groups that had benefitted from the boom, as well as homeowners. The losing side was essentially comprised of vulnerable groups and those who did not own property. As Drudy argued, the property market had thus produced a significant degree of intergenerational inequality. While he rightly described the wealth gains accruing to homeowners as essentially notional unless they downsized, the additional costs to new buyers were far from abstract. Although there were impressive contributions made in the Dáil about the intergenerational implications of the boom and of housing policy, nobody recognised the full extent of the cumulative impact of all of the choices made, which was to the marked advantage of established homeowners at the expense of prospective buyers. This cannot be attributed solely to the age profile of the House, since as we shall see the most vocal and insightful contribution on the topic came from a rather surprising source.[37]

Some of the key intergenerational outcomes of the housing boom were raised by Deputies across the political spectrum. Labour's Sean Ryan pointed out that young couples with two incomes struggled to afford the same houses that their parents had bought on a single salary a generation earlier. Similarly, Seán Fleming argued that the boom constituted a massive intergenerational transfer of wealth, 'to the phenomenal disadvantage of young people and to the tremendous advantage of the elderly'.[38]

One of the most discussed legislative initiatives of the period was Part V of the 2000 Planning and Development Bill, which required developers to allocate up to 20% of new houses to social or affordable use. Martin Cullen was widely accused of having caved in to vested interests and significantly diluted the provision shortly after his appointment as Minister for the Environment. The left-wing independent Deputy Tony Gregory was particularly critical, arguing that Cullen had destroyed 'the most socially progressive measure to have come through the House in many years'. While the positive social aspects of the initiative rightly attracted significant praise, there was a fundamental objection that received far less attention. As several Fine Gael TDs observed, it effectively transferred the responsibility for paying for social and affordable housing from the Government to buyers of new houses. In the absence of price controls, protestations that the cost was intended to be absorbed by the developer were risible. Meaningful efforts to develop more social and affordable houses were of course to be welcomed, particularly their integration into private developments. The problem with Part V was that it absolved established homeowners with significant net wealth from paying for it through general taxation, and acted as a sizeable de facto premium targeted at new buyers.[39]

[37] P. J. Drudy, 'Housing: The Case for a New Philosophy', in B. Reynolds and S. Healy (eds.), *Securing Fairness and Well-Being in a Land of Plenty* (Dublin, 2005), 43–44.

[38] *Dáil Eireann Debate 2003*, vol. 575, no. 3: Private Members' Business—Local Government Funding: Motion, Sean Ryan, 25 November 2003 and *Dáil Eireann Debate 2004*, vol. 579, no. 5: Finance Bill 2004: Second Stage, Seán Fleming, 11 February 2004.

[39] *Dáil Eireann Debate 2004*, vol. 582, no. 6: Private Members' Business—Confidence in the Minister for the Environment, Heritage and Local Government: Motion, Tony Gregory, 30 March 2004; *Dáil Eireann Debate 2003*, vol. 575, no. 3: Private Members' Business—Local Government Funding, Billy Timmins, 25 November 2003; and *Dáil*

A related issue was the imposition of substantial taxes on houses at the point of purchase, particularly stamp duty, development levies and VAT. These were maintained largely intact throughout the period, evidently on the basis of the revenue they generated for the Exchequer. Ciarán Cuffe from the Green Party argued that it in the absence of domestic rates it was inequitable to fund affordable housing provision and local Government projects that benefited everyone simply by levying significant taxes on new developments. He instead advocated taxing undeveloped zoned lands and second homes. John Bruton was even more fervent, arguing that 'our system of tax on property is the most anti-youth system of tax on property one could possibly design'. Bruton criticised the imposition of multiple charges on young people trying to buy their first house, while exempting those with minimal outstanding mortgage debt from any form of property tax. He observed that 'we tax the young to exempt middle aged and older people from any form of property taxation', suggesting that the evident bias might be attributable to the age profiles and income levels of influential members in the dominant political parties. One can question what it said about the conservatism of the House that the role of enfant terrible was left to a former Taoiseach on the eve of his retirement from Irish politics.[40]

The Kenny Report was the subject of significant attention during the boom years. The report was commissioned in 1971 by Bobby Molloy as Minister for Local Government and was published three years later. The Commission was instructed to consider measures to control the price of development land, which had increased rapidly during the 1960s. It concluded that without the provision of key services by local authorities, particularly sewerage and drainage, potential building land would have continued to command agricultural prices. Since these price increases were thus largely attributable to investments made by the community, the Commission argued that the community had a legitimate claim to

Eireann Debate 2000, vol. 516, no. 5, Planning and Development Bill, 1999 [Seanad]: Second Stage (Resumed), 23 March 2000.

[40] *Dáil Eireann Debate 2001*, vol. 531, no. 4, Finance Bill, 2001: Second Stage (Resumed), Charlie McCreevy, 28 February 2001; *Dáil Eireann Debate 2003*, vol. 531, no. 4, Private Members' Business—Local Government Funding: Motion (Resumed), Ciarán Cuffe, 26 November 2003; and *Dáil Eireann Debate 2004*, vol. 579, no. 5: Finance Bill 2004: Second Stage, John Bruton, 11 February 2004.

the profit. The Kenny Report's central proposal was therefore that local authorities should be empowered to compulsorily purchase undeveloped land in areas designated by a High Court judge, at agricultural prices plus a premium of 25% to capture other factors of price appreciation. The Commission concluded that such legislation would not be constitutionally repugnant and suggested it would stabilise prices and end the practice of speculators profiting from services provided at the public expense.[41]

The Kenny proposal was predictably politically contentious and was never implemented. After a failed attempt by the Labour Party to pass the initiative in 1980, it was again revived when it was recommended by the party's Housing Commission in 1999. Thereafter Labour, Green Party and independent TDs frequently argued for the implementation of the report, most notably Eamon Gilmore who was easily the strongest contributor on housing in the period. The proposal received a further boost when it was promoted by the All-Party Committee on the Constitution in 2004, for the same reasons outlined by the Kenny Committee. On the basis of expert advice the All-Party Committee also supported Kenny's contention that the measure would likely be deemed constitutional, adding that if anything Kenny had been too conservative in suggesting the need for High Court involvement.[42]

As Gilmore argued, the boom had made the issue of land prices far more pressing, given that the proportion of house prices attributable to site costs had risen to 42.5% nationally, almost treble the European norm or the early 1990s Irish level of 15%. He pointed to the availability of enough zoned and serviced land in Dublin for 100,000 new units, suggesting that the Government should push ahead and legislate without waiting for the report of the All-Party Committee. While he expected a constitutional challenge to such legislation to fail, he argued that even a successful case would clarify the constitutional amendments required. Significantly, the All-Party Committee explicitly supported this approach

[41] Committee on the Price of Building Land, *Report to the Minister for Local Government* (Dublin, 1974), 1, 3, 9, 23–24, 35–42, 61.

[42] Labour Party Housing Commission, *Housing: A New Approach* (Dublin, 1999), 9; *Dáil Eireann Debate 2000*, vol. 521, no. 1: Private Members' Business—Housing Policy: Motion, Eamon Gilmore, 13 June 2000; and The All-Party Oireachtas Committee on the Constitution, *Ninth Progress Report: Private Property* (Dublin, 2004), 39–40, 137, 142–144.

in its report the following year. The biggest advance for the Kenny proposal seemed to arrive in October 2003, when the Taoiseach suggested that it was a pity that the report had not been implemented. Crucially, he also affirmed his willingness to 'go down the constitutional road' in order to address the land price issue. The Government's stated position was it was considering the best course to take and was awaiting the publication of relevant reports due over the coming months.[43]

The following year Martin Cullen and Mary Harney both affirmed their support for the Kenny/All-Party Committee recommendation, with the former deeming it 'necessary', and the latter expressing her hope that it would be legislated for 'sooner rather than later'. Cullen, however, explained that his department was still considering all recommendations and awaiting the publication of a major study from the NESC (National Economic and Social Council). Dick Roche, upon succeeding Cullen as Minister for the Environment, similarly stressed that he did not want to 'see any undue delay' on the issue, and promised action once he had received the NESC report. The evident contradiction between this ongoing inactivity and the professed support for the measure by senior Ministers was duly criticised by the Opposition, as was the prolonged delay before the Government allowed a Dáil debate on the issue. In February 2005, three months after receiving the NESC report, Noel Ahern suggested that some key changes in housing policy 'may be made shortly'. The Kenny/All-Party Committee recommendation was never implemented, and nor was a convincing rationalisation offered. Labour in particular understandably criticised the Government's strategy of waiting for successive reports for some eighteen months as a delaying tactic.[44]

[43] *Dáil Eireann Debate 2003*, vol. 571, no. 4: Private Members' Business—Planning and Development (Acquisition of Development Land) (Assessment of Compensation) Bill 2003: Second Stage, Eamon Gilmore and Martin Cullen, 7 October 2003; The All-Party Oireachtas Committee on the Constitution, *Ninth Progress Report: Private Property* (2004), 39; *Dáil Eireann Debate 2003*, vol. 572, no. 1: Questions—Constitutional Amendments, Bertie Ahern, 8 October 2003; *Dáil Eireann Debate 2003*, vol. 572, no. 5: Other Questions—House Prices, Noel Ahern, 16 October 2003; and Department of the Environment, Heritage and Local Government (Ireland), *Annual Housing Statistics Bulletin 2006* (Dublin, 2007), 44.

[44] *Dáil Eireann Debate 2004*, vol. 586, no. 6: Priority Questions—Building Lands, Martin Cullen, 2 June 2004; *Dáil Eireann Debate 2004*, vol. 586, no. 6: Leaders' Questions, Mary Harney, 29 June 2004; *Dáil Eireann Debate 2004*, vol. 589, no. 2: Other Questions—House Prices, Dick Roche, 30 September 2004; *Dáil Eireann Debate 2004*,

In the absence of leaked documents or a surprise revelation it is impossible to definitively conclude that the Government, and particularly the Taoiseach, had either never intended to implement the Kenny proposal, or alternatively had intended to and had then changed its mind. Nonetheless, the contemporary discourse does give a good insight into the political tensions facing the Government and perhaps helps to explain the strategy it pursued. One clue is in the All-Party Committee report itself. The report states that in 2000 the Taoiseach wrote to the Committee and asked it to consider the need to update the constitution in respect of property rights, specifically pertaining to infrastructure development and planning controls. The Committee took this to encompass a re-examination of the Kenny proposals. However, it is not clear that this had been the Taoiseach's intention, and in his letter he made no explicit reference to the Kenny Report or even to housing. One plausible explanation then, is that by reviving the issue of the Kenny Report and supporting Labour's stance, the All-Party Committee had provided Ahern with a solution that he did not wish to implement but which was too politically charged to reject upfront. The tactic of professing support for the proposal and then delaying its implementation until it fell down the political agenda would clearly make sense under these circumstances.[45]

In determining why the enactment of the Kenny proposal was unpalatable for the Government, the Opposition predictably pointed to factors such as Fianna Fáil's relationship with developers and the revenue generated for the Exchequer by high house prices. Conspicuously, the Taoiseach himself suggested that one of the key groups to oppose it would have been the farming lobby. However, the most compelling explanation was offered by Fine Gael's Liam Twomey, who contended that speculators were too small in number to mount a significant protest to the proposal, and that builders could continue to make a profit regardless. He instead suggested that the people who would be most impacted were recent buyers, as it would cause their houses to depreciate

vol. 595, no. 1: Other Questions—House Prices, Noel Ahern, 9 December 2004; and *Dáil Eireann Debate 200*, vol. 597, no. 3: Other Questions—Housing Policy, Noel Ahern, 9 December 2005.

[45] The All-Party Oireachtas Committee on the Constitution, *Ninth Progress Report: Private Property* (2004), 17, A5–6.

significantly in value. He thus came to the troubling conclusion that it was too late to address the issue, and that 'the very people we seek to protect are those who would suffer the most'. This of course presupposed that local authorities would pass on the savings, but this was implicitly assumed across the debates. The same motive presumably underpinned declarations from Pat Rabbitte and Liz McManus that they wished to see a stabilisation of prices rather than nominal falls and a risk of negative equity. Throughout the period Government Ministers similarly stated that the objective was price stability, without any reference to the desirability of a fall. Politicians were thus committed to promoting the interests of prospective buyers only insofar as action did not cause commensurate harm to existing homeowners, even if that meant sustaining high prices into the medium term. While there was a professed appetite for radical intervention, in reality any action would be severely limited if measures that risked nominal falls were precluded. The perverse consequence was to sustain some of the highest land prices in Europe in one of the continent's most sparsely populated countries.[46]

Summary

Both the house price boom and housing policy created winners and losers, with existing homeowners generally in the first camp and prospective buyers decidedly in the second. Some Deputies did recognise that the boom constituted a significant transfer of wealth from the old to the young. Others argued that decisions like the Part V measures on social and affordable housing and the imposition of transactional rather than annual housing taxes were inequitable. However, no Deputy appreciated the collective impact of these issues, and how the inequities in the housing system repeatedly fell along generational lines. We cannot definitively explain why the key proposal of the Kenny Report was never implemented despite the widespread professed support it received. Although

[46] *Dáil Eireann Debate 2003*, vol. 572, no. 1: Questions—Constitutional Amendments, Bertie Ahern, 8 October 2003; *Dáil Eireann Debate 2003*, vol. 571, no. 4: Private Members' Business—Planning and Development (Acquisition of Development Land) (Assessment of Compensation) Bill 2003: Second Stage, Eamon Gilmore and Martin Cullen, 7 October 2003; *Dáil Eireann Debate 2004*, vol. 586, no. 2: Private Members' Business—Housing Provisions: Motion, Liz McManus, 25 May 2004; *Dáil Eireann Debate 2004*, vol. 586, no. 3: Private Members' Business—Housing Provisions: Motion (Resumed), Pat Rabbitte, 26 May 2004; and Data from Eurostat. Available from http://ec.europa.eu/eurostat. Accessed 15 October 2015.

the dependency of the Government parties on funding and support from the construction sector or other landowners may have been a factor, it is likely that if the discounts on land prices were passed on by local authorities the cost to existing homeowners would have been very substantial. The expressed desire of senior Government and Opposition Deputies to see a stabilisation of house prices, rather than fall, becomes much more meaningful in this light. The Kenny proposal would have negatively impacted landowners and potentially existing homeowners, while benefitting new buyers. The political objections to its implementation were therefore far more comprehensible than they first appear.

7 The Financial Sector

One explanation that has been offered for the evident shortcomings of the economic analysis published by the Irish newspapers was that many journalists had inadequate specialist knowledge and were not sufficiently interested to set about acquiring it. The same criticism is even more applicable to the Dáil debates in the period, and given Michael Ring's contention that constituency rather than legislative work was the path to electoral success this should perhaps not come as a major surprise. While politicians would periodically reference the broad findings from Central Bank reports, there was no meaningful engagement with the analysis or data provided. Some TDs did raise concerns about the rate of credit growth, but were decidedly unforthcoming with opinions about how it should be addressed. While there were a number of strong contributions on financial stability issues, there was no standout contributor akin to Eamon Gilmore on the property sector.[47]

Some of the Government's arguments in support of the apparent health of the financial sector should have been scrutinised far more robustly by the Opposition. One particularly dubious defence was the Taoiseach's argument that 'Irish residential property stock is worth €500 billion and the loan book is €100 billion so I do not see why that should create a shock'. Given that a large proportion of homeowners had no outstanding mortgages, the €100 billion debt was held disproportionately by recent buyers. In the event of a shock the €500 billion figure

[47] Mark O'Brien, 'The Irish Press, Politicians, and the Celtic Tiger Economy' in Shane Schifferes and Richard Roberts, *The Media and Financial Crises: Comparative and Historical Perspectives* (2014), 81.

would clearly have been irrelevant to the banks, and Ahern would have been far better off focusing on the assets owned by those who actually owed the debt. Rather than worrying him, the longevity of the housing boom seemed to bolster the Taoiseach's confidence, and he went on to observe that 'every year I had to listen to reports that the bottom would fall out of the market and we would build fewer houses but that is not the case'. Brian Cowen also exhibited questionable logic when he argued that one would expect consumers to make use of historically low interest rates and that credit allowed households to smooth out their consumption over time. The problem was that far from smoothing out their consumption, households were amplifying its fluctuations by borrowing heavily during an economic boom. In the likely event that borrowers would have less access to credit once the economic cycle turned, the role of debt would almost certainly be to exacerbate the downturn.[48]

Insofar as any regulatory ideology was articulated in the house, it was that financial regulation should not be burdensome to the point that it acted as a disincentive to foreign investment. Nonetheless, there certainly were worthwhile concerns aired about the scale of credit growth in the period. Fine Gael's Gay Mitchell warned about the risks posed by excessive mortgage lending and the prospect of negative equity, while Eamon Ryan argued that the 'massive credit explosion' could cause difficulties when the economy turned. The Green Party's Trevor Sargent pointed to the OECD's contention that house prices were overvalued, and like Mitchell broached the prospect of negative equity in the event of house price falls. Conspicuously, Noel Ahern expressed concern about excessive mortgage lending and its impact on prices, adding that his Department had contacted the Central Bank and some of the institutions involved. However, there was essentially no demand within the House for the Bank or the Financial Regulator to actively intervene in the market, and little evidence that Deputies understood the powers available to the joint authority. Similarly, isolated warnings about the banks' exposures to the

[48] *Dáil Eireann Debate 2006*, vol. 619, no. 83: Leaders' Questions, Bertie Ahern, 17 May 2006; Keen, *Debunking Economics* (2011), 6, 14, 335–336, 341–346; and *Dáil Eireann Debate 2005*, vol. 612, no. 105: Priority Questions—Fiscal Policy, Brian Cowen, 13 December 2005.

construction industry were not followed up with any meaningful debate or action.[49]

The general perception of the Opposition was that McCreevy and the Department of Finance had beaten Harney at Enterprise in the battle to control the financial regulatory framework, and had ensured that the Central Bank would continue to play a central supervisory role. From an institutional perspective, Jim Mitchell expressed concern that the lines of demarcation between the Department and the Bank were too blurred to ensure that the latter acted as an independent critic of Government policy, particularly given the continued tradition of appointing senior officials from the Department. Ironically, the primary grievance from the Opposition in relation to the new structure was that consumer issues would be given secondary priority to prudential regulation, with Joan Burton contending that the Department of Finance seemed determined to 'protect the financial institutions at all costs'. To the extent that the Financial Regulator dealt exhaustively with consumer issues it was entirely in keeping with the prevailing political priorities of the day. By contrast, the need for robust prudential supervision received remarkably little political attention.[50]

Labour's Kathleen Lynch was palpably dismissive of the need to concentrate on financial stability, arguing that 'all the scandals of recent years indicate that the consumer needs to be protected rather than the banks and financial institutions. The banks and financial institutions are capable of protecting themselves'. While recognising that prudential regulation

[49] *Dáil Eireann Debate 2002*, vol. 553, no. 3, Central Bank and Financial Services Authority of Ireland Bill, 2002: Second Stage (Resumed), Conor Lenihan, 19 June 2002; *Dáil Eireann Debate 2004*, vol. 578, no. 6, Central Bank and Financial Services Authority of Ireland Bill, 2003: Second Stage (Resumed), Seymour Crawford, Gay Mitchell, and Eamon Ryan, 29 January 2004; *Dáil Eireann Debate 2006*, vol. 623, no. 124, Leaders' Questions, Trevor Sargent, 4 July 2006; *Dáil Eireann Debate 2004*, vol. 595, no. 3, Housing (Miscellaneous Provisions) Bill 2004 [Seanad]: Second Stage, Arthur Morgan, 15 December 2004; *Dáil Eireann Debate 2006*, vol. 614, no. 18, Priority Questions—House Prices, Noel Ahern, 14 February 2006; and *Dáil Eireann Debate 2004*, vol. 585, no. 6, Central Bank and Financial Services Authority of Ireland Bill, 2003: Report Stage (Resumed), Ned O'Keefe, 19 May 2004.

[50] *Dáil Eireann Debate 2004*, vol. 586, no. 6, Central Bank and Financial Services Authority of Ireland Bill 2003: Report Stage (Resumed) and Final Stage, Joan Burton, 2 June 2004; *Dáil Eireann Debate 2002*, vol. 548, no. 5, Priority Questions—Governorship of the Central Bank, Jim Mitchell, 19 February 2002; and Nyberg Commission, *Misjudging Risk* (2011), viii.

was important, the Green Party's Dan Boyle also asked that it be put 'on the back-burner' in order to give greater priority to consumer protection. To McCreevy's credit he refused this outright, arguing that the prudential function must be given priority and pointing to the outcry there would be if an institution failed. The focus of the discourse during the establishment of the Central Bank and Financial Services Authority is perhaps best conveyed quantitatively. In a single three-hour debate, the word 'consumer' was used 142 times, a remarkable average of once every 76 seconds. By contrast, the words 'stability' and 'prudential' were used three and four times respectively. In the same debate both Lynch and Richard Bruton called for the appointment of somebody with consumer protection experience to the board of the regulator. There were no corresponding demands for someone with prudential expertise, despite the rather troubling fact that nobody appointed to the board had any experience of bank regulation.[51]

In the debates on the establishment of the new joint regulatory authority there were frequent references to high-profile financial scandals, such as Enron and Allfirst, an American subsidiary of AIB. Deputies similarly pointed to the recent tribunals and the Ansbacher scandal as cases of potential institutional malfeasance. What is striking about the examples used, however, is that they were all household names in Ireland. As a base of historical experience on which to draw in constructing a regulatory system these episodes were totally inadequate. There was essentially no discussion about the 112 financial crises that had occurred internationally in just the two immediately preceding decades, including those in three Nordic countries and Japan. An enormous wealth of relevant experience was thus ignored, save the occasional reference to England in the 1980s. It is highly likely that TDs were not aware of the enormous historical prevalence of such crises, and that this informed their apathy towards prudential supervision. One must then question how well-equipped the Dáil was to consider this type of legislation. Nor did Deputies exhibit much evidence of attempting to bridge

[51] *Dáil Eireann Debate 2004*, vol. 585, no. 6, Central Bank and Financial Services Authority of Ireland Bill, 2003: Report Stage, Kathleen Lynch, Richard Bruton, and Dan Boyle, 19 May 2004 and Houses of the Oireachtas, *Joint Committee of Inquiry into the Banking Crisis*, vol. 2, no. 27, Brian Patterson, 11 June 2015, 59.

the gap, and there were virtually no references to the relevant studies that might have improved the debate.[52]

Summary

During the debates on financial regulation Deputies exhibited minimal technical expertise or knowledge of global financial history. While some TDs had proved sufficiently interested and capable to make worthwhile contributions on other issues, particularly property, the Dáil was evidently poorly-placed to debate the formation of the new joint regulatory authority. For the same reason Government Ministers could present highly questionable arguments supporting the view that the banking system was secure without fear of robust contradiction. It is apparent from the Dáil Debates that, like the newspapers, Deputies were unaware of the prudential powers available to the Central Bank and Financial Regulator to curtail credit growth. This is particularly difficult to justify since TDs were uniquely well-placed to find out by submitting a parliamentary question. The lack of political pressure exerted on the Bank to act in these years reflects one of the key failings of any of the Irish institutions. Without any working knowledge of the history of financial crises Deputies were likely oblivious of how high-risk the rate of private credit growth actually was.

Deputies explicitly focused on the importance of consumer protection over the less immediate but potentially far more impactful issue of financial stability. The single TD who was most concerned with preventing the failure of a financial institution was almost certainly McCreevy himself. This is of course somewhat incongruous given the marked limitations of the regulatory framework that he introduced, and the attention that he paid to prudential supervision was notable only because it was such a low priority for other Deputies. Across the House prudential supervision had no champions and its importance was either largely ignored or even explicitly downplayed. The fact that there was nobody appointed to the board of the new Financial Regulator with any experience of banking regulation was clearly deeply problematic. The evident insouciance of the Opposition was perhaps even more so.

[52] *Dáil Eireann Debate 2002*, vol. 553, no. 2, Central Bank and Financial Services Authority of Ireland Bill, 2002: Second Stage, Richard Bruton, Pat Rabbitte, Caoimghín Ó Caoláin, and Denis Naughten, 18 June 2002.

8 Conclusion

It is clear that Government Ministers could justify the pursuit of policies that would garner widespread popular support if they chose to believe three convenient truths. Firstly, the position adopted by McCreevy, McDowell, Harney, Ahern and Cowen meant that far from having to choose between tax cuts or additional spending, they could increase spending on the strength of the additional revenue generated by lower yields. To put it mildly this was a minority view among commentators on the Irish economy, and Ministers were clearly misattributing the effects of an historic economic boom. Secondly, McCreevy contended that he could simultaneously cut taxes and increase spending without fuelling inflation. Again, this line of argument was seemingly devoid of adherents outside of Irish officialdom. Lastly, Ministers consistently argued that the ultimate solution to high house price inflation was to increase supply. While this belief was quite rational in the late 1990s it became increasingly untenable as time went on, given the continued rate of price growth in the face of output that Cullen recognised to be 'probably well ahead of anything taking place elsewhere in the world'. Again, the fact that much of the supply was being delivered in places where there was little demand received remarkably little attention.[53]

In theory the Dáil should have provided a forum where these ideas were challenged and debated. In reality, the Opposition largely side-lined the key issue of pro-cyclical spending and never meaningfully challenged the contention that lower tax rates would continue to generate higher yields. On both fronts it appears that more politically attractive positions on fiscal policy were given precedence. However, Eamon Gilmore's consistent and informed criticism of housing policy should give pause for thought. Gilmore did question why the Government continued to promote higher housing output as the solution to prices when it had clearly been of limited success hitherto. Despite this objection the Government continued unflinchingly with the same approach, and made no meaningful efforts to implement the superior alternative policies proposed by the Opposition, particularly the Kenny recommendation. The unusually stringent enforcement of the party whip in Ireland clearly played a role here. A majority Government was impervious to the arguments

[53] *Dáil Eireann Debate 2003*, vol. 560, no. 3, Other Questions—House Prices, Martin Cullen, 4 February 2003.

made in the House as long as none of its own Deputies were sufficiently convinced or motivated to defect. Even if the Opposition had been more rigorous in challenging the questionable ideas informing policy, there was thus no guarantee that different decisions would have been made.[54]

The precedence given to the immediate impact of policy choices on people over systems or institutions was a constant throughout the debates. Of course the direct human impact of decisions was crucial, but the crash of 2007/2008 serves as a stark reminder that systemic failures can cause far greater societal damage than the issues that preoccupied Deputies at the time. The shortfall of relevant expertise certainly played a significant role in this respect. Again however, the exception to the rule is key. Richard Bruton had worked as both as an economist both with the ESRI (Economic and Social Research Institute) and in the private sector, and held relevant graduate degrees from both UCD (University College Dublin) and Oxford. He explicitly expressed concern about the vulnerability of the construction sector, and accordingly of the Exchequer and the macroeconomy. While there is no evidence that Bruton appreciated the scale of the risk, one would have expected him to advocate greater prudence on the part of the Government. Instead, he continued to focus on what more the Government should have done for people in successive Budget debates. By expressing concern about economic mismanagement without advocating any unpalatable solutions, Bruton was therefore making political gain on both fronts. Isolated TDs with relevant economic expertise clearly faced an uphill struggle to change the nature of the debate and Irish political culture. However, there is no compelling evidence that Bruton made much attempt in this respect.[55]

No analyst proposed a solution to the housing crisis that was more radical or potentially effective than the Kenny Report. The contributions by Labour, the Green Party and Independents on the proposal represented the high-water mark of the debates on housing. However, the fact that senior Labour Deputies avowed their desire for price stability rather than price falls was crucial. Their rationale was that static nominal prices would allow for real falls over time through inflation. The duration that such a process would take was never explicitly considered, nor were the ethical implications of allowing new buyers to pay excessive prices in the interim.

[54] *Dáil Eireann Debate 2003*, vol. 560, no. 3, Other Questions—House Prices, Eamon Gilmore, 4 February 2003.

[55] https://www.linkedin.com/in/richardbruton. Accessed 23 October 2015.

The core subtext of the housing debates in the period was thus a disagreement over whether radical intervention should be made on behalf of new buyers if such action would negatively impact on existing homeowners. If this had been addressed explicitly it would presumably have generated heated disagreement even within parties. More broadly, the Dáil Debates in the period were characterised by Deputies prioritising political gain over economic stability. This was observable in both the widespread demands for fiscal largesse and the championing of consumer protection over prudential regulation. The fact that housing policy routinely favoured established homeowners over the young most likely emanated from the same mentality, and a habitual preference for the path of least political resistance.

The most striking limitation of the political discourse on the Irish economy was the dearth of theoretical, international or long-term historical perspectives evident in the debates. As we have seen, the worldviews of several senior Ministers were heavily informed by perceived recent Irish experience. For the most part Opposition TDs did not make compelling, evidence-based arguments to challenge this double-insularism. However, there is a strong sense that Harney, McDowell and McCreevy had strong ideological predispositions towards a low-tax regime, and that they readily attributed the boom to tax rate reductions because it confirmed the veracity of their established beliefs. If one genuinely believed that lower taxes had liberated the talents of the citizenry, then such reforms were justifiable on ethical grounds alone. Even if Opposition Deputies had made convincing arguments to disprove the causal relationship between lower tax rates and the boom, it is therefore doubtful that several key decision-makers would have changed their minds. Similarly, it is difficult to imagine a scenario whereby Bertie Ahern would have endorsed a radical shift of economic policy on the basis of a well-informed argument alone. Nor does it seem likely that macroeconomic concerns could have induced Fianna Fáil or PD Deputies to defect in sufficient numbers to threaten the Government. Therefore, from a tactical perspective, even if an Opposition Deputy or party was sufficiently concerned about the risk of a crash, they would need to have convinced a large proportion of the electorate of the need for measures to reign in the boom in order to mount an effective challenge to prevailing policy. This would clearly have been a formidable undertaking and a high-risk political strategy, and the fact that Deputies across the House continued to stoke demands and expectations in spite of the various economic vulnerabilities that they recognised is actually quite comprehensible, if not particularly uplifting.

CHAPTER 8

Conclusion

Nothing beside remains. Round the decay
Of that colossal Wreck, boundless and bare
The lone and level sands stretch far away.

Percy Bysshe Shelly, *Ozymandias*

On the basis of the material examined it is possible to identify the degree to which commentators recognised the extent of the various risks facing the Irish economy. Many analysts understood that eroding cost competitiveness represented a vulnerability, though showed little appreciation of the primary cause of the problem. David McWilliams was particularly strong in this respect, arguing from the start of the decade that the inflationary impact of the credit boom dwarfed that of fiscal policy. There was far too little recognition of the extent to which credit growth was the key factor elsewhere in the discourse and even less attempt to propose how it could be meaningfully restricted. As we have seen, there almost no cognisance among commentators of the powers available to the joint regulatory authority in this respect. This of course proved a major shortfall of the discourse on financial stability, but was perhaps equally significant in terms of the solutions proposed to control inflation.[1]

[1]David McWilliams, 'This Borrowing Binge Is Blowing Our Bubble', *The Sunday Business Post*, 2 December 2000.

C. M. Casey, *Policy Failures and the Irish Economic Crisis*,
https://doi.org/10.1007/978-3-319-90182-4_8

In terms of house prices, the two most accurate quantitative predictions came from academics, namely Constantin Gurdgiev and particularly Morgan Kelly. McWilliams was of course very sceptical about the house price boom from much earlier, but in the articles examined was slow to explicitly predict the extent of potential falls. The 2000 IMF mission was clearly also very concerned, warning that it would be unprecedented if the Irish price boom ended without a fall. Kelly was again the most prescient analyst in terms of predicting the employment and fiscal consequences of a property and construction crash, warning of a collapse in Government revenue and unemployment levels in excess of 15%.[2]

Commentators were particularly late in recognising the extent to which the Irish financial institutions were exposed to the fortunes of the property and construction sectors and to international wholesale funding markets. The Central Bank's Financial Stability Reports did qualitatively identify the key risks, but analysts made minimal explicit use of international precedent to gauge the extent of these threats, and were far too sanguine about the fundamental resilience of the financial sector. McWilliams did express some concern in 2003, suggesting that if land prices fell the banks could face a share price collapse. However, there were no liquidity or solvency warnings issued about the Irish banks in the period studied. Table 1 presents some key warnings and predictions issued about the Irish economy in the 2000–2006 period.[3]

As argued in Chapter 2, both the history of asset booms and Philip Tetlock's analysis of expert prediction strongly suggest that the failure of most commentators to accurately anticipate how the Irish boom would end was far from atypical. However, this certainly does not mean that the crash was not predictable, and Kelly's use of international precedent informed a remarkably accurate forecast. The Honohan report has since contended that Kelly's analysis lacked an 'in depth econometric analysis of the Irish situation', while Honohan has elsewhere suggested that the most satisfactory econometric analysis of Irish house prices was conducted by Anthony Murphy in 2005. Murphy's analysis was clearly

[2] Morgan Kelly, 'How the Housing Corner Stones of Our Economy Could go into Rapid Freefall', *The Irish Times*, 28 December 2006.

[3] Patrick Honohan, 'Resolving Ireland's Banking Crisis', UCD Economic Workshop Conference 'Responding to the Crisis', Dublin, 12 January 2009a, 6 and Morgan Kelly, 'Banking on very Shaky Foundations', *The Irish Times*, 7 September 2007.

Table 1 Notable warnings and predictions, 2000–2006

Analyst	*Warning or prediction*	*Date*
House prices		
• IMF 2000 Mission	Unprecedented if prices level off without a significant fall	August 2000
• David McWilliams (Sunday Business Post)	Ireland looks like Japan before the bubble burst	October 2000
• *The Economist*	20% price falls over four years (nominal)	May 2003
• IMF 2003 Mission	Prices potentially 50% over long-run equilibrium	August 2003
• Constantin Gurdgiev (Irish Times)	Anyone who bought after 2001 will see negative equity	December 2005
• Morgan Kelly (IT)	Real falls of 40–50%	December 2006
Construction activity		
• Jim O'Leary (IT)	Hallmarks of a pyramid scheme	October 2005
• Mark Coleman (IT)	Potentially 100,000 job losses	June 2006
• Morgan Kelly (IT)	A collapse of house building activity	December 2006
Commercial property		
• Caroline Gavin (Central Bank)	Significant price falls likely if the economy slows	December 2000
Exchequer revenue		
• Morgan Kelly (IT)	A collapse of Government revenue	December 2006
Banks' exposure to property and construction		
• David McWilliams (Sunday Business Post)	Collapsing bank shares and takeovers if land prices fall	October 2003
Bank funding		
• Patrick Honohan (ESRI)	Huge reliance on overseas funding	December 2006

highly authoritative, and his critique of the other models used to assess Irish house prices has been invaluable to this study. Nonetheless, he was quite candid about the difficulty involved in assessing the extent of the deviation of Irish prices from fundamentals. Furthermore, there is no empirical evidence in the contemporary literature on the Irish economy that suggested that prices would necessarily revert to their fundamental values. If irrational exuberance had driven prices above this level it was quite possible that a widespread panic could encourage prices to fall below it. Even more significantly, to the extent that the fundamentals were buoyed by the housing boom itself, one would logically expect them to weaken as the boom abated. Finally, as observed in Chapter 6, even a small increase in interest rates was liable to increase the measured overvaluation dramatically.[4]

Criticising Kelly's article because it lacked sufficient econometric analysis of the Irish situation was therefore to miss the central point. International precedent strongly suggested that after house price booms peaked they would revert towards their pre-boom levels, rather than their boom-time fundamental values. Similarly, the OECD's 2006 study of construction booms demonstrated that investment in residential construction tended to rapidly revert towards its pre-boom level once a boom had peaked. Nonetheless, analysts overwhelmingly forecast the future for the construction sector on the basis of anticipated demand. Again, there was no historical evidence provided to suggest that this was the level at which activity could be expected to stabilise. The forecasts were also highly questionable insofar as they assumed continued high net immigration and demand for second homes, both of which were to a significant extent functions of the construction boom itself.[5]

The contemporary discourse was replete with examples of analysts ignoring, misinterpreting or disregarding pertinent historical episodes. The widespread perception that nominal house price falls had been rare was a case in point, and in a Western European context they had been anything but. Similarly, Maurice Roche's contention that the Irish housing boom in the 1970s and early 1980s had ended without a crash was deeply problematic given that real prices fell by 27% from 1981. Most striking of all were the Central Bank's explicit dismissals of the relevance of past experience in the 2004 and 2007 Financial Stability Reports. The belief that the world had changed and that countries like Ireland had graduated from the threat of a financial or asset market collapse had remarkably little factual basis, and even recent Irish history

[4] Patrick Honohan, *The Irish Banking Crisis: Regulatory and Financial Stability Policy 2003–2008. A report to the Minister for Finance by the Governor of the Central Bank* (2010), 84; Patrick Honohan, 'Resolving Ireland's Banking Crisis', UCD Economic Workshop Conference 'Responding to the Crisis', Dublin, 12 January 2009a, 6; Anthony Murphy, 'Modelling Irish House Prices: A Review and Some New Results' (2005), 10–17, 21, 23. Available from http://www.nuff.ox.ac.uk/users/murphya/Centre.htm; John Maynard Keynes, *The General Theory of Employment, Interest and Money* (BN Publishing, 2008), 97, 104–105.

[5] Morgan Kelly, 'On the Likely Extent of Falls in Irish House Prices', ESRI, *Quarterly Economic Commentary*, Summer 2007, 42.

offered evidence to this effect. At an analytical level, observers of the Irish economy could be accused of having operated on the basis of false assumptions and looking for instruction in the wrong places.

It is clear from the source material examined that many of the commentators on the Irish economy were poorly placed to correctly identify and warn about the degree of the risk. The impediments facing the formal institutions stemmed from both political sensitivities and the fear that strong warnings from these agencies could precipitate a market crash. Tom O'Connell, as former Chief Economist of the Central Bank, has spoken explicitly about how the Irish authorities scrutinised reports from the IMF and OECD for negative findings before they were published. He has also stressed that in its own publications the Bank was required to 'pull its punches' and 'put a positive gloss on things rather than frightening the horses'. As we have seen, academics were not incentivised to examine the contemporary Irish economy in their journal publications. Nor is there much evidence of senior policymakers seeking their advice in a meaningful way. Neither the newspapers nor the Dáil enjoyed an abundance of relevant expertise, and they were thus highly dependent on externally produced analysis. This left relatively few appropriately trained analysts who were both sufficiently incentivised to analyse the Irish economy in detail and free to speak their minds.[6]

Although the impact of institutional impediments on the discourse was significant it was certainly not decisive. The fact that the ESRI published Kelly's paper in 2007 is crucial, and suggests both that the institute enjoyed a significant degree of autonomy and that it was sufficiently high-minded to risk the associated fallout. While the international organisations were presumably restricted from warning about a property price crash they were certainly not obliged to predict a soft landing, as the IMF did in 2005 and the OECD did in 2006. Most compellingly, several highly regarded academics published articles on the contemporary Irish economy without recognising anything like the extent of the risk. Flawed analysis played a central role even notwithstanding the institutional curtailments which many commentators faced.[7]

[6] Houses of the Oireachtas, *Joint Committee of Inquiry into the Banking Crisis*, vol. 2, no. 26, Tom O'Connell, 10 June 2015, 83–84, 92, 134.

[7] Houses of the Oireachtas, *Joint Committee of Inquiry into the Banking Crisis*, vol. 2, no. 26, Tom O'Connell, 10 June 2015, 84 and Houses of the Oireachtas, *Joint Committee of Inquiry into the Banking Crisis*, vol. 2, no. 33, John McCarthy, 24 June 2015, 6–7, 9–10.

As we saw in Chapter 2, the history of financial and asset bubbles suggests that after a period of perceived economic tranquillity societies commonly conclude that the world has fundamentally changed, which is a key precondition for a speculative boom. The fact that so many observers succumbed to the prevailing narrative of the boom is therefore not the most noteworthy feature of the contemporary discourse on the Irish economy. Of much more interest are the characteristics shared by those who strongly dissented from the prevailing view of what was happening and what was to come. Many commentators raised concern about the trajectory of certain aspects of the Irish economy, though this did not necessarily constitute dissent. The dissenters in the fuller sense of the term were those who issued strong warnings about a potentially very deleterious outcome for the Irish economy or property market. The most striking examples include Morgan Kelly, David McWilliams, the IMF's 2000 mission, Caroline Gavin and *The Economist*.

A notable characteristic shared by McWilliams and Kelly was that they both came to the Irish boom with a relatively fresh perspective and were thus perhaps less inured than other commentators. McWilliams returned to Ireland when the housing boom was already well under way, while Kelly has suggested that he had been totally disinterested in the Irish economy for most of the period. They were both highly qualified to challenge the prevailing view: Kelly was a university professor and McWilliams had worked as a senior economist for an international financial services firm. As argued in Chapter 5, Kelly also had potentially less to lose by making a bold prediction than somebody whose core area of expertise was the contemporary Irish economy. McWilliams has suggested that issuing public warnings did not make him popular, which is certainly credible. However, this did not prevent him from establishing a highly successful career as an economic commentator.[8]

While an international perspective was an important attribute, it alone was insufficient to alert analysts to the precariousness of the Irish situation. As noted in Chapter 5, many of the key academic commentators on the Irish economy had been educated abroad. Prominent contributors to the newspapers had worked overseas, yet did not recognise anything

[8]https://ie.linkedin.com/in/damcwilliams. Accessed 27 January 2016; Michael Lewis, *Boomerang: The Biggest Bust* (London, 2011), 89, 90; and Houses of the Oireachtas, *Joint Committee of Inquiry into the Banking Crisis*, vol. 1, no. 10, David McWilliams, 26 February 2015, 500–501.

like the extent of the threat to the Irish economy. On various occasions the IMF and the OECD came to remarkably sanguine conclusions, despite the fact that their missions were comprised of external analysts. Given that many observers had implicitly concluded that advanced economies in general had become more tranquil this is perhaps unsurprising. What was unusual about the five key dissenters listed above is that they all exhibited a combination of strong international *and* historical perspectives, and in each case explicitly looked to international precedent to inform their analyses. This evidently encouraged them to consider deep economic market crashes as an ever-present possibility rather than an unlikely abstraction. On the publication of the fourth edition of 'Manias, Panics and Crashes' in 2001, an *Irish Times* article suggested that the book was 'the last word by a distinguished scholar on the history of financial crises and should be on the desks of bankers everywhere'. One could make the same argument for the desks of many of the contemporary commentators on the Irish economy.[9]

Since there is so little evidence that these dissenters secured policy changes it is reasonable to conclude that dissent failed in this instance. But of course this does not mean that the fault lay with the dissenters themselves. To have achieved any meaningful changes they would either had to have persuaded key decision-makers of the veracity of their views, or else subjected them to sufficient pressure by convincing others. One theoretically possible option would have been to convince enough Deputies on the Government backbenches of the risks to encourage a significant revolt. Given the level of disinterest in macroeconomic stability issues exhibited by many TDs in the period, this was never likely to be achievable. Persuading either of the major Opposition parties to champion the pessimistic view would have been similarly difficult given how high risk this would have been as a political strategy. A third option was to convince a significant proportion of the electorate that the economy was in a precarious position, thereby making it an election issue. McWilliams clearly went to significant efforts to publicise the risks to the property market, spending 'the best part of a decade trying to warn as many people as possible on as many platforms as possible'. The longevity of the price boom, contemporary survey data, and the 2007 General

[9] John Mulqueen, 'Brought to Book', *The Irish Times*, 27 July 2001, 54.

Election results all strongly suggested that the public was relatively impervious in this respect.[10]

A more plausible alternative would have been to convince enough expert analysts of the risks to significantly alter the public discourse. This raises an important question: if more commentators had been highly pessimistic would senior decision-makers or the broader public have acted differently? While it is impossible to know for certain, such an approach might have been more fruitful than those already outlined. Even still, dissenters would have been vigorously contradicted by the spokespeople from the banks and real estate agencies who played such an integral role in setting the agenda in the Irish newspapers. Whatever the strategy, the dissenters undoubtedly faced a formidable uphill struggle.

A key question then, is how and why the optimists remained so unreceptive to the warnings issued. One reason that we have already considered is that their confidence grew as the boom years went on and the day of reckoning never came. A good example of this was in April 2006, when Bertie Ahern criticised those who had issued warnings about a 'huge downturn' the previous year, observing the need for 'an examination into why so many people got it so wrong'. A second possible explanation is the affect heuristic, and the common propensity to ignore unwelcome advice. In September 2006 a Fianna Fáil parliamentary party meeting was addressed by a prominent economist. Perhaps unsurprisingly the economist in question was Dan McLaughlin, who predicted a good medium-term outlook for the Irish economy, no reduction in Government revenue, no fall in house prices due to rising interest rates, and no major economic slowdown in 2007. It is almost unimaginable that Fianna Fáil would have invited an economist who was deeply concerned about the future to address the meeting. One could of course suggest that doing so might conceivably have triggered public alarm, but this is deeply problematic in itself. Seeking out and giving a fair hearing to analysts with opposing views should not have been considered noteworthy in a healthy democracy. Additionally, that even an action on

[10] Houses of the Oireachtas, *Joint Committee of Inquiry into the Banking Crisis*, vol. 1, no. 10, David McWilliams, 26 February 2015, 500–501 and Paul Melia, 'Survey Sees no End to Boom in Property', *The Irish Independent*, 21 March 2005.

this scale could potentially have upset the property market should have served as a significant warning.[11]

Both Government and Opposition Deputies were clearly concerned about the rate of house price increases from the late 1990s. Although this primarily stemmed from affordability rather than market stability concerns, it does seem quite plausible that reducing the rate of price growth was a genuine Government objective. The degree of responsiveness to the recommendations of the first Bacon Report corroborates this view, although the subsequent retraction of the Bacon measures does suggest that price stability was a secondary concern. It also seems clear from the contemporary Dáil debates, Bertie Ahern's subsequent testimony to the Banking Inquiry, and the measures implemented, that the Government's strategy to deal with price increases from 1998 onwards was to increase supply to the point that it satiated demand while avoiding a house price crash in the interim. Unfortunately the intended cure of abundant supply proved to be considerably more damaging than the original disease. If policymakers had elected to dampen the housing market from the outset, even at the risk of a price crash, the employment, fiscal and financial consequences would have been far less severe than those subsequently endured. The dilemma was akin to that which had faced US policymakers in the 1920s: 'the real choice was between an immediate and deliberately engineered collapse and a more serious disaster later on'.[12]

The financial and fiscal measures that could have been taken to dampen housing demand have already been examined. On the financial side, the CBFSAI (Central Bank and Financial Services Authority of Ireland) could have achieved meaningful results by enforcing the existing sectoral concentration limits on property and construction lending, directly restricting the rate of credit growth, or by imposing high lending standards. Successive Governments could have mitigated the problem by permanently withdrawing tax incentives and subsidies for property investors and homeowners, by implementing the Kenny Report

[11] 'No Indication of Property Downturn, Says Ahern', *The Irish Times*, 8 April 2006 and Liam Reid, 'Inflation and Rising Interest Rates Are Biggest Challenges', *The Irish Times*, 5 September 2006, 9.

[12] Houses of the Oireachtas, *Joint Committee of Inquiry into the Banking Crisis*, vol. 2, no. 48, Bertie Ahern, 16 July 2015, 82, 83, 100 and Galbraith, *The Great Crash 1929* (2009), 52.

recommendations, or by running counter-cyclical Budgets. However, there is another approach that could have been adopted, which has received minimal attention since and would have been unthinkable to Ministers at the time. The Government could have chosen to actively talk down the housing market and publicise its concerns about potential price falls. While successive Governors of the Central Bank had done just this, they enjoyed nothing like the collective public profile of the senior Ministers who were actively promoting the opposite view. A key political objection to the strategy of talking down the market would be that the effects could be so readily 'attributed with the greatest of precision to the person or persons who uttered the words'. Nonetheless, it would have had a dramatic impact on the public discourse and potentially on the property market.[13]

It is quite apparent that the depth of the Irish crisis was attributable to both analytical shortcomings and poor policy. The fact that no contemporary commentators considered the risks posed by the rate of Irish private-sector credit growth and the degree of sectoral lending concentration in a global historical context was crucial. Although some commentators did recognise that plentiful credit was the key driver of the Irish property and construction booms, this was of limited value given the remarkable lack of discussion about the remedial powers available to the regulatory authorities. Nonetheless, much better policies could have been pursued on the basis of the advice that was given. Far from implementing 'the best advice available at the time', decision-makers adopted high-risk strategies even in the face of mainstream Opposition. Key examples included the rapid fiscal expansion in the run-up to the 2002 General Election, the reinstatement of tax incentives for property investors, and the refusal to introduce additional charges or taxes for homeowners. If policymakers had acted more prudently within the parameters of the available advice the bubble could have been somewhat curtailed, though certainly not avoided without measures to reduce credit growth. Nor can we assume that policymakers would have been more prudent even if there had been more ominous predictions. The official responses to the warnings that were issued about the property market were often dismissive and occasionally hostile. Policymakers were oblivious to the rarity of what they inadvertently achieved in 2001: an apparent soft

[13] Galbraith, *The Great Crash 1929* (2009), 59.

landing. With a better grounding in financial history they would have recognised this as the remarkably fortuitous outcome that it was, and made significant efforts to consolidate it.[14]

The reforms that have been made since the onset of the crisis have done little to address the institutional shortfalls that impaired the policy debate during the boom. We will turn very briefly to the types of structural changes suggested by the findings of this book. As already discussed, a temporarily restricted memorandum to policymakers outlining any market-sensitive risks would be a significant step in the right direction for all of the formal organisations. These bodies should also be far more frank about both the limits of what they can say and the fallibility of their conclusions. Perhaps counterintuitively, the reports should be less structured and formulaic. If the purpose is to warn of systemic risks then there is little point in allocating comparable attention to a very minor risk and one that jeopardises the entire financial system. In several instances this practice helped to blunt the edge of the warnings issued. Similarly, the formal organisations should be much more open-minded about the types of analysis that constitute the bedrock of their publications. If econometric estimates of fundamental house prices told little about what would happen in the future then there was no reason to continue treating this as the 'core' analysis and past precedent as supplementary or somehow less empirically robust.

Much better use could have been made of academic economists in the period, both in terms of increasing the amount of analysis they published on the contemporary Irish economy and ensuring that what was published was absorbed by policymakers and the general public. Addressing the first issue requires restacking the incentives facing academics within university departments, and researchers could be encouraged to publish at least periodically with explicit reference to Irish policy issues. There is already a policy section in the *Economic and Social Review*, but the establishment of a new annual journal akin to the *Irish Banking Review* could be helpful here. Of course, decision-makers would then need to be both encouraged and equipped to read the publication, which likely requires

[14]Frank Barry, 'Towards Improved Policymaking in Ireland: Contestability and the Marketplace for Ideas', *Irish Journal of Public Policy* (2011), vol. 3, no. 2. Available from http://publish.ucc.ie/ijpp/2011/02. Accessed 2 February 2016; 'Taoiseach Apologises for Suicide Comments', *The Irish Times*, 4 July 2007; and 'No Indication of Property Downturn, Says Ahern', *The Irish Times*, 8 April 2006.

at least a change in senior job descriptions in relevant Government departments and the Central Bank.

Academic economists should also be encouraged and facilitated in publishing at least one newspaper comment piece a year. This would help to offset some of the dependence on industry representatives on the part of these publications, though they evidently also need a much more radical overhaul. Economics journalists should be responsible for thorough and critical engagement with third-party publications and analyses. This type of work is very time-consuming and therefore costly. But the lesson from *The Economist* is that the Irish newspapers would serve their readers far better by sacrificing quantity for the sake of quality. Nor does robust economic analysis have to be impenetrable for the typical reader, and international comparisons would likely have resonated better than just the reported conclusions of various experts. Furthermore, no industry claims should be published without at least an accompanying recognition of the conflicts of interest at play, and preferably with a rebuttal from an internal or external analyst with an opposing view.

The limitations of the Dáil as a forum for debating and improving economic policy were stark, and suggest that any piecemeal reforms would almost certainly be inadequate. Like economic observers in other spheres, Deputies operated according to a set of incentives that did little to encourage deep engagement with potential macroeconomic vulnerabilities. Whatever reactions Michael Ring's claim that his seat was secured through constituency work might provoke, few could question its veracity. TDs are currently required to perform two demanding and distinct roles, which necessitate very different skill sets. It would be an unusual person who could perform in both to their full potential, and those familiar with Irish political history might struggle to identify many Deputies who have been up to the task. There is no compelling logical reason for constituency and national responsibilities to be vested in the same people. For parliamentarians to concentrate on the national good they need to be elected specifically to do so, prohibited from addressing the concerns of their individual constituents or constituencies. These localised roles could be fulfilled by separate elected representatives, who would hopefully act on behalf constituents with the same energy and commitment which has characterised TDs in this respect to date.

Bibliography

Printed Primary Sources

Reports and Research Papers

Bacon, Peter & Associates, Fergal MacCabe, and Anthony Murphy. *An Economic Assessment of Recent House Price Developments: Report Submitted to the Minister for Housing and Urban Renewal.* April, 1998.

Committee on the Price of Building Land. *Report to the Minister for Local Government.* Dublin, 1974.

Goodbody Economic Consultants in Association with Mazars and HKR. *Review of Area-Based Tax Renewal Incentive Schemes.* November 2005. Available from http://taxpolicy.gov.ie/wp-content/uploads/2011/03/Taxrev2006vol2.pdf. Accessed 7 October 2015.

Labour Party Housing Commission. *Housing: A New Approach.* Dublin, 1999.

Murphy, Anthony. *Housing and National Competitiveness: A Report for the National Competitiveness Council.* Unpublished, 2004.

The All-Party Oireachtas Committee on the Constitution. *Ninth Progress Report: Private Property.* Dublin, 2004.

CBFSAI

CBFSAI. *Financial Stability Reports*, 2004–2006.

CBFSAI. *2004–2006 Strategic Plan of the Central Bank and Financial Services Authority of Ireland*, 2004.

Central Bank of Ireland. *Annual Reports 1999–2005*, 2000–2006.

Central Bank of Ireland. *Quarterly Bulletins*, 2000–2006.

Financial Regulatory Authority of Ireland. *Annual Report 2003/2004*, 2005.

Geraldine Slevin. 'Is There a "New Economy" in Ireland?'. Technical Paper 3/RT/02, 2002.

C. M. Casey, *Policy Failures and the Irish Economic Crisis*,
https://doi.org/10.1007/978-3-319-90182-4

McQuinn, Kieran. 'A Model of the Irish Housing Sector'. Research Paper 1/RT/04, 2004.

ESRI

ESRI. *Quarterly Economic Commentaries*, January 2000–December 2006.

ESRI. *Medium-Term Review: 2001–2007*, 2001.

ESRI. *Medium-Term Review: 2003–2010*, 2003.

ESRI. *Medium-Term Review: 2005–2012*, 2005.

European Commission

Čech, Zdeněk. 'Ireland: No Place Like (My Own) Home'. *EcFin Country Focus*, vol. 3, no. 13, European Commission, 2006.

Čech, Zdeněk and John Macdonald. 'The "Celtic Tiger" Learns to Purr'. *EcFin Country Focus*, vol. 1, no. 18, European Commission, 2004.

European Commission, Directorate General for Economic and Financial Affairs. *European Economy: Public Finances in EMU*, 2000–2006.

IMF

IMF. *Ireland: Staff Reports for the Article IV Consultations.* Washington: IMF, 2000–2006.

IMF. *Selected Issues and Statistical Appendix 2000.* Washington: IMF, 2000.

IMF. *Selected Issues.* IMF Staff Country Report No. 02/171, Washington: IMF, 2002.

IMF. *Selected Issues.* IMF Staff Country Report No. 04/171, Washington: IMF, 2004.

IMF. *Ireland: Staff Report for the 2005 Article IV Consultation*, 11, 2005.

IMF. *Ireland: Financial System Stability Assessment Update*, IMF Country Report No. 06/292, Washington: IMF, 2006.

OECD

OECD. *Economic Surveys: Ireland*, OECD, 1999.

OECD. *Economic Surveys: Ireland*, OECD, 2001.

OECD. *OECD Economic Outlook*, vol. 2002, no. 2, OECD, 2002.

OECD. *Economic Surveys: Ireland*, OECD, 2003.

OECD. *OECD Economic Outlook*, vol. 2003, no. 1, OECD, 2003.

OECD. *OECD Economic Outlook*, vol. 2005, no. 2, OECD, 2005.

OECD. *Economic Surveys: Ireland*, OECD, 2006.

Academic Articles and Book Chapters

Baker, Terry, John Fitzgerald, and Patrick Honohan. 'Economic Implications for Ireland of EMU'. ESRI Policy Research Series Paper no. 28. Dublin, 1996.

Barry, Frank. 'Dangers for Ireland of an EMU Without the UK: Some Calibration Results'. *Economic and Social Review*, vol. 28, no. 4 (October 1997): 333–349.

Barry, Frank. 'The Celtic Tiger Era: Delayed Convergence or Regional Boom?'. *ESRI, Quarterly Economic Commentary* (Summer 2002): 35–42.

Barry, Frank. 'FDI, Transfer Pricing and the Measurement of R&D Intensity'. *Research Policy: Policy and Management Studies of Science, Technology and Innovation*, vol. 34, no. 5 (2005): 673–681.

Barry, Frank. 'Future Irish Growth: Opportunities, Catalysts, Constraints'. *ESRI, Quarterly Economic Commentary* (Winter 2005): 33–58.

Barry, Frank, Aoife Hannan, and Eric A. Strobl. 'The Real Convergence in the Irish Economy and the Sectoral Distribution of Employment Growth'. In *Understanding Ireland's Economic Growth*, edited by Frank Barry, 13–24. Basingstoke: Macmillan, 1999.

Drudy, P.J. 'Housing: The Case for a New Philosophy'. In *Securing Fairness and Well-Being in a Land of Plenty*, edited by B. Reynolds and S. Healy, 36–49. Dublin: CORI Justice Commission, 2005.

Fahey, Tony. 'The Housing Boom in Ireland: Causes, Effects on Affordability and Policy Responses'. *Housing Finance International*, vol. 18, no. 4 (2004): 11–17.

Fitzgerald, John. 'Comment on "Dangers for Ireland of an EMU Without the UK: Some Calibration Results" by Frank Barry'. *Economic and Social Review*, vol. 29, no. 1 (January 1998): 99–102.

Fitzpatrick, Trevor, and Kieran McQuinn. 'House Prices and Mortgage Credit: Empirical Evidence for Ireland', *Manchester School*, vol. 75, no. 1 (2007): 82–103.

Foley, Patrick. 'Are Irish House Prices Driven by Fundamentals?', University College Cork Working Paper, 2004. Available from https://www.ucc.ie/en/media/academic/economics/documents/research/wp04-01.pdf.

Goodhart, Charles A.E. 'What Can Academics Contribute to the Study of Financial Stability'. *Economic and Social Review*, vol. 36, no. 3 (Winter 2005): 189–203.

Hogan, Vincent, and Patrick O'Sullivan. 'Consumption and House Prices in Ireland', *ISSC Discussion Paper Series*, Working Paper 2003/15, 2003.

Honohan, Patrick. 'To What Extent Has Finance Been a Driver of Ireland's Economic Success?'. *ESRI, Quarterly Economic Commentary* (Winter 2006): 59–72.

Honohan, Patrick, and Anthony J. Leddin. 'Ireland in EMU: More Shocks, Less Insulation'. *Economic and Social Review*, vol. 37, no. 2 (Summer/Autumn 2006): 263–294.

Honohan, Patrick, and Brendan Walsh. 'Catching Up with the Leaders: The Irish Hare'. *Brookings Papers on Economic Activity*, no. 1 (2002): 1–57.

Kelly, Morgan. 'On the Likely Extent of Falls in Irish House Prices', UCD Centre for Economic Research, Working Paper 07/01. Dublin, 2007.

Krugman, Paul R. 'Good News from Ireland: A Geographical Perspective'. In *International Perspectives on the Irish Economy*, edited by Alan W. Gray, 38–53. Dublin, 1997.

Lane, Philip R. 'Profits and Wages in Ireland, 1987–1996'. *Journal of the Statistical and Social Inquiry Society of Ireland*, vol. xxvii, part v (May 1998): 223–252.

Lane, Philip R. 'What Should We Do with The Surpluses', Administration, XXX, October, 1999.

Lane, Philip R. 'Assessing Ireland's Fiscal Strategy: Recent Experiments and Future Plans'. In *Budget Perspectives 2004*, edited by Tim Callan et al., 4–22, 2003.

Lane, Philip R., and Patrick Honohan. 'Divergent Inflation Rates in EMU'. IIIS Discussion Paper no. 5, July 2003.

McAleese, Dermot. 'The Celtic Tiger: Origins and Prospects'. In *Policy Options*, 46–50, July–August 2000.

McAleese, Dermot. 'The Irish Economy: Recent Growth, European Integration and Future Prospects', Address at Cantro Informação Europeia Jacques Delors, Lisbon, October 12, 2001.

McAleese, Dermot. Review of *The Making of the Celtic Tiger: The Inside Story of Ireland's Boom Economy*, by Ray MacSharry and Padraic White. *Studies: An Irish Quarterly Review*, vol. 90, no. 359 (Autumn 2001): 333–335.

McDowell, Moore. 'The Rationale and Scope for Privatisation in Ireland'. *Journal of the Statistical and Social Inquiry Society of Ireland*, vol. xxix (January 2000): 48–64.

McGunnigle, Patrick, and David McGuire. 'Why Ireland? A Qualitative Review of the Factors Influencing the Location of US Multinationals in Ireland with Particular Reference to the Impact of Labour Issues'. *Economic and Social Review*, vol. 32, no. 1 (January 2001): 43–67.

Murphy, Anthony. 'Modelling Irish House Prices: A Review and Some New Results'. Available from http://www.nuff.ox.ac.uk/users/murphya/Centre.htm.

Murphy, Antoin E. 'The "Celtic Tiger"—An Analysis of Ireland's Economic Growth Performance'. RSC no. 2000/16, European University Institute, 2000.

Neary, J. Peter. 'An Interview with Brendan Walsh'. *Economic and Social Review*, vol. 37, no. 2 (Summer/Autumn 2006): 295–302.

Neary, J. Peter, and D. Rodney Thom. 'Punts, Pounds, and Euros: In Search of An Optimal Currency Area', *Irish Business Administration Research*, November 1997. Available from http://researchrepository.ucd.ie/bitstream/handle/10197/707/ibar1997.pdf?sequence=3.

Norris, Michelle, and Patrick Shiels. 'Irish Housing in the European Context'. In *Housing Contemporary Ireland: Policy, Society and Shelter*, edited by Michelle Norris and Declan Redmond, 364–388. Dublin, 2005.

Ó Gráda, Cormac. 'Is the Celtic Tiger a Paper Tiger?'. *ESRI, Quarterly Economic Commentary* (Spring 2002): 51–62.

Ó Gráda, Cormac, and Kevin H. O'Rourke. 'Living standards and Growth'. In *The Economy of Ireland: Policy and Performance of a European Region*, edited by J.W. O'Hagan, 198–227. Dublin, 2000.

O'Leary, Jim. 'Benchmarking the Benchmarkers'. *ESRI, Quarterly Economic Commentary* (Winter 2002): 1–13.

Palcic, Donal, and Eoin Reeves. 'An Economic Analysis of Privatisation in Ireland, 1991–2003'. *Journal of the Statistical and Social Inquiry Society of Ireland*, vol. xxxiv (October 2004): 1–27.

Power, Jim. 'One Year of the Euro'. *Irish Banking Review* (Spring 2000).

Power, Jim. 'The Changing Dynamics of Irish Inflation'. *Irish Banking Review* (Spring 2003): 33–48.

Roche, Maurice J. Irish House Prices: Will the Roof Cave In?'. *Economic and Social Review*, vol. 30, no. 4 (1999): 343–362.

Roche, Maurice J. 'The Rise in House Prices in Dublin: Bubble, Fad or Just Fundamentals'. *Economic Modelling*, vol. 18, no. 2 (2001): 281–295.

Roche, Maurice J. 'Will There Be a Crash in Irish House Prices?'. *ESRI, Quarterly Economic Commentary* (Winter 2003): 1–16.

Roche, Maurice J., and Kieran McQuinn. 'Testing for Speculation in Agricultural Land in Ireland'. *European Review of Agricultural Economics*, vol. 28, no. 2 (2001): 95–115.

Walsh, Brendan. 'The Irish Economic 'Miracle': How Do We Explain the Timing of the Boom?'. *New Economy*, vol. 6, no. 4 (December 1999): 223–228.

Walsh, Brendan. 'The Role of Tax Policy in Ireland's Economic Renaissance'. *Canadian Tax Journal*, vol. 48, no. 3 (2000): 658–673.

Walsh, Brendan. 'Taxation and Foreign Direct Investment in Ireland'. In *Tax Reform in Canada: Our Path to Greater Prosperity*, edited by H.G. Grubel, 207–230. Vancouver: Fraser Institute, 2003.

Walsh, Brendan. 'The Transformation of the Irish Labour Market: 1980–2003'. *Journal of the Statistical and Social Inquiry Society of Ireland*, vol. xxxiii (May 2004): 83–115.

Newspapers

Sunday Business Post, David McWilliams articles, 1 January 2000 to 31 December 2006. Available from *Factiva*, https://global.factiva.com/.

The Economist, 1 January 2000 to 31 December 2006. Available from *The Gale Group*, https://www.gale.com/.

The Irish Times and *Irish Independent*, 1 January 2000 to 31 December 2006. Available from *Factiva*, https://global.factiva.com/.

Parliamentary Debates

Dáil Eireann Debates, 1 January 2000 to 31 December 2006. Available from http://www.oireachtas.ie/parliament/.

Printed Secondary Works

Ahearne, Alan, Finn Kyland, and Mark A. Wynne. 'Ireland's Great Depression'. *Economic and Social Review*, vol. 37, no. 2 (Summer/Autumn, 2006): 215–243.

Akerlof, George A., and Robert J. Shiller. *Animal Spirits*. Princeton, 2010.

Anton R. Valukas. Report of Anton R. Valukas. 2010. Available from http://jenner.com/lehman/lehman/VOLUME%201.pdf. Accessed 15 September 2014.

Baldwin, Richard et al. 'Rebooting the Eurozone: Step 1—Agreeing a Crisis Narrative', Centre for Economic Policy Research, Policy Insight No. 85, November 2015.

Barret, Alan, and Brian Lucey. 'An Analysis of the Journal Output of Irish-Based Economists, 1970–2001'. *Economic and Social Review*, vol. 34, no. 2 (Summer/Autumn 2003): 109–143.

Barry, Frank. 'Towards Improved Policymaking in Ireland: Contestability and the Marketplace for Ideas'. *Irish Journal of Public Policy*, vol. 3, no. 2 (2011). Available from http://publish.ucc.ie/ijpp/2011/02. Accessed 2 February 2016.

Bezemer, Dirk J. '"No One Saw This Coming": Understanding Financial Crisis through Accounting Models', Munich Personal RePEc Archive Paper no. 15892, June, 2009.

Breen, Michael. 'IMF Surveillance of Ireland during the Celtic Tiger'. In *Irish Political Studies*, vol. 27, no. 3 (2012): 431–439.

Byrne, Elaine A. *Political Corruption in Ireland, 1922–2010: A Crooked Harp?* Manchester, 2012.

Calomiris, Charles W., and Stephen H. Haber. 'Why Banking Systems Succeed—and Fail: The Politics Behind Financial Institutions', *Foreign Affairs*, November/December 2013. Available from www.foreignaffairs.com. Accessed 24 September 2014.

Calomiris, Charles W., and Stephen H. Haber. *Fragile by Design: The Political Origins of Banking Crises and Scarce Credit*. Princeton, 2014.

Cardiff, Kevin. *Recap: Inside Ireland's Financial Crisis*. Dublin 2016.

Carswell, Simon. *Anglo Republic: Inside the Bank that Broke Ireland*. London, 2011.

Central Bank of Ireland. *The Financial Measures Programme Report*, March, 2011.

Central Statistics Office. *Proceedings of Conference on Measuring Economic Growth Organised by Central Statistics Office and Irish Economic Association 9 November 1995*. Dublin, 1996.

Christensen, Johan. *The Power of Economists Within the State*. Stanford: Stanford University Press, 2017.

Collins, Liam. 'Just Who Is Morgan Kelly'. In *Irish Independent*, 30 November, 2012. Accessed 4 June, 2014. http://www.independent.ie/opinion/analysis/just-who-is-morgan-kelly-26699342.html.

Collins, Stephen. *Breaking the Mould: How the PDs Changed Ireland*. Dublin, 2006.

Comptroller and Auditor General. *National Asset Management Agency: Progress Report 2010–2012*, Report No. 81. Dublin, 2014.

Corcoran, Paul, Eve Griffin, Ella Arensman, Anthony P. Fitzgerald, and Ivan J. Perry. 'Impact of the Economic Recession and Subsequent Austerity and Suicide on Self-harm in Ireland: An Interrupted Time-Series Analysis'. *International Journal of Epidemiology*, vol. 44, no. 3 (June 2015): 969–977.

Cowen, Brian. 'The Euro: From Crisis to Resolution? Some Reflections from the Road Thus Far', at the BMW Centre of German and European Studies, Georgetown University, Washington, March, 2012.

Cruise O'Brien, Conor. *States of Ireland*. London, 1979.

Daly, Mary E. *Industrial Development and Irish National Identity, 1922–1939*. Syracuse, 1992.

Delany, Sarah, Richard Sinnott, and Niall O'Reilly. 'The Extent of Clientelism in Irish Politics: Evidence from Classifying Dáil Questions on a Local–National Dimension'. *AICS: Proceedings of 21st Irish Conference on Artificial Intelligence and Cognitive Science*, NUI Galway, 30 August–1 September 2010.

Department of the Environment, Heritage and Local Government (Ireland). *Annual Housing Statistics Bulletin 2006*. Dublin, 2007.

Donovan, Donal, and Antoin E. Murphy. *The Fall of the Celtic Tiger: Ireland and the Euro Debt Crisis*. Oxford: Oxford University Press, 2013.

Dowd, Kevin, and Martin Hutchinson. *Alchemists of Loss: How Modern Finance and Government Intervention Crashed the Financial System*. Hoboken, NJ: Wiley, 2006.

Duffy, David. 'User Cost and Irish House Prices'. *ESRI, Quarterly Economic Commentary* (Autumn 2011): 1–14.

Eichengreen, Barry. *Hall of Mirrors: The Great Depression, The Great Recession, and the Uses—and Misuses—of History*. Oxford: Oxford University Press, 2016.

Elton, Matt. 'History? It Started a Second Ago', 28 October 2009. Available from http://www.historyextra.com/feature/history-it-started-second-ago.

Elton, Matt. 'When Does History End?', 28 October 2009. Available from http://www.historyextra.com/feature/when-does-history-end.

Fahy, Declan, Mark O'Brien, and Valerio Poti. 'From Boom to Bust: A Post-Celtic Tiger Analysis of the Norms, Values and Roles of Irish Financial Journalists'. *Irish Communications Review*, vol. 12 (2010): 5–20.

Fahy, Declan. 'A limited focus? Journalism, Politics, and the Celtic Tiger'. In *Political Communication in the Republic of Ireland*, Liverpool, Mark O'Brien and Donnacha Ó Beacháin, eds. (2014): 129–146.

Fitzgerald, John. 'The Irish Economy Today: Albatross or Phoenix?', ESRI Working Paper no. 384 (2011).

Fonseca Galvis, Ángela, James M. Snyder Jr., and B.K. Song. 'Newspaper Market Structure and Behavior: Partisan Coverage of Political Scandals in the United States from 1870 to 1910'. *Journal of Politics*, vol. 78, no. 2 (2016).

Friedman, Milton. *Capitalism and Freedom*, Fortieth Anniversary Edition, Chicago, 2002.

Gentzkow, Matthew, Edward Glaeser, and Claudia Goldin. 'The Rise of the Fourth Estate: How Newspapers Became Informative and Why It Mattered'. In *Corruption and Reform: Lessons from America's Economic History*, Glaeser and Goldin, eds., 187–230. Chicago, 2006.

Gentzkow, Matthew, and Jesse M. Shapiro. 'What Drives Media Slant? Evidence from U.S. Daily Newspapers'. *Econometrica*, vol. 78, no. 1 (2010): 35–71.

Galbraith, John Kenneth. *The Great Crash 1929*. London, 2009.

Garvin, Tom. *Preventing the Future: Why Was Ireland so Poor for so Long?* Dublin, 2004.

Hayek, F.A. *The Road to Serfdom*. New York: Routledge, 2001.

Herman, Edward S., and Noam Chomsky. *Manufacturing Consent: The Political Economy of the Mass Media*. London, 2008.

Honohan Commission. *The Irish Banking Crisis: Regulatory and Financial Stability Policy 2003–2008. A Report to the Minister of Finance by the Governor of the Central Bank*. Dublin, 2010.

Honohan, Patrick. 'Resolving Ireland's Banking Crisis', UCD Economic Workshop Conference 'Responding to the Crisis'. Dublin, 12 January 2009a.

Honohan, Patrick. 'What Went Wrong in Ireland?', Prepared for the World Bank, May, 2009b.

Houses of the Oireachtas. *Joint Committee of Inquiry into the Banking Crisis*, vol. 1, no. 6, William Black, 5 February 2015.

Houses of the Oireachtas. *Joint Committee of Inquiry into the Banking Crisis*, vol. 2, no. 26, Tom O'Connell, 10 June 2015.

Houses of the Oireachtas. *Joint Committee of Inquiry into the Banking Crisis*, vol. 1, no. 16, Paul Mulligan, 26 March 2015.

Houses of the Oireachtas. *Joint Committee of Inquiry into the Banking Crisis*, vol. 2, no. 38, Charlie McCreevy, 1 July 2015.

Houses of the Oireachtas. *Joint Committee of Inquiry into the Banking Crisis*, vol. 1, no. 10, David McWilliams, 26 February 2015.

Houses of the Oireachtas. *Joint Committee of Inquiry into the Banking Crisis*, vol. 2, no. 48, Bertie Ahern, 16 July 2015.

Houses of the Oireachtas. *Joint Committee of Inquiry into the Banking Crisis*, vol. 1, no. 7, John Fitzgerald, 11 February 2015.

Houses of the Oireachtas. *Joint Committee of Inquiry into the Banking Crisis*, vol. 2, no. 33, John McCarthy, 24 June 2015.

Houses of the Oireachtas. *Joint Committee of Inquiry into the Banking Crisis*, vol. 2, no. 19, John Hurley, 21 May 2015

Houses of the Oireachtas. *Joint Committee of Inquiry into the Banking Crisis*, vol. 2, no. 27, Liam O'Reilly, 11 June 2015.

Houses of the Oireachtas. *Joint Committee of Inquiry into the Banking Crisis*, vol. 2, no. 12, Pat McArdle, 7 May 2015.

Houses of the Oireachtas. *Joint Committee of Inquiry into the Banking Crisis*, vol. 2, no. 27, Brian Patterson, 11 June 2015

Houses of the Oireachtas. *Report of the Joint Committee of Inquiry into the Banking Crisis*, vol. 1 (January, 2016).

IMF. *Ireland: Staff Report for the Article IV Consultation*, IMF Staff Country Report No. 12/264. Washington: IMF, 2012.

Independent Evaluation Office of the IMF. *IMF Performance in the Run-Up to the Financial and Economic Crisis: IMF Surveillance in 2004–2007.* Washington: IMF, 2011.

Kahneman, Daniel. *Thinking, Fast and Slow.* London, 2011.

Kanda, Daniel. 'Asset Booms and Structural Fiscal Positions: The Case of Ireland', IMF Working Paper WP/10/57, March, 2010.

Keen, Steve. *Debunking Economics: The Naked Emperor Dethroned.* London, 2011.

Kelly, Morgan. 'The Irish Credit Bubble', UCD Centre for Economic Research Working Paper, WP 09, December, 2009.

Kelly, Morgan. 'What Happened to Ireland? (The Hubert Butler Annual Lecture)'. *Irish Pages*, vol. 6, no. 1 (2009): 7–19.

Kennedy, Gerard, and Kieran McQuinn. 'Why are Irish House Prices Still Falling?'. Central Bank of Ireland Economic Letter Series, no. 5 (2012).

Kindleberger, Charles P., and Robert Z. Aliber. *Manias, Panics and Crashes: A History of Financial Crises*, 5th ed. Hampshire, 2005.

Kinsella, Stephen, and Anthony Leddin. Understanding *Ireland's Economic Crisis.* Dublin, 2010.

Komito, Lee. 'Irish Clientelism: A Reappraisal'. *Economic and Social Review*, vol. 15, no. 3 (1984): 173–184.

Krugman, Paul. *The Return of Depression Economics.* London, 2008.

Lane, Philip R. 'The Irish Crisis'. IIIS Discussion Paper no. 356, February 2011.

Lane, Philip R. 'International Financial Flows and the Irish Crisis'. IIIS Discussion Paper no. 444. March, 2014.

Laffer, Arthur B. 'The Laffer Curve: Past, Present and Future', Backgrounder no. 1765, Published by the Heritage Foundation. Available from www.heritage.org.

Lawrence, Dena, Federica Pazzaglia, and Karan Sonpar. 'The Introduction of a Non-traditional and Aggressive Approach to Banking: the Risks of Hubris'. *Journal of Business Ethics*, vol. 102, no. 3 (2011): 401–420.

Lee, J.J. *Ireland: 1912–1985, Politics and Society*. Cambridge: Cambridge University Press, 1989.

Lewis, Michael. *Boomerang: The Biggest Bust*. London: Penguin Books, 2011.

Lunn, Pete. 'The Role of Decision-Making Biases in Ireland's Banking Crisis'. ESRI Working Paper no. 389, May, 2011.

Lynch, Suzanne. 'Ireland Remains Fastest-Growing Economy in Europe'. *The Irish Times*, 4 February 2016.

Lyons, Tom, and Brian Carey. *The Fitzpatrick Tapes*. Dublin: Penguin Ireland, 2011.

Madden, David. 'Winners and Losers on the Roller-Coaster: Ireland, 2003–2011'. *Economic and Social Review*, vol. 45, no. 3 (2014): 405–421.

Madden, David. 'Health and Wealth on the Roller-Coaster: Ireland, 2003–2011'. *Social Indicators Research*, vol. 121, no. 2 (2015): 387–412.

Manton, Richard. 'Spokes or Strokes? Clientelism and Cycling Funding in Ireland'. *Irish Political Studies*, published online 10 February 2016.

McCabe, Conor. *Sins of the Father: Tracing the Decisions that Shaped the Irish Economy*. Dublin: The History Press Ireland, 2011.

Mercille, Julien. 'The Role of the Media in Sustaining Ireland's Housing Boom'. *New Political Economy*, vol. 9, no. 2 (2014): 282–301.

Ministry of Infrastructure of the Italian Republic. *Housing Statistics in the European Union 2005/6*. Available from http://www.bluomelette.net/bluomelette/wp-content/uploads/hs_annual2006.pdf. Accessed 5 November 2015.

Minsky, Hyman P. *Stabilising an Unstable Economy*. New York; London: McGraw-Hill, 2008.

Newstalk. 'Sinn Féin calls on Fianna Fáil to Apologise for Lenihan's "We all partied" line', at www.newstalk.com, 28 January 2016. Available from https://www.newstalk.com/Dil-debate-on-Banking-Inquiry-report-today. Accessed 3 February 2016.

Nyberg Commission. *Misjudging Risk: Causes of the Systemic Banking Crisis in Ireland. Report of the Commission of Investigation into the Banking Sector in Ireland*, March, 2011.

O'Brien, Mark. 'The Irish Press, Politicians, and the Celtic Tiger Economy'. In *The Media and Financial Crises: Comparative and Historical* Perspectives, edited by Shane Schifferes and Richard Roberts, 75–86, 2004.

O'Leary, Eoin. 'Reflecting on the Celtic Tiger: Before, During, and After'. *Irish Economic and Social History*, vol. 38 (2011): 73–88.

O'Leary, Jim. 'External Surveillance of Irish Fiscal Policy During the Boom', July 2010. Available from http://www.irisheconomy.ie/Notes/IrishEconomyNote11.pdf. Accessed 24 May 2014.

Ó Riain, Seán. 'The Crisis of Financialisation in Ireland'. *Economic and Social Review*, vol. 43, no. 4 (2012): 497–533.

Ó Riain, Seán. *The Rise and Fall of Ireland's Celtic Tiger: Liberalism, Boom and Bust*. Cambridge: Cambridge University Press, 2013.

OECD. *Economic Surveys: Ireland*, OECD, 2008.

Regling, Klaus, and Max Watson. *A Preliminary Report on the Sources of Ireland's Banking Crisis*. Dublin, 2010.

Reinhardt, Carmen M., and Kenneth S. Rogoff. *This Time is Different: Eight Centuries of Financial Folly*. Princeton: Princeton University Press, 2011.

Savage, Michael, Tim Callan, Brian Nolan, and Brian Colgan. 'The Great Recession, Austerity and Inequality: Evidence from Ireland'. ESRI Working Paper no. 499. Dublin 2015.

Schoenmaker, Dirk. 'Stabilising and Healing the Irish Banking System: Policy Lessons', 19 January 2015. Available from https://www.imf.org/external/np/seminars/eng/2014/ireland/pdf/Schoenmaker_IrishBanking.pdf. Accessed 4 February 2016.

Shiller, Robert J. *Irrational Exuberance*. Princeton: Princeton University Press, 2000.

Shiller, Robert J. 'Long-term Perspectives on the Current Boom in Home Prices'. *Economist's Voice*, 1–11. The Berkeley Electronic Press, 2006.

Skidelsky, Robert. *Keynes: The Return of the Master*, London: Allen Lane, 2010.

Stigler, George L. 'The Theory of Economic Regulation'. *Bell Journal of Economics and Management Science*, vol. 2 (1971): 3–21.

Taleb, Nassim Nicholas. *The Black Swan*, London: Penguin Books, 2010.

Taylor, George. 'Risk and Financial Armageddon in Ireland: The Politics of the Galway Tent'. *The Political Quarterly*, vol. 82, no. 4 (October–December 2011): 596–608.

Tetlock, Philip E. *Expert Political Judgement: How Good Is It? How Can We Know?* Princeton: Princeton University Press, 2005.

The Hague: Ministry of the Interior and Kingdom Relations. *Housing Statistics in the European Union 2010*. Available from http://www.bmwfw.gv.at/Wirtschaftspolitik/Wohnungspolitik/Documents/housing_statistics_in_the_european_union_2010.pdf. Accessed 23 March 2016.

Walsh, Brendan, and Dermot Walsh. Suicide in Ireland: The Influence of Alcohol and Unemployment. *Economic and Social Review*, vol. 42, no. 1 (2011): 27–47.

Wetherell, Margret. 'Themes in Discourse Research: The Case of Diana'. In *Discourse Theory and Practice: A* Reader, edited by Margaret Wetherell, Stephanie Taylor, and Simeon J. Yates, 14–20. London: Sage, 2001.

Whelan, Karl. 'Policy Lessons from Ireland's Latest Depression'. *Economic and Social Review*, vol. 41, no. 2, (Summer 2010): 225–254.

Whelan, Karl. 'Ireland's Economic Crisis: The Good, The Bad and The Ugly'. UCD Centre for Economic Research Working Paper, WP 13/06, July, 2013.

White, Timothy J. 'Celtic Collapse, or Celtic Correction? Ireland's Recession in Historical Perspective', *New Hibernia Review*, vol. 14, no. 4 (2011): 27–43.

Wright, Rob et al. 'Strengthening the Capacity of the Department of Finance: Report of the Independent Review Panel' (December 2010).

Index

C. M. Casey, *Policy Failures and the Irish Economic Crisis*,
https://doi.org/10.1007/978-3-319-90182-4

The manufacturer's authorised representative in the EU is Springer Nature Customer Service Centre GmbH, Europaplatz 3, 69115 Heidelberg, Germany. If you have any concerns regarding our products, please contact ProductSafety@springernature.com

Printed and bound by CPI Group (UK) Ltd, Croydon, CR0 4YY
05/10/2026
02228140-0007